The Decline
and Fall of
Ancient Greece

Other Books in the Turning Points Series:

Turning Points
IN WORLD HISTORY

The Decline and Fall of Ancient Greece

Don Nardo, *Book Editor*

David L. Bender, *Publisher*
Bruno Leone, *Executive Editor*
Bonnie Szumski, *Editorial Director*
David M. Haugen, *Managing Editor*

Greenhaven Press, Inc.; San Diego, California

Every effort has been made to trace the owners of copyrighted material. The articles in this volume may have been edited for content, length, and/or reading level. The titles have been changed to enhance the editorial purpose.

No part of this book may be reproduced or used in any form or by any means, electrical, mechanical, or otherwise, including, but not limited to, photocopy, recording, or any information storage and retrieval system, without prior written permission from the publisher.

Library of Congress Cataloging-in-Publication Data

The decline and fall of ancient Greece / Don Nardo, book editor.
    p.   cm. — (Turning points in world history)
    Includes bibliographical references and index.
    ISBN 0-7377-0241-9 (lib. : alk. paper)
    ISBN 0-7377-0240-0 (pbk. : alk. paper)
    1. Greece—Civilization—To 146 B.C. 2. National characteristics, Greece. 3. City-states—Greece—History, Military. 4. Military history, Ancient—Greece. 5. Military history, Ancient—Rome. I. Nardo, Don, 1947– . II. Series: Turning points in world history (Greenhaven Press)
DF78 .D42 2000
938—dc21

2355 9395 6/00

99-36891
CIP

©2000 by Greenhaven Press, Inc.
P.O. Box 289009, San Diego, CA 92198-9009

Printed in the U.S.A.

Contents

Chapter 1: A Long History of Disunity

Chapter 4: The Coming of Rome and Downfall of the Greeks

time only the Ptolemaic Kingdom remained, a third-rate power in a world dominated by Rome. Against all odds, Cleopatra, last of the Ptolemies, made a bold bid for world power; unsuccessful, she gained instead another realm—that of legend.

Epilogue: The Survival of Greek Culture

The demise of independent Greek political states in antiquity did not signal the end of Greek influence; for the Romans, who were mightily impressed by Greek culture, absorbed it and passed it on to future ages. In this way, the Greek spirit became an intrinsic part of Western civilization's fabric.

Foreword

Certain past events stand out as pivotal, as having effects and outcomes that change the course of history. These events are often referred to as turning points. Historian Louis L. Snyder provides this useful definition:

> A turning point in history is an event, happening, or stage which thrusts the course of historical development into a different direction. By definition a turning point is a great event, but it is even more—a great event with the explosive impact of altering the trend of man's life on the planet.

History's turning points have taken many forms. Some were single, brief, and shattering events with immediate and obvious impact. The invasion of Britain by William the Conqueror in 1066, for example, swiftly transformed that land's political and social institutions and paved the way for the rise of the modern English nation. By contrast, other single events were deemed of minor significance when they occurred, only later recognized as turning points. The assassination of a little-known European nobleman, Archduke Franz Ferdinand, on June 28, 1914, in the Bosnian town of Sarajevo was such an event; only after it touched off a chain reaction of political-military crises that escalated into the global conflict known as World War I did the murder's true significance become evident.

Other crucial turning points occurred not in terms of a few hours, days, months, or even years, but instead as evolutionary developments spanning decades or even centuries. One of the most pivotal turning points in human history, for instance—the development of agriculture, which replaced nomadic hunter-gatherer societies with more permanent settlements—occurred over the course of many generations. Still other great turning points were neither events nor developments, but rather revolutionary new inventions and innovations that significantly altered social customs and ideas, military tactics, home life, the spread of knowledge, and the human condition in general. The developments of writing, gunpowder, the printing press, antibiotics, the electric light, atomic energy, television, and the computer, the last two of which have recently ushered in the world-altering information age, represent only some of these innovative turning points.

Each anthology in the Greenhaven Turning Points in World History series presents a group of essays chosen for their accessibility. The anthology's structure also enhances this accessibility. First, an introductory essay provides a general overview of the principal events and figures involved, placing the topic in its historical context. The essays that follow explore various aspects in more detail, some targeting political trends and consequences, others social, literary, cultural, and/or technological ramifications, and still others pivotal leaders and other influential figures. To aid the reader in choosing the material of immediate interest or need, each essay is introduced by a concise summary of the contributing writer's main themes and insights.

In addition, each volume contains extensive research tools, including a collection of excerpts from primary source documents pertaining to the historical events and figures under discussion. In the anthology on the French Revolution, for example, readers can examine the works of Rousseau, Voltaire, and other writers and thinkers whose championing of human rights helped fuel the French people's growing desire for liberty; the French *Declaration of the Rights of Man and Citizen*, presented to King Louis XVI by the French National Assembly on October 2, 1789; and eyewitness accounts of the attack on the royal palace and the horrors of the Reign of Terror. To guide students interested in pursuing further research on the subject, each volume features an extensive bibliography, which for easy access has been divided into separate sections by topic. Finally, a comprehensive index allows readers to scan and locate content efficiently. Each of the anthologies in the Greenhaven Turning Points in World History series provides students with a complete, detailed, and enlightening examination of a crucial historical watershed.

Introduction: Disunity and the Decline of the Greeks

From the outset, it must be understood that when discussing the decline and fall of ancient Greece, the term "Greece" refers to a general geographic region, and also a civilization, not to a country. At no time in antiquity (ancient times) was Greece a unified nation in the modern sense. Instead, mainland Greece and various neighboring Aegean and Mediterranean islands and coasts were divided into hundreds of small, independent city-states (and later several larger kingdoms), each of which viewed itself as a separate nation. And in fact, it was principally the very inability of these states to unite into a strong nation that brought about their eventual downfall.

Modern historians have long speculated about why the Greeks so stubbornly failed to unite. Some have suggested that Greece's geography played a major role. Because it is riddled by rugged mountains and numerous islands, physically it is naturally divided into many small regions; and according to this view, the localized nature of these regions promoted the growth of not only small city-states, but also a fierce spirit of independence. Other scholars point to the Greeks' intense devotion to competition. "The Greeks were one of the most competitive peoples in history," writes historian Robert J. Littman.

> Everything was made into a contest, from athletics to the great drama festivals. . . . Competition was formalized in the great *agones*, public festivals at which competitors contended. . . . Much of the competition, however, was non-productive. . . . The Greeks regarded any kind of defeat as disgraceful, regardless of circumstances. . . . Egoism, the need to excel, to gain honor and glory at the expense of others, helped to produce a society incapable of unity. The individual would not risk sacrificing himself for the city-state, nor the city-state for the welfare of Greece.[1]

The Greeks' competitiveness may have been one reason why the ancient city-states never formed a strong, central union.

Whatever kept the Greeks from forming a strong, centralized nation, their continued disunity led them to fight among themselves almost incessantly. These conflicts culminated in the disastrous Peloponnesian War (431–404 B.C.), which engulfed and exhausted most of the Greek world. In retrospect, this watershed event can be seen as the beginning of the decline of Greek power and independence in the Mediterranean. In the two turbulent centuries that followed, the dominance of city-states in Greek affairs gave way to that of large monarchies. Having failed to learn the lesson of unity, these states, too, quarreled among themselves, leaving the Greek sphere open to outside aggression.

Sure enough, in the second and first centuries B.C., Rome, master of the Italian peninsula, picked off the Greek states one by one and absorbed them into its expanding empire. It was, therefore, the Romans, and not the Greeks, who subsequently went on to unite the whole Mediterranean world into a vast commonwealth administered by one central government. And for this reason, the end of independent Greek political power in antiquity marks one of history's pivotal turning points.

The Struggle for Supremacy

The Peloponnesian War, which initiated Greece's decline, was no sudden or isolated event. Rivalry and warfare among the city-states, which had been going on for centuries, began to increase in intensity in the mid-fifth century B.C., shortly after the close of the Persian Wars. The Persians, whose empire, centered in what is now Iran, was then the world's largest and most powerful, had invaded Greece in 490 and again in 480. In both instances, much smaller Greek armies or navies had decisively defeated the invaders. These momentous victories had instilled in the Greeks a tremendous sense of accomplishment and self-confidence, which in turn

Although geographically close, the Greek city-states were separated by rugged terrain.

had helped to inspire the cultural renaissance of that century for which they are justly renowned.[2]

Another outcome of the Greco-Persian conflicts was the increased power and prestige of the two Greek states that had led the resistance and largely engineered the victories—Athens and Sparta. Athens (located on the Attic Peninsula, on the mainland's eastern flank) had Greece's strongest navy; while Sparta (in the Peloponnesus, the large peninsula that makes up the mainland's southern third) possessed its most formidable land army. In the wake of the victory over Persia, each of these two states became convinced that it alone should enjoy supremacy in Greece. To this end, Athens swiftly built a maritime empire that at its height included over a hundred city-states. (Though still independent, these states were largely dominated by the Athenians, whose navy ruled the Aegean seaways.) And Sparta responded by forming its own bloc of allies and continually attempting to contain Athenian political ambitions.

By the late 430s, after several decades of mutual distrust and small-scale fighting, each side finally reached a point where it was willing to wage a major war to gain overall supremacy. "The preparations of both the combatants were in every department in the last state of perfection," wrote Thucydides, the contemporary Greek historian who chronicled the war,

> and [I] could see the rest of the Hellenic [Greek] race taking sides in the quarrel; those who delayed doing so at once having it in contemplation. Indeed, this was the greatest movement [event] yet known in history. . . . If both sides nourished the boldest hopes and put forth their utmost strength for the war, this was only natural. Zeal is always at its height at the commencement of an undertaking; and on this particular occasion the Peloponnesus and Athens were both full of young men whose inexperience made them eager to take up arms, while the rest of Greece stood straining with excitement at the conflict of its leading cities.[3]

The so-called "great war" ended up dragging on for twenty-seven grueling years and ultimately proved ruinous for all involved. Athens went down to defeat in 404, ending its

The ruins of the Parthenon stand as a reminder of the Golden Age of Athens.

golden age, in which it had expanded its democracy (established in 508); constructed the magnificent Parthenon and other temples atop its Acropolis; and enjoyed the hegemony (dominance) of much of Greece.

The Spartan and Theban Hegemonies

The great war had caused widespread death and destruction, to be sure. But a far worse consequence was that those who had waged it had failed to learn from it the lesson that continued disunity and rivalry was futile and dangerous. The result was that the fourth century B.C. proved to be a period of further war-weariness and also political decline for the Greek city-states. At first, because it had defeated Athens, Sparta dominated Greek affairs. But the Spartans failed to maintain their hegemony of Greece, partly because they were not able administrators, and also because they were insensitive and heavy-handed in their dealings with other states. Athens responded to what most Greeks viewed as overt Spartan aggressions by building up another bloc of its own allies. And soon the two sides were at each other's throats again.

It was not Athens, however, that ended the Spartan hegemony. In the 370s, a brilliant military innovator named Epaminondas rose to prominence in Thebes (located a bit over thirty miles northwest of Athens). Epaminondas was also known for his exceedingly noble character. The first-century B.C. Greek historian Diodorus Siculus said of him:

> He surpassed his contemporaries not only in skill and experience in the art of war, but in reasonableness and generosity as well. For among the generation of Epaminondas were famous men. . . . If you should compare the qualities of these with the generalship and reputation of Epaminondas, you would find [his] qualities far superior. . . . For in strength of body and eloquence of speech . . . elevation of mind . . . fairness, and, most of all, in courage and shrewdness in the art of war, he far surpassed them all.[4]

Under the guidance of Epaminondas, Thebes overhauled its military and surprised everyone by crushing Sparta's army at Leuctra, west of Thebes, in 371. Soon afterward, the Thebans invaded the Peloponnesus, where the political climate now changed drastically. Supported by Thebes, most of the Peloponnesian cities, which had long followed Sparta out of fear, threw out their Spartan-backed regimes and instituted new governments (usually some form of democracy).

But Thebes did not retain its leading place in Greek affairs for long. Less than a decade after gaining it, the Thebans fought a major battle at Mantinea, in the central Peloponnesus, against an unlikely (and decidedly temporary) coalition led by Athens and Sparta. Epaminondas was killed; Theban influence rapidly waned; and afterwards, according to the Athenian historian Xenophon (pronounced ZEN-uh-phon), "There was even more uncertainty and confusion in Greece . . . than there had been previously."[5]

Philip and Alexander

Decades of bickering, war, destruction, and shifting political alliances had left the major mainland city-states exhausted, weakened, and vulnerable to outside attack. This time, however, the threat did not come from Asia, as it had in the previous century, but from Macedonia, a kingdom in extreme northern Greece. Its tribes had themselves long been disunited and militarily weak. The city-state Greeks had generally viewed them contemptuously as backwoods types living outside the mainstream of the civilized world and for the most part had ignored them, which turned out to be a grave mistake. In the mid-fourth century B.C., just as Theban power was on the decline and exhaustion and confusion reigned in southern Greece, a brilliant and capable young man ascended the Macedonian throne. He was Philip II, who in an amazingly short time united the Macedonian tribes, forming a strong nation with a powerful army.

Eventually, Philip set his sights on making himself master of all the Greeks. Over the course of several years, he employed a highly effective combination of diplomacy, deceit, and naked aggression to seize large tracts of territory in northern and central Greece. In the summer of 338, accompanied by his eighteen-year-old son, Alexander (who would later be called "the Great"), he marched his army to Chaeronea, northwest of Thebes. There, the Macedonian forces clashed with those of a hastily organized coalition led by Athens and Thebes. In the face of Philip's superior strategy and tactics (some of them borrowed from Epaminondas), most of the allies eventually broke ranks and fled, Philip's victory was complete, and the Greek city-states now faced the dawn of a new political order.

In the wake of Chaeronea, Philip attempted to create a confederacy of Greek states, in effect to unite the Greeks at last into a single political unit (although it was intended to be an alliance of small nations rather than a single large nation). In September 338, Philip presided over an assembly attended by delegates from many mainland and island city-states (the principal absentee being Sparta, which remained stubbornly aloof). "The Greek states were to make a common peace . . . with one another," noted classical historian Peter Green explains, and constitute themselves into a federal Hellenic League. This league would take joint decisions by means of a federal council . . . on which each state would be represented according to its size and military importance. . . . Simultaneously, the league was to form a separate alliance with Macedonia, though Macedonia itself would not be a member. This treaty was to be made with "Philip and his descendants" in perpetuity [forever]. The king would act as "leader" (hegemon) of the league's joint forces, a combined civil and military post designed to provide for the general security of Greece.[6]

The city-states also found themselves swept along in the tide of Philip's grandiose plans for invading Persia. In a twist of fate, however, he was assassinated in 336 and his son ended up leading this fateful expedition.

In 334, Alexander crossed the Hellespont (the narrow strait separating northern Greece from Asia Minor, what is now Turkey) at the head of a small but, as it turned out, very formidable army. The first of his long series of victories and territorial gains occurred at the Granicus River, in northwestern Asia Minor, where he encountered an army commanded by some of the local Persian governors. In the following few years, he twice defeated the Persian king, Darius III; besieged and captured the island city of Tyre; liberated Egypt (which had been under Persian rule for two centuries) and there established a new city in the Nile Delta, naming it Alexandria after himself; occupied the three Persian capitals—Babylon, Susa, and Persepolis; and continued eastward, eventually reaching India. He may have gone on to further conquests. However, his exhausted troops, many of whom had not seen home and family in many years, mutinied and demanded that he turn back. This proved to be the end of the road for Alexander, for shortly after returning to Persia, he died, at the age of thirty-three, in Babylon on June 10, 323.

Wars of the Successors

In just ten years, Alexander had conquered the vast Persian domain, in the process spreading Greek language, political administration, and culture to many parts of the Near East.

But the huge kingdom he had created was immediately torn asunder as his leading generals and governors faced off and eventually came to death grips. Alexander's rightful heirs (a retarded half-brother, a son by his Persian wife, Roxane, and his mother, Olympias) were in time swept aside and murdered; and for the next forty-odd years, these men, who came to be called the *Diadochoi* ("Successors"), waged almost unrelenting war.

Among the most powerful and/or successful of the Successors were Perdiccas (ca.360–321 B.C.), whom Alexander had given his royal seal and who, likely hoping to control the empire himself, tried but failed to hold it together; Perdiccas's trusted lieutenant, Eumenes (ca.360–316); Antipater (ca.398–319), who commanded Macedonia and Greece in the years immediately following Alexander's death; Cassander (ca.355–297), Antipater's son, who ruled these domains after his father's death; Lysimachus (ca.361–281), who tried to carve out a section of Asia Minor for himself; Antigonus, "the One-Eyed" (ca.382–301), the first of the Successors to take the title of king; his colorful but brutal son, Demetrius, "the Besieger" (336–283), who for a while controlled Athens and other parts of mainland Greece; Seleucus (ca.358–281), who created his territorial niche in Syria and other sectors of the Near East; and Ptolemy (pronounced TAW-luh-mee; ca.360–284), who became master of Egypt. During the many, complex, and, to modern eyes, confusing rounds of rivalry and warfare among these men, they frequently made, broke, and shifted alliances. And all the while they and their armies spread fear, chaos, and destruction throughout the eastern Mediterranean–Near Eastern sphere.

Finally, by about 280, three major new Greek kingdoms had emerged in that sphere. These so-called successor-states included the Ptolemaic Kingdom, founded by Ptolemy, consisting mainly of Egypt and parts of nearby Palestine; the Seleucid Kingdom, established by Seleucus, encompassing the lands north and west of the Persian Gulf—the heart of the old Persian Empire—and parts of Asia Minor; and the Macedonian Kingdom, created by Antigonus Gonatas (grandson of Antigonus the One-Eyed), made up mostly of Macedonia and portions of the Greek mainland. Among the smaller but still influential states of the day were the kingdoms of Pergamum (in western Asia Minor) and Epirus (in extreme northwestern Greece); the Aetolian League (in western Greece) and Achaean League (in the Peloponnesus), federations of cities that had banded together for mutual protection; and some powerful independent city-states, notably the island of Rhodes (off the coast of Asia Minor) and Byzantium (on the Propontis, the waterway on the far side of the Hellespont).

The "Inhabited World"

Historians refer to these realms as Hellenistic, meaning "Greek-like," since their societies often consisted of various Eastern languages, customs, and ideas overlaid by a veneer of Greek ones. Likewise, the period lasting from Alexander's death in 323 B.C. to the death of the last Hellenistic ruler, Cleopatra VII, in 30 B.C., is called the Hellenistic Age. Historically speaking, this era, the last period of major Greek political independence in antiquity, was the hinge, so to speak, between the Greek Mediterranean domination of the past and the Roman domination of the future. Yet, as the prolific historian Michael Grant points out, the age

> must emphatically not be seen as just the forerunner of the Roman epoch [era], any more than it must be seen as a sort of appendix of classical Greece. For the epoch was rich and fertile in versatile creations which, despite all debts to the past, were very much its own.[7]

Indeed, it is perhaps ironic that, though Greek autonomy ended in Hellenistic times, it was an era of widespread experimentation, new horizons, and notable achievement in the arts, sciences, and numerous social institutions. Greek scientists, for example, especially those working in Alexandria, which had become the known world's foremost commercial and intellectual center, made significant strides in anatomy, astronomy, and other fields. One of these men, Eratosthenes, correctly measured the earth's circumference to within one percent of the value accepted by modern science.[8] This spirit of searching for the underlying truth of things found further expression in the arts, as poets, sculptors, and

During the Hellenistic Age, Greek scholars made notable achievements in the sciences, especially astronomy.

painters achieved levels of vividness and realism unknown in prior ages. The new spirit also generated, in Grant's words,

> a greatly enhanced interest in the individual human being and his mind and emotions, an interest given vigorous expression by biographers and portrait artists. And this concern for the individual was extended not only to men but to women, whose position in society, literature and art underwent an unprecedented transformation that was one of the most remarkable evolutionary changes of the age.[9]

Perhaps more remarkable still was the transformation of society itself. Some scholars have suggested that Alexander dreamed of creating a sort of "world society," or "brotherhood of humanity," in which all people under his rule, regardless of ancestry, would share a universal culture. Whether or not this accurately reflects his vision, what might be described as a modified version of such a society emerged in the eastern Mediterranean and Near East during the Hellenistic Age. This was the *oikoumene* (pronounced ee-koo-MEH-nee), or "inhabited world." Almost all of the Hellenistic realms, whether large or small, bore common political, economic, and cultural institutions that blended Greek and Near Eastern elements; so a traveler might feel more or less at home anywhere he or she went in the Hellenistic sphere.

Repeating the Same Mistakes

It would be a mistake, however, to view this cultural blend, or Hellenistic society in general, as equal, fair, or classless. It was, in fact, a highly classist society that heavily favored Greeks, which is not surprising considering that Greeks established and controlled virtually all the states in the *oikoumene*. Greek Koine (a dialect that developed from the Attic, or Athenian, dialect) became the "lingua franca," the universal language of administration and business; and those who could not speak, read, and write it found it difficult, if not impossible, to get ahead in life. "In Alexandria, Antioch [in Syria], and the great Babylonian center of Seleucia-on-the-Tigris alike," remarks scholar Chester G. Starr, "groups of relatively few Greeks constituted an upper crust much as did the English masters of Bombay, Singapore, or Hong Kong in the nineteenth century."[10] In his definitive study of the Hellenistic world, Peter Green elaborates:

> In all instances what the Successors set up were enclaves of Greco-Macedonian culture in an alien world, governmental ghettos for a ruling elite. When we come to assess the ubiquitous [existing seemingly everywhere] Greek temples, Greek theaters, Greek gymnasia, Greek mosaics, and Greek-language inscriptions scattered through the *oikoumene,* we should never forget that it was for the Hellenized Macedonian ruling minority and its Greek supporters . . . that such home-from-home luxuries . . . were . . . provided.[11]

One might assume that, since the various Hellenistic rulers, aristocrats, and their supporters were all cut from the same cloth, so to speak, they would get along with one another. But the political reality of the era was exactly the opposite. The Hellenistic Greeks proceeded to repeat the same fatal mistake the city-states had; in short, they constantly argued and fought among themselves. The reasons for their disputes were many and complex. But the principal goal of the great monarchies, one that continually led to conflict, was to keep open and control the communication and travel lines to and from the Aegean Sea. This was partly to ensure a steady flow of Greek administrators, colonists, and mercenary (hired) soldiers from Greece. (Hired armies were especially important, for all of the Hellenistic rulers used them and the ready availability of mercenary generals became one of the chief hallmarks of the age.) It was also essential from an economic standpoint to have access to the Mediterranean ends of the great trade routes that ran west to east through the *oikoumene;* so when one ruler tried to monopolize those routes, one or more of the others moved to stop him.

Pyrrhus's Italian Adventure

Needless to say, the frequent bickering and warfare among the Hellenistic states inevitably reinforced their disunity and led to weakness and vulnerability to an outside power. In the mid-third century B.C., as they squabbled, far to the west that power, Rome, was engaged in its first war against the maritime empire of Carthage (centered in Tunisia, in North Africa). Shortly before, one of the Hellenistic rulers, Pyrrhus of Epirus, had briefly fought the Romans. He had answered a plea for aid from the most prosperous and important of the Greek cities that had for several centuries dotted southern Italy.[12] Tarentum (its Latin name; the Greeks called it Taras), located in the "instep" of the Italian boot, had recently sunk a small fleet of Roman ships that had violated its territorial waters. And the Tarentines feared that Rome would retaliate by sending troops against them.

In crossing to Italy with his army in the spring of 280, Pyrrhus was likely motivated by more than just sympathy for fellow Greeks. His first-century A.D. Greek biographer, Plutarch, attributes the following remarks to him (which Pyrrhus may never have actually said, but which probably summarize what he was thinking at the time):

> If we can conquer the Romans, there is no other Greek or barbarian [non-Greek] city which is a match for us. We shall straightaway become the masters of the whole of Italy. . . . After Italy, [we will take] Sicily, of course. . . . We can make it the spring-board for much greater enterprises. How could we resist making an attempt upon Libya and Carthage?[13]

Motivated by these dreams of conquest, Pyrrhus met the Romans in battle at Heraclea, not far from Tarentum, and scored a victory. But it was a costly one; for the Romans showed themselves to be stubborn and courageous fighters and slew some 4,000 of Pyrrhus's men, over a sixth of his army. He fought the Romans again the following year at Ausculum, in southeastern Italy, and won again. But this time his losses were so great that he is said to have joked: "One more victory like that over the Romans will destroy us completely!"[14] Ever since, an excessively costly win has been called a "Pyrrhic victory."

After fighting still another costly battle against the Romans in 275, Pyrrhus decided to cut his losses and return to Epirus. The failure of his Italian adventure had extremely ominous overtones; the fact that he, one of the greatest Greek generals of that or any day, could not decisively defeat the Romans did not bode well for either Carthage's or Greece's future.

The Greek Phalanx Versus the Roman Legion

Indeed, just eleven years after Pyrrhus had vacated Italy, Rome engaged and defeated Carthage in the First Punic War (264–241 B.C.), the most destructive conflict the world had yet seen. The Second Punic War (218–202) soon followed. In this truly stupendous conflict, Macedonia's king, Philip V, made the mistake of allying himself with the ultimate loser—Carthage. (The Romans later referred to their involvement with him as the First Macedonian War, a subconflict of the greater war with Carthage.) And just two years after their victory, the Romans were ready to punish Philip for his interference in their affairs. In this way, Rome, which had recently become master of the western Mediterranean sphere, now turned its attention to the Greek states in the sea's eastern sphere.

Largely because these states remained disunited, their fates were virtually sealed. The so-called Second Macedonian War (200–197) was noteworthy because it pitted the Mediterranean world's two most prestigious and feared military systems against each other. (Pyrrhus's battles with Rome had done the same, but because they had ended in a draw, more or less, they were seen as inconclusive.) The Greeks employed a unique battle formation known as the Macedonian phalanx, consisting of thousands of soldiers arrayed in ranks, one behind the other. Each man in the front rank held a long spear, or battle pike, and the men in the next few succeeding rear ranks held increasingly longer pikes, so that the tips projected outward from the front of the formation. The result was an impenetrable and frightening mass of spear points that resembled a giant porcupine with its quills erect. When this formation marched forward, it usually demolished all before it.

By contrast, Rome's armies consisted of legions, groups of about 4,500 to 5,000 soldiers. On the battlefield, each le-

Despite being the most dominant form of land warfare for centuries, the Macedonian phalanx proved ineffective against more mobile Roman legions.

gion broke down into smaller units called maniples, having from 60 to 120 men each, which could move around in various ways to form strategic patterns, the most common resembling a checkerboard. Each individual maniple or group of maniples was less formidable than a large Greek phalanx. Yet the Roman units could move back, forward, and around quickly at a commander's order, giving the Roman army a degree of flexibility that the stiff, monolithic phalanx lacked. According to the second-century B.C. Greek historian Polybius:

> Nothing can withstand the frontal assault of the phalanx so long as it retains its characteristic formation and strength. What then is the factor which enables the Romans to win the battle and causes those who use the phalanx to fail? The answer is that . . . [the phalanx can only operate effectively on flat ground unencumbered by obstacles] . . . and [also that] the phalanx soldier cannot operate either in smaller units or singly, whereas the Roman formation is highly flexible. Every Roman soldier, once he . . . goes into action, can adapt

himself equally well to any place or time and meet an attack from any quarter.[15]

The final, decisive battle of the Macedonian War took place in 197 at Cynoscephalae ("Dog's Heads"), in Thessaly in central Greece. The outcome fully confirmed Polybius's astute analysis and showed that the Greek system, which had largely dominated Mediterranean land warfare for centuries, had become outmoded. First, the ground was uneven, which seriously hindered the cohesiveness of Philip's phalanx. And although the troops on his right wing overcame the Romans they faced, a resourceful Roman officer led several maniples around to the rear of the phalanx, outflanking it. Unable to wheel their huge pikes around quickly enough to protect their backs, the Greek troops were slaughtered in their ranks.

Dreams of Empire Dashed

The results of the Greco-Roman battles and wars of the ensuing decades were hauntingly similar. In 189 B.C., the Romans soundly defeated the ruler of the Seleucid Kingdom, Antiochus III, at Magnesia (in Asia Minor); the Third Macedonian War (171–168), against Philip's son, Perseus, ended with the abolition of the Macedonian Kingdom (Rome annexed the area as a new province in 148); and in 146, after a courageous but futile military resistance by the Achaean League, the Romans brutally destroyed the once great city of Corinth as an object lesson to other Greeks who might dare to rebel.

Meanwhile, the rulers of the Ptolemaic kingdom wisely submitted to Roman domination without a fight. For the next century, Egypt remained independent, but was in reality no more than a Roman client state (or vassal), allowed to pursue its own local affairs as long as it did Rome's bidding in the international scene. The Ptolemies of the first century B.C., who were weak, pale shadows of the formidable Greek general who had founded their dynasty, did their best to appease Rome and maintain their autonomy. But Egypt, with its vast stores of grain and royal treasure, increasingly became a prize coveted by the ambitious leading Romans of the day, who were vying for mastery of Rome's domains. Cleopatra VII, sister of the young and inept Ptolemy XIII, boldly allied herself with two of these men—Julius Caesar (who was assassinated in 44) and Marcus Antonius (Mark Antony).

For a while, Antony and Cleopatra seemed on the verge of consolidating the whole East, including large portions of Alexander's former empire and the now defunct Hellenistic monarchies. Had they succeeded, the course of Western history would undoubtedly have been quite different. As it was, however, a third powerful Roman, Octavian (later Augustus Caesar, the first Roman emperor), decisively defeated them at Actium, in western Greece, in 31. With her ally/lover dead and her dreams of empire dashed, the famous queen, last of the Ptolemies, as well as the last Hellenistic ruler, committed suicide shortly afterward.

Back in 213 B.C., when the Romans were fighting Carthage and positioning themselves for Mediterranean mastery, a Greek orator, Agelaus of Aetolia, had recognized the potential danger and warned:

> It would be best of all if the Greeks never went to war with one another, if they could regard it as the greatest gift of the gods for them to speak with one voice, and could join hands like men who are crossing a river; in this way they could unite to repulse the incursions of the barbarians and to preserve themselves and their cities.[16]

At the time, the Hellenistic world's great powers could have and certainly should have joined forces, as Agelaus urged, and presented a united front against the Roman threat. But his warning went unheeded. And though the Romans absorbed much of Greece's cultural legacy and subsequently passed it on to later ages, ensuring its survival, independent Greek rule in antiquity died with Cleopatra.

Notes

1. *The Greek Experiment: Imperialism and Social Conflict, 800–400 B.C.* London: Thames and Hudson, 1974, pp. 13–14, 20.

2. The Persian Wars were themselves an important historical turning point because they prevented Europe from coming under Asian domination, and thereby made possible the development of Greco-Roman civilization and the

Western cultures that grew from it. For a concise overview of the Greco-Persian conflicts, see Don Nardo, *The Battle of Marathon*. San Diego: Lucent Books, 1996; an excellent, more detailed account is Peter Green, *The Greco-Persian Wars*. Berkeley: University of California Press, 1996.

3. *The Peloponnesian War*, published as *The Landmark Thucydides: A Comprehensive Guide to the Peloponnesian War*. Trans. Richard Crawley, ed. Robert B. Strassler. New York: Simon & Schuster, 1996, pp. 3, 93.

4. *Library of History*. 12 vols. Various trans. Cambridge, MA: Harvard University Press, 1962–1967, vol. 7, pp. 197–199.

5. *Hellenica*, published as *A History of My Times*. Trans. Rex Warner. New York: Penguin Books, 1979, p. 403.

6. *Alexander of Macedon, 356–323 B.C.: A Historical Biography*. Berkeley: University of California Press, 1991, p. 86.

7. *From Alexander to Cleopatra: The Hellenistic World*. New York: Charles Scribner's Sons, 1982, p. xiii.

8. Eratosthenes of Cyrene (ca.276–194 B.C.) served for many years as the chief librarian of Alexandria's famous university, the Museum. For an account of how he measured the earth, as well as other achievements of Hellenistic scientists, see Don Nardo, *Greek and Roman Science*. San Diego: Lucent Books, 1997.

9. *From Alexander to Cleopatra*, p. xiii.

10. *A History of the Ancient World*. New York: Oxford University Press, 1991, p. 408.

11. *Alexander to Actium: The Historical Evolution of the Hellenistic Age*. Berkeley: University of California Press, 1990, p. 319.

12. These cities, including Sybaris, Croton, Rhegium, and Tarentum, among many others, had been established in an intensive burst of Greek colonization spanning the period ca.750–550 B.C. In Pyrrhus's day, some were larger, and all were more cultured, than Rome.

13. *Life of Pyrrhus*, in *The Age of Alexander: Nine Greek Lives by Plutarch*. Trans. Ian Scott-Kilvert. New York: Penguin, 1973, p. 399.

14. Plutarch, *Pyrrhus*, in *Age of Alexander*, p. 409.

15. *Histories*, published as *Polybius: The Rise of the Roman Empire*. Trans. Ian Scott-Kilvert. New York: Penguin Books, 1979, pp. 511–13.

16. Quoted in Polybius, *Histories*, trans. Scott-Kilvert, pp. 299–300.

Chapter 1

A Long History of Disunity

Was Disunity Part of the Greek Character?

Robert J. Littman

In the final analysis, disunity, more than any other single factor, contributed to the decline and fall of the independent Greek states of antiquity. As explained here by University of Hawaii scholar Robert J. Littman, historians have long speculated about why the Greeks found it so difficult to achieve any kind of lasting unity. He explores the various possible factors, including geography (which played at least some role in the development of the polis, or city-state), the intense Greek competitive spirit, the prevalence of extreme personal narcissism (conceit) and ambition, and antagonism between the sexes. Ultimately, all or none of these factors may have contributed to the Greeks' inability to get along. What is certain is that disunity was ingrained in them.

Historians of ancient Greece have tended to dwell on its achievements, on the legacy of ideas it handed down to Europe, on its culture and civilization and on the contribution of Athens to political thought. . . .

But a one-sided emphasis on the Greek cultural legacy is apt to obscure other aspects of Greek experience, and there is as much to be learned from a critical analysis of Greek society—from studying the problems with which it had to cope and seeing how far it came up with valid answers, and, where it did not, why not—as there is from the more conventional attempt to allot it a place in the development of 'Western tradition'. . . .

Anyone approaching classical Greece in this way is at once confronted by a great paradox. . . . Politically the Greek city state—the political unit in which [the Greek] spirit was born—was ultimately a failure. Its history is one of dissent and disunity, of war between Greek cities and within the cities themselves. During the ninth and eighth centuries BC the polls flourished as a kinship-based agricultural society, divided into aristocrats and peasants. So long as trade and commerce were minimal the fragmentation and factionalism which existed did not prevent the polls from being an effective unit. But in the late eighth and early seventh centuries rapid increases in the size of population and the rise of trade forced the polis out of its isolation; it could no longer function efficiently as an individual agricultural state, cut off from its neighbours. However, the polls had little flexibility. As a unicellular organism, incapable of growth except by subdivision, it could reproduce indefinitely; but its offspring could not combine with it to form a united creature. Consequently it could not successfully adapt to a changing world.

Economic and social developments in Greece during the seventh and sixth centuries plunged the polis into political and social chaos. The fifth century saw the beginnings of new forms of government, which transcended the polis and were capable of uniting several states: the Athenian empire and the Peloponnesian League, to be followed in the fourth century by Panhellenism and further attempts at union through powerful leagues. These experiments failed: disunity was so ingrained that even the descending armies of Philip of Macedon could not induce the Greek city states to stand together. Unification had to come from without, imposed by Philip and after him Alexander. Even then, a truly stable unity did not come to Greece until the country was garrisoned by Rome in 146 BC.

Was Geography a Factor?

The disunity of Greece has been explained by many theories, but none is altogether satisfactory. Many have suggested that the geography of the land was a major factor in preventing unity. Greek settlements extended through Asia Minor, the islands of the Aegean and mainland Greece. The coast of the entire area is jagged and the land broken by bays and gulfs; the interior is full of mountains and mountainous districts, producing many small separated regions. This physical fragmentation is believed to have prompted the development of highly individual city states.

Though such a view is attractive, it is simplistic. Geography doubtless played some part in Greece's political development, but the extent of its influence is easy to overrate. The patterns of Greek settlement throw some light on the question. Regardless of the nature of the land, wherever Greeks settled they were disunited. The colonies they founded in southern Italy, such as Croton and Tarentum, became independent states. Yet when Rome expanded south in the third century BC she had little difficulty in welding southern Italy into a cohesive area. Step by step, Rome assimilated and incorporated first Italy and then the entire Mediterranean into the Roman state. Inherently the Romans unified and the Greeks produced only disunity. A further flaw in the geographical theory is the fact that it was in just those regions where the physical barriers were minimal that the polis flourished best, while in the more mountainous regions, such as Arcadia, it was slow in developing. Many other lands and countries fragmented by nature never formed a polis system.

The Competitive Spirit

Furthermore, though geography may have encouraged fragmentation in Greece and the nature of the land may be consistent with the formation of many independent states, still unexplained is the constant strife and dissension that was ingrained in every Greek city, where class struggles, civil war, treason, betrayal and constant contention were the norm. Many factors contributed to disunity. It is beyond the scope of this study to analyse the Greek character, but one facet of it stands out as at least partly responsible for disunity, both on a national level and on that of the individual city. The Greeks were one of the most competitive peoples in history. Everything was made into a contest, from athletics to the great drama festivals, such as the Dionysia at Athens, where playwrights vied for prizes. Competition was formalized in the great *agones*, public festivals at which competitors contended. The prizes for victory were generally of symbolic value only, though the victor might incidentally receive rich rewards from his city. According to the historian Herodotus, certain Arcadians who had deserted the Greek cause for the Persian and been brought before Xerxes, King of Persia, were asked what the Greeks were doing at that moment; they replied that they were celebrating the Olympic festival and viewing sports and horse-races. Xerxes then inquired as to the prize. When the Arcadians responded that it was a crown of olive, a Persian broke into the inquisition: 'My god, Mardonius, what sort of men are these against whom you have brought us to fight? They do not compete for money, but for glory.' Usually these competitions were religious in origin, under the patronage of some god. The best known were the Panhellenic athletic contests, the Olympian, Pythian, Nemean and Isthmian Games. The Greeks even competed in singing, in riddle-solving, in staying awake, in dancing.

Much of the competition, however, was nonproductive. The Greeks had a shame culture, rather than a guilt culture. In the former one's sense of worth is entirely determined by the opinion of others, while in the latter an internalized set of standards control behaviour. As in many shame cultures, the Greeks regarded any kind of defeat as disgraceful, regardless of circumstances. Yet no victory was possible unless someone else lost. The glory of winning accrued to the victor from the lost glory of the defeated. The loser could not leave the contest with as much prestige as he entered. Contributing to this contentiousness was the Greek obsession with fame, honour and achievement.

The Struggle for Personal Glory

The competitiveness of the Greeks was rooted in their narcissism, which led them into a continuing struggle for personal glory and fame, as well as for the wealth and power by means of which these were to be acquired. Personal ambition was unquenchable. Such men as the Athenian Alcibiades were paradigmatic [illustrative] of the Greek ideal and of the tragic self-destructiveness which was inherent in that ideal.

During the Peloponnesian War, for example, to create opportunities for his own self-aggrandizement, Alcibiades encouraged Athens to send him to open a second front with the Sicilian Expedition at a time when renewed war with Sparta might erupt at any moment. Then one night, shortly before the Expedition was to depart for Sicily, the faces and phalli of the small stone statues called 'herms', which stood in front of many houses, were found to have been mutilated. . . .

His involvement in the ensuing accusations of sacrilege caused Alcibiades to be relieved of his command of the Sicilian venture, whereupon, his sense of personal worth violated, he deserted to Sparta to fight against Athens. After seeking glory in this arena for a time, however, he left Sparta for Persia, and finally returned to Athens. But he quit Athens once again, this time to fight as a privateer in the Thracian region, in which capacity he made one last attempt to regain the honour he desperately sought by coming to the aid of his native city. His proffered help was rejected, however, and within a short time, while on his way to Persia, he was killed (at the instigation of the Spartans, who wanted him out of the way as an ever possible saviour of Athens).

Alcibiades was a loyal Athenian, but loyal to Athens only when Alcibiades was running its affairs. The same motivation is seen in the actions of the oligarchs at Athens, who in 404 BC preferred to betray their city to Sparta rather than see democrats rule it. Betrayal and treason were national pastimes of the Greeks. When deposed, Hippias, tyrant of Athens, went over to the Persians and fought with them at the battle of Marathon against Athens and Greece. When Demaratus, King of Sparta, was expelled by his co-monarch, he fled to Persia and aided invading Persian armies against his homeland. Themistocles, who had been the architect of the Persian defeat in the Persian War, eventually deserted Athens for Persia, where he enjoyed a successful career. 'I fear the Greeks, even bearing gifts' had much basis in reality.

The Greeks were obsessively concerned with the admiration and approval of their peers. This fostered a character which was vain, boastful, ambitious, envious and vindictive. Above all the arousal of envy and the obtaining of revenge were esteemed most highly. Thucydides, the historian of the Peloponnesian War, observes in connection with civil strife:

> Words had to change their ordinary meaning and to take that which was now given them. Reckless audacity came to be considered the courage of a loyal ally; prudent hesitation, specious cowardice; moderation was held to be a cloak for unmanliness; the ability to see all sides of a question, a sign of incapacity to act on any. Frantic violence became the attribute of manliness. . . . Revenge also was held of more account than self-preservation. Oaths of reconciliation . . . only held good so long as no other weapon was at hand; but, when opportunity offered, he who first ventured to seize it and to take his enemy off his guard thought this perfidious vengeance sweeter than an open one, since, considerations of safety apart, success by treachery won him the palm of superior intelligence. Indeed it is generally the case that honest men are readier to call rogues clever than simpletons honest. . . . The cause of all these evils was the lust for rule arising from greed and ambition.

Mothers and Sons

It has recently been suggested by Philip Slater in *The Glory of Hera* (Boston, 1968) that narcissism in Greek society may have been a product of the family structure. Women, together with slaves, were considered inferior by nature, as Aristotle so bluntly put it. Consequently they were relegated to child-bearing and domestic duties. They had few legal rights, received little or no education, were excluded from male society, and were largely confined to the home. . . . In the house, however, she was supreme: she controlled the women's quarters, the inhabitants of which included the children and slaves.

At a young age the Greek girl passed from her father's house to that of her husband, who had been chosen by her father. Since the Greek male married late and the woman early, a typical bride might be sixteen and her husband thirty. Often a brother-sister instead of a connubial relationship existed between husband and wife. The wife was usually ignored by her husband, whose real love might be public life, business, his male social companions or the *hetairai*, educated courtesans similar in many ways to the Japanese geisha. So Pericles, entranced by the *hetaira* Aspasia, left his wife for her. Slater asserts that the wife could and did take out on her male child the resentment she felt towards her husband. There was great antagonism between the sexes and the mother thus became ambivalent towards her son. She tried to make him a replacement for her husband, but at the same time she made him a scapegoat. She thus at the same time exalted and belittled her son, and fed on and destroyed him. On the one hand she accepted him as a hero and on the other she rejected him. This produced a person overly concerned with his image in the minds of others and with an unstable self-concept: a person who was fearful of women. This fear is reflected in the terrifying and vengeful portraits of women in Greek tragedy and myth, women such as Medea, who murders her children, and Clytemnestra, who kills her husband. Most of the monsters of mythology are earth-born females—the Medusa, Scylla and Charybdis, the Furies. When Zeus decided to punish man because Prometheus had stolen fire, the worst penalty he could devise was 'the damnable race of women . . . a plague with which men must live'. Uranus was castrated by Cronos while he was having intercourse with Gala, who provided her son with the weapon and set the ambush. The Greek man felt that he was a hero or nothing. Pride, prestige and honour were paramount. In short the Greek male became the classic narcissist. . . .

Competition Also Bred Creativity

Egoism, the Greek need to excel, to gain honour and glory at the expense of others, helped to produce a society incapable of unity. The individual would not risk sacrificing himself for the city state, nor the city state for the welfare of all Greece. This facet of Greek character must be regarded as a major contribution to Greek contentiousness [inability to get along].

While the competitive nature of the Greeks may have generated innumerable political problems, it also stimulated creative genius in art, literature, philosophy and science in certain respects never since equalled. The concentration of achievement in fifth- and fourth-century Greece was astounding. Socrates, Plato, Hippocrates, Polycleitus, Praxiteles, Thucydides, Herodotus, Aeschylus, Sophocles and Euripides were all products of Greek society, along with its contentiousness, factionalism, civil wars and disunity.

Many factors encouraged disunity in Greece, among them the social framework and the economic and political patterns of development. The character of the Greeks may have been consonant with disunity, but the cause and effect is impossible to determine. The Romans were superb at organization and unification, yet many centuries after the fall of Rome Italy polarized into numerous powerful city states. Did the 'character' of the Italians change or did different political and socio-economic factors cause the city-state system to develop in Italy? Greek contentiousness and competitiveness contributed to disunity, but at the same time the political, economic and social structure encouraged and fostered those very traits. Thus, while the competitive nature of the Greek character can be considered neither as the cause of Greek disunity, nor necessarily as a direct result of it, their political system formed a fertile culture medium in which contentiousness could breed.

The Devastating Peloponnesian War

Charles Freeman

Charles Freeman, author of several recent, widely-read books about ancient Greece and Rome, begins this overview of the so-called "great war" by examining the Greek historian who chronicled the conflict. Without Thucydides' honest reporting, attention to detail, and vivid writing, Freeman points out, later ages would be left with no record of much of the event that left the Greek world shattered and exhausted. He then goes on to summarize the war's highlights, including the ill-fated Sicilian expedition, Alcibiades' treachery, and Athens's eventual defeat after a decisive Spartan naval victory on the Hellespont.

The Peloponnesian War began with the declaration of war by Sparta on Athens in 431 BC. . . . Almost immediately Athens suffered a devastating blow when plague broke out. Its spread was aggravated by the large number of country-dwellers who had crowded into the city. It is possible that a quarter of the population died, including, a year later, Pericles himself, probably from an associated disease. This is perhaps the turning-point in the history of Athens, the moment when the optimism expressed so confidently by Pericles begins to fade.

Thucydides' Vivid Account of the War

The full horror of the plague is detailed by the historian Thucydides (c.460–c.399), and it is he who provides the only full history of the war to survive. It is a magnificent one, one of the great intellectual achievements of the fifth century.

Excerpted from *Egypt, Greece, and Rome: Civilizations of the Ancient Mediterranean,* by Charles Freeman. Copyright ©1996 by Charles Freeman. Reprinted with the permission of the Oxford University Press, Inc.

Thucydides was born in Athens but his father's name suggests the family was Thracian in origin. He served in the war, but when, as a commanding general, he failed to save the important Athenian outpost at Amphipolis from capture by Sparta he was exiled. This gave him the opportunity to visit Sparta and to collect the material for his history while the war was still being fought. He completed the story to 411, dying himself some time after 404. The bulk of his book is therefore technically a documentary account rather than a history.

Thucydides writes vividly. Many of his descriptions of the war haunt the reader. (I can still remember, as a halting Greek scholar aged 14, the impact of my first reading of his description of the Sicilian expedition.) His account is so detailed and seemingly authoritative compared to any other that exists that it has set the image of the war for every later generation. Thucydides prides himself on his accuracy, deriding those such as Herodotus who used evidence too loosely. He tries to set out the chronology of the war year by year, in what is almost a scientific way, and with the expressed ambition to provide a narrative that would last. It is only recently that there has been serious critical analysis of Thucydides' approach (whether, for instance, his description of Pericles is not too flattering and that of Cleon too harsh, and whether the expedition to Sicily was quite such a turning-point as he suggests). Nevertheless, no account of the war at all would be possible without his account and it will continue to dominate the source material for the period as well as providing a compulsive read.

No historian, however detached, works without an ideological framework. Thucydides is very much a man of the fifth century. Man is the 'measure of all things', and the gods play no direct part in Thucydides' understanding of how the war happened and the course it followed. He takes it upon himself to penetrate the causes of the war and find the different levels at which antagonism between states was fostered. It is this fascination with the motivations of men, their fears, and the factors which shape decision-making that makes his work so much than mere narrative.

Thucydides has no illusions about human behaviour. No one before and few after have detailed quite so vividly the appalling cruelty with which men can act when under stress. There is little in the history of the twentieth century which would have surprised him. He is particularly adept at showing how words are manipulated by those in power. . . . In the famous debate he reports between the people of Melos, whom Athens was trying to force into her empire, and the Athenians in Book Five of his *History*, he shows how the Athenians ruthlessly exploit their superior strength. 'You know as well as we do,' say the Athenian representatives to the hapless Melians, 'that when these matters are discussed by practical people, the standard of justice depends on the equality of power to compel and that in fact the strong do what they have to do and the weak accept what they have to accept.' (Translation: R. Warner) Reality, suggests Thucydides, is structured by those who have power, an idea with enormous implications for philosophers and social scientists.

Thucydides' detached analysis of the war does not mean that he takes no moral stance. The famous Funeral Oration of Pericles, which extols the self-confidence of the Athenian state, is presented alongside his account of the plague, as if to suggest the fragility of its supremacy. . . . He may have dwelt on the ruthlessness of the Athenians at Melos in 416 (the men of Melos were all executed, their women and children enslaved) so that the Athenian disaster in Sicily which followed could be presented as their just deserts.

The War's Opening Years

The fundamental problem of the war was how a naval power such as Athens could defeat land-locked Sparta and how Sparta, with no effective navy, could hope to capture the well-defended Athens. The first years of the war were marked by a series of ineffective raids on each other's territories. Spartan troops ravaged Attica almost every year (but could never actually storm the city itself, which, protected by its Long Walls, maintained open access to the sea). Athens launched raids on the Peloponnesian coast and one on Megara, an ally of Sparta's. Her hope was perhaps to stimulate the helots [the Spartan serfs, who were essential to Sparta's economy] into revolt and destabilize Sparta's alliances. She also revived her old policy of the 450s and attempted to win control of the plains of Boeotia [the Theban-controlled region lying just north of Attica]. The policy ended in failure after a decisive defeat at the hands of Thebes and her allies at Delium in 424.

In 425, however, the Athenians had a lucky break that ended the stalemate. They managed to capture a group of some 120 Spartans who had become stranded on the island of Sphacteria on the western coast of the Peloponnese when their supporting fleet had been destroyed by the Athenians. The shock effect of the Spartan capitulation was immense, not only on Sparta but on the Greek world. Traditionally Spartans died in battle rather than capitulate and the city's reputation was seriously damaged. Sparta was ready to surrender and would probably have done so immediately if a raid by a Spartan general Brasidas in 524 had not succeeded in capturing a number of Athenian cities along the Chalcidice peninsula and the northern Aegean, including the vital centre of Amphipolis. After an Athenian counter-attack saw the death of Brasidas, both sides were willing to come to terms. The Peace of Nicias was signed in 421 with each side agreeing to give up their gains. Amphipolis, however, chose to stay independent of Athens.

Sparta appeared, at first, the more vulnerable of the two states. Her manpower was in decline, one reason why the loss at Sphacteria was so significant, and her control over the Peloponnese seemed to be faltering. Her ally Corinth refused to sign the treaty when land she had lost was not included in it. Athens, under the influence of a persuasive young aristocrat, Alcibiades, now began interfering directly in the Peloponnese, making treaties of mutual defence with two important cities, Argos and Elis. (Elis oversaw the Olympic Games and even banned Spartan athletes from them in 420.) Alcibiades claimed later that his strategy was to force Sparta to counter-attack and risk losing everything in one battle. The battle came in 418, at Mantineia, but it was a crushing Spartan victory. It was to be another thirty years before the Peloponnesian cities risked confrontation with Sparta again.

The Sicilian Expedition

Athens' hopes of direct control of the Peloponnese now seemed thwarted, and her next move was to launch an expedition to the west, to Sicily and southern Italy, as a means of strengthening her position as a Mediterranean power. Her trading interests in the west were well established and there had been an earlier expedition to Sicily in 427. This new venture was largely the brainchild of Alcibiades. Alcibiades was a complex character, egocentric and ambitious, and shrewd enough to use his status as a successful competitor in the Olympic Games (he won the chariot race in 416) and his personal magnetism to manipulate the Assembly into support for the expedition. Thucydides considered his motives were largely personal ones, the desire to make his name as a military commander and to tap the wealth of the west for himself.

The problems involved in achieving and holding even a foothold in Sicily when the opposition of such wealthy and well-protected cities as Syracuse was bound to be aroused were immense. Yet such was the confidence of Athens that there was even talk of conquering the whole island. . . . Shortly before the fleet sailed, however, the Herms, marble pillars bearing the head of the god Hermes and an erect phallus, which were used as boundary markers and signposts and whose phallic properties were a token of good luck, were mysteriously mutilated. The hysteria that resulted and the witch-hunt that followed in the effort to find the perpetrators shows that Athens remained a deeply superstitious city despite the intellectual revolutions of the fifth century. A number of aristocrats were rounded up (and Alcibiades himself later recalled from Sicily to face trial) but the matter was never satisfactorily explained. The city was left haunted by a sense of ill omen.

The story of the expedition is Thucydides' masterpiece and deserves to be read in his own words. His account starts with a magnificent description of the fleet of 134 triremes and 5,000 hoplites setting off to the west in 415. Once the fleet had arrived in Sicily, however, . . . it soon became clear that conflict with Syracuse was inevitable. There were three commanders, among them Alcibiades himself, and they disagreed as to whether to launch an immediate attack, delay until they had found more allies, or return home after making a show of strength. Alcibiades was then summoned home (to defend himself against a charge of involvement in the mutilation of the Herms), but defected to Sparta instead. His loyalties to his home community turned out to be much shallower than those to himself. By then Athens was in direct conflict with Syracuse, and another of the commanders, Lamarchus, was killed in skirmishing around the city. Nicias, who was left in charge, was the commander least committed to direct confrontation with Syracuse, whose fine position, large resources, and well-defended harbour made her a formidable enemy.

The Horrific Athenian Retreat

In fact, there was a time when Athens might have triumphed. Her fleet gave her the initiative at sea and she captured Syracuse's harbour. The construction of siege walls around the city was put in hand. The morale of Syracuse was, however, transformed when a Spartan commander, Gylippus, managed to infiltrate a small force into the city. Athens lost her chance. Even though reinforcements arrived from home (bringing the total commitment to half of Athens' entire navy) a land attack failed. Eventually the decision was made to evacuate the harbour, whose entrance was now blocked by the Syracusan fleet.

In one of his most gripping passages Thucydides describes the emotional impact of this decisive battle as the Athenian hoplites waited to see if they would be saved:

> As the struggle went on indecisively, the Athenian soldiers revealed the fear in their hearts by the swaying of their bodies; it was a time of agony for them, for escape or destruction seemed every moment just at hand. So long as the issue of the sea-battle was in doubt, you could have heard every kind of sound in one place, the Athenian camp: lamentation, shouting, 'We're winning!', 'We're losing!', all the cries wrung from a great army in great peril. The feelings of the

men on the ships were much the same, until at last, when the battle had gone on for a long time, the Syracusans and their allies routed the Athenians and fell upon them, decisive winners, yelling and cheering, and chased them to the land. And then the Athenian sailors, as many of them as had not been captured afloat, beached their ships wherever they could and poured into the camp. The soldiers were not in two minds any more, but all with one impulse, groaning, wailing, lamenting the outcome of the battle, rallied—some of them close to the ships, others to guard the rest of their defensive wall, while the greater part of them began to think now about themselves, about how they were going to survive.

(Translation: Kenneth Dover)

A final attempt to urge the Athenians to give battle again with their surviving ships was met with mutiny and the only option left was to escape overland. The description Thucydides gives is one of his most gripping and heart-rending. The dead were left unburied. The wounded, desperate at being left, dragged themselves after their comrades as they moved off, overcome themselves by their own shame of betrayal. The plight of the retreating army, without food and with continual harassment by Spartans and Syracusans, was horrific. When they came to water the hoplites were so thirsty they rushed forward to drink even though enemy missiles rained down on them. They lay in a stream drinking what was turning into a mess of mud and blood before the final surrender. The survivors were herded back to Syracuse and then imprisoned in appalling conditions in the quarries which surrounded the city.

Athens Rebounds, the Fighting Continues

There was no doubt that this was a catastrophe. Forty thousand men may have been lost as well as half the city's fleet. Athens' democracy came under severe strain, overthrown in 411 by an oligarchical government of Four Hundred who were in favour of making peace with Sparta. The empire was also in revolt. One rebel, Mytilene, was recaptured but the island of Chios had to be abandoned after a blockade which failed. In 411 Euboea revolted and joined Sparta. However, some historians . . . argue that Thucydides inflated the importance of the Sicilian disaster, partly to create a literary impact. The fact is that Athens was able to continue the war. The Four Hundred were overthrown when they tried to make peace on behalf of Athens and replaced by a semi-democratic government of Five Thousand. The navy remained loyal to the democracy throughout and gradually new ships were built. Despite some defections, the empire survived largely intact. The will to resist remained amazingly strong.

Once again, however, it looked as if there would be deadlock with neither city able to deliver a death-blow to the other. Sparta, on the advice of Alcibiades, had set up a fortified base at Deceleia, half-way between Athens and her frontier with Boeotia, which meant that Spartan soldiers could dominate and ravage land in Attica all the year round. They could also lure slaves away from Athens, and twenty thousand are recorded as escaping from the city, a severe drain on its human resources but not enough to defeat it. Somehow new resources had to be found to bring the conflict to an end.

The only major source was Persia, and in fact from the 420s both Athens and Sparta had been hoping to secure her support. The Athenians ruined their chances by unwisely backing two satraps [Persian governors] who were in rebellion against the monarchy and, from 411, it was Sparta who gained the money to build and equip a fleet. In return the Spartans acquiesced in the achievement of Persia's main objective since the Persian Wars, the return of the Greek cities of Asia to her control. This was the end of any pretence that Sparta was fighting for the liberation of Greece.

The closing years of the war (411–404) saw the experienced Athenian fleet locked in conflict with the newer but better-resourced Spartan one. The ambition of Sparta was now to close off Athenian supplies of grain from the Hellespont. A Spartan fleet was there in 411 and managed to capture the city of Byzantium. The Athenian were not finished, however, and won two major victories in 411 and 410 and another at Arginusae (near Lesbos) in 406. Byzantium was regained in 408. In 410 the Spartans even sued for peace, but Athens refused to negotiate.

The Spartans Victorious

For Athens, however, a final victory remained elusive. The Spartans now always had enough resources to rebuild their fleet. In 405 the Spartans, under their commander Lysander, captured the town of Lampsachus in the Hellespont and were able to shelter their fleet in its harbour. The Athenian fleet arrived to challenge them but had to beach on the other side of the strait at Aigospotamae where there was no harbour. This left them dangerously exposed. They sailed out day after day to challenge the Spartans, who would not come out. Lysander noticed, however, that once the Athenian ships returned across the strait they were left on the beach unmanned. He launched a sudden attack achieving complete surprise. One hundred and seventy ships out of Athens' fleet of 180 were captured. When the news reached Athens, a howl of despair spread up from the Piraeus [Athens's port town] to the city as the implications were realized. With the Hellespont now under Spartan control, Athens was starved and forced into surrender (404). The Long Walls were pulled down, the fleet reduced almost to nothing, and a Government of Thirty imposed on the city by the victorious Spartans. Against all expectations, Athens had actually been comprehensively defeated, even though the Spartans did not destroy the city completely, afraid perhaps of creating a power vacuum in the area.

New Struggles for Supremacy Leave the Greeks Exhausted

Michael Grant

It had been Persian money that had enabled the Spartans to build the fleet with which their general, Lysander, had defeated Athens, bringing the calamitous Peloponnesian War to a close in 404 B.C. But almost immediately after the war, Sparta turned on the Persians, one of several imprudent moves it made in the next three decades, during which it was Greece's dominant power. In this excerpt from his book *The Classical Greeks*, Edinburgh University scholar and prolific writer Michael Grant begins with an overview of Sparta's diplomatic blunders. He then chronicles the fall of the Spartan hegemony and the rise and fall of the Theban one, pointing out how years of shifting political alliances and incessant fighting finally left the Greeks war-weary, demoralized, and easy prey for a would-be outside aggressor.

After the Persian viceroy in Asia Minor, Cyrus the younger, had provided the funds which enabled Sparta to win the Peloponnesian War against Athens, Cyrus decided to contest the Persian throne with his brother Artaxerxes II Mnemon, and mobilized 13,000 Greek mercenaries.

He also asked for Spartan help (401); and, in response, Sparta furnished naval support and a military commander Clearchus. This aid was only unofficial; all the same, it represented a grave and rash step, since it meant that the Spartans were jettisoning the Persian alliance—which had won them the Peloponnesian War—at a time when their own control over their newly acquired 'empire' was maladroit [inept] and

Excerpted from *The Classical Greeks*, by Michael Grant. Copyright ©1989 by Michael Grant Publications, Ltd. Reprinted with the permission of Scribner, a division of Simon & Schuster.

precarious. The hand of Lysander, their victorious general, may be seen in the intervention, for he was Cyrus' intimate friend, and this consideration evidently prevailed, in his mind, over the undesirability of breaking with the Great King. Besides, Spartans had a bad conscience, and an awareness of unfavourable publicity, because they had relinquished the Asian Greeks to Persian intervention and control.

Cyrus was killed at Cunaxa, as Xenophon's *March Up Country (Anabasis)* so brilliantly recounts, but Sparta nevertheless made an alliance with Egypt (in revolt against Persia), and raided Persian territory. In 399 there was an open state of war between the Spartans and Persians, and in 396, amid Panhellenic propaganda (if that is not a later embellishment), the new Spartan King Agesilaus II arrived with reinforcements. In spite of two effective campaigns, however, he failed to check the increasing Persian naval menace.

The Spartan Bully

Meanwhile, in the homeland, a coalition comprising the Boeotian League (Thebes), Athens, Corinth and Argos rebelled against the heavy-handed conduct of Sparta, and launched the 'Corinthian War' (395). Persia, with pleasure, financed the confederates, and in the following year the Athenian Conon, sharing the command with Pharnabazus, the satrap [Persisan governor] of Dascylium, inflicted a naval defeat on the Spartans at Cnidus. Meanwhile, however, Agesilaus had been recalled, and proceeded overland to Boeotia, but although victorious at Coronea (394) was obliged to return to the Peloponnese.

The Persians allowed Conon to rebuild the Long Walls at Athens—which thus achieved a rapid recovery from the Peloponnesian War, accelerated by an inventive commander of light-armed troops, Iphicrates. Next, however, . . . Persia changed sides, transferred its support to Sparta after all, and in 387/386 compelled all Greek contestants to adhere to the King's Peace or Peace of Antalcidas. . . .

Athens was willing to make peace because of threats to its grain supply (blocked by a Spartan, Persian and Syracusan fleet), and Spartan supremacy was confirmed; but only on the condition that, whereas other Greek city-states would remain 'autonomous', those in Asia Minor and Cyprus were to be subject to the Great King. This was not a new requirement, but its formal inclusion in the treaty meant that the subordination of those Greek states to Persia had been underlined with humiliating clarity—as if the Persian Wars had never happened.

Convinced, however, of the backing of the Persians, Sparta flagrantly interfered with other city-states of the Greek mainland. Phoebidas was sent to capture Thebes by treachery and install an oligarchic regime. This new government was backed by a Spartan garrison, and others were planted at Thespiae, and Plataea, and Heraclea in Trachis. But Thebes fought back in 379, when seven exiles, led by Pelopidas, returned by night and led a successful revolt against Spartan control. This moment can be seen, in retrospect, as a historical landmark, marking the approaching end of Sparta's hegemony and the inauguration of a brief period during which the Boeotian League in central Greece, dominated by the Thebans, took its place as the principal mainland power. . . .

A State of Deadlock

Following Sparta's coup at Thebes (382) and the ejection of its garrison three years later, it was decided that the League [which the Spartans had recently dissolved to curb Theban power] should once again be revived. And there was a time, too, when the Athenian recovery from the Peloponnesian War assumed a concrete form. First, the Spartans repeated their Theban gesture by dispatching Sphodrias to make an unsuccessful attack on Athens (378). The Athenians, although no longer the political leaders of the Greek world, were still a power to be reckoned with. . . . And now Sphodrias' stupid action so greatly infuriated and alarmed them that they founded a Second Athenian League of maritime cities, offering more tempting terms than the first (in the previous century). Moreover, they also took the unusual step of forming an alliance with the Boeotians, which Agesilaus' invasions of Boeotia in that and the following year failed to disrupt.

Seeing that the Athenians were now reviving and increasing their naval potentialities, Sparta hastened to do the same. However, the alliance between Athens and Thebes did not last after all, and a split developed between them. Greece was now in a state of complete deadlock; and Persia saw an opportunity to intervene once again. In 371, therefore, its representatives came to Sparta to meet envoys of the belligerent Greek states, and the result was the 'Peace of Callias'. . . .The new Peace was made on the basis of 'independence', according to which no city-state should maintain a garrison on another's territory, and all should disarm.

The Spartans duly took the oath on behalf of their own city and their allies, but the delegates of Athens and other states swore separate and individual oaths. Thebes, too, did the same. But then the Theban delegates, led by [the brilliant military innovator] Epaminondas, claimed to be recognized as acting for the Boeotian League as well; and this Sparta refused to allow. So the Thebans withdrew from the negotiations, and this . . . 'Peace of Callias' came to nothing.

Shattering the Myth of Spartan Invincibility

The Theban obstruction, which nullified it, was the work of Epaminondas, the most important public figure that his city ever produced, who thus appears at the head of his city's affairs for the first time. He became the subject of many eulogies, for everyone agreed about his qualities. The nobility and uprightness of his modest, unambitious character were impressive and even Athenians had to admire his eloquence and culture, which he had acquired as a pupil of Lysis, a Pythagorean philosopher in exile.

Epaminondas was said to have assisted Spartan troops in their siege of Mantinea in 385 (although this remains doubtful), and also, perhaps, helped in the restoration of Theban power six years later. Now, in 371, he was one of the generals (Boeotarchs) elected as leaders of the Boeotian confederacy. In its new form, the earlier system of indirect government by proportional representation was abandoned in favour of a broadly democratic federal Assembly, meeting at Thebes, which took its decisions by direct vote. Three of the 'wards', however (reduced from eleven to seven), were still dominated by the Thebans, and it was this pre-eminence which prompted Epaminondas' demand that Thebes should act for the League.

The result, as he had probably hoped and intended, was immediate war against Sparta. The Spartan army, under the Agiad King Cleombrotus I, was already in the territory of the Thebans' neighbour Phocis, and now it made a rapid move—before Thebes could mobilize its allies—arriving in the middle of Boeotia by a surprise march through the glens of Mount Helicon, and forcing battle at Leuctra. The Spartans enjoyed a numerical advantage, marshalling 10,000 hoplites, including 700 Spartiates [Spartan citizens], against a total of 6,000 Thebans (though the Theban cavalry enjoyed a slight superiority).

But the decisive factor was Epaminondas himself, who was serving as one of the Theban generals—and proved more than a match for the invaders. Behind the Spartans' cavalry—drawn up, like that of their opponents, in the front line—their hoplite phalanx stood twelve deep. On the Theban side, however, Epaminondas massed hoplites fifty deep to constitute his left wing, which advanced not in the customary continuous front aligned with the rest of the army, but ahead of the other units in a slanting, oblique formation. Then, after the Thebans' cavalry had driven its enemy counterpart back on its own phalanx, this strengthened left wing, led by the Sacred Band (of devoted homosexual couples) under Pelopidas—Epaminondas' closest associate—charged forward at the double. King Cleombrotus I, attempting to oppose the charge, was struck down and killed, and four hundred Spartiates died with him. Those of his followers who survived fled in disorder, and so did the rest of his force, leaving nearly a thousand dead.

'The most famous of all victories won by Greeks over Greeks' [according to the second-century A.D. Greek writer Pausanias], this engagement proved for the first time, and once and for all, that the Spartans' phalanx was not invincible. Their conduct as an imperial power had been inefficient and brutal, at a time when diminishing manpower had augmented their already grave social stresses; and now, this stunning reversal of their military reputation announced the end of their thirty-three-year-old predominance in Greece.

Despite Epaminondas' previous lack of experience as commander-in-chief, the battle of Leuctra had shown him to be a masterly strategic and tactical planner and commander. True, the Thebans had tried out something like this heavily weighted wing before, notably at Delium in 424 (and at Coronea in 394 a deep phalanx had fought well), so that it should not therefore have taken the Spartan king by surprise. But no doubt, like most of his compatriots, he was conservative in his military thinking, and, besides, the scheme had never before been put into effect on so formidable a scale. Epaminondas had also displayed himself as an adroit coordinator of infantry and cavalry, and co-ordinator, also, of the diverse forces that various states had placed under his command. He goes down to history as the most professional military genius that the Greek city-states of the mainland ever produced, and one of the mentors of Philip II and Alexander.

The Short-Lived Theban Supremacy

Thebes was now the leading land-power in Greece, though it had to keep a careful watch on a potential rival, Jason of Pherae in Thessaly, who had recently brought all the other Thessalian states under his control. After Leuctra Epaminondas diplomatically invited him to join up with the Theban forces, Jason refused to lend his well-trained mercenaries for the purpose, and instead negotiated an armistice between the Thebans and Spartans. Athens, which Epaminondas had also asked for help, organized a conference seeking a renewed Common Peace, under the auspices of its own confederacy, and Persia sponsored the plan.

But this did not prevent Epaminondas from pressing ahead with the destruction of Sparta's hegemony, amid a chaotic outburst of factional strife in numerous cities. In 370/369 he invaded the Peloponnese, helped the Arcadians to throw off Spartan control (building Megalopolis as their new federal capital), and led the first recorded invasion of

Sparta's own Eurotas valley, penetrating into the barricaded streets of the unwalled city itself. Next he liberated Messenia—where many Spartiates had owned their rich land—and founded a new fortified town of Messene beside the ancient Ithome. Before long (366), the long-lived, famous Peloponnesian League had ceased to exist. . . .

At some time during this period, Epaminondas' position was threatened by his political opponents in Thebes itself. However, he survived the challenge, and moved north to defeat Alexander, Jason's nephew and successor at Pherae, though Pelopidas, the architect of this diplomatic and military penetration of Thessaly, was killed in the battle. Then in 364, despite the relative inaccessibility of Boeotia's ports, Epaminondas decided, in what was for Thebes a revolutionary innovation, to challenge the Athenian supremacy at sea, leading a fleet as far as Byzantium.

However, learning that the Arcadian League had broken away from his coalition, he returned, with unprecedented speed of movement, to the Peloponnese, where his force, consisting of troops from Argos, Sicyon, Messenia, together with Arcadian dissidents, had to confront a coalition of Spartans, Athenians, Eleans and Achaeans. In the battle of Mantinea that followed (362)—the largest battle yet fought between one Greek force and another—Epaminondas, employing tactics similar to those of Leuctra, was well on the way to an overwhelming victory when he fell, mortally wounded.

After his death, the Boeotians and their allies halted in their tracks, and concluded peace. For the Greek mainland states were exhausted; and although yet another and even more ambitious Common Peace (excluding only Sparta) was attempted, [the contemporary historian] Xenophon gloomily observed that, from now on, the confusion was more hopeless than ever. He was writing, admittedly, as a disillusioned pro-Spartan, but what he said was not far wrong.

And the Roman biographer [Cornelius] Nepos, too, was right to say that Epaminondas counted more than his state. For Thebes and Boeotia had nothing to fall back upon once he was dead. True, whatever future eulogists might say, his successes had not been unlimited: despite his military talents, he had not achieved extensive, positive results in the political field. Certainly, he had overthrown the incompetent Spartan predominance. But the 'Panhellenic' liberation which he evidently sought to establish in its place, envisaging a utopian coalition of self-governing leagues (linked somehow with a novel Boeotian overseas confederacy), came to nothing—and may, indeed, be little more than a later fiction.

A Vacuum Waiting to Be Filled

Instead, all that had replaced the Spartan hegemony was a vacuum, which the Boeotian League proved unfitted to fill. True, Boeotia's agricultural economy was strong. But the manpower of the territory was insubstantial, and its professional army (once Pelopidas and Epaminondas had died) fell short of Spartan standards. Nor did Thebes (except in mythology) have a distinguished past to live up to, unlike Sparta and Athens. But Sparta was shattered, and the Second Athenian League, too, lacked sufficient strength to survive. So now there was no mainland city capable of taking the lead—and, without a lead, the Greek states were too divisive and quarrelsome to maintain any stable equilibrium, or any combined resistance to a threat from outside. That threat would very soon be presented with formidable effect, not this time by Persia, but by Philip II, who came to the Macedonian throne three years after Epaminondas had fallen at Mantinea.

Philip II and the Rise of Macedonia

N.G.L. Hammond

The sudden, spectacular rise of the Macedonian monarch Philip II in the mid-fourth century B.C. and his subsequent mastery of Greece's leading city-states is one of history's most remarkable success stories. When he assumed power as a young man, his country was backward and divided (into Lower and Upper Macedonia, the latter being more backward than the former). And his northern borders were threatened by Illyrians (or Dardanians), Paeonians, and other fierce tribal peoples. Yet in an amazingly short time he overcame these obstacles and forged Europe's first national standing army. As detailed in this essay, by N.G.L. Hammond, professor emeritus at Bristol University, it was this effective fighting force that enabled Philip to penetrate central and southern Greece. His first major victory in this strategic region was over the Phocians (of the city-state of Phocis, northwest of Thebes). The Phocians had recently seized the sacred sanctuary at Delphi (in central Greece), home of the famous oracle. Most members of the Amphyctyonic League, a loose alliance of nearby states who sent representatives to administer the sanctuary, objected and the so-called Sacred War ensued. The ambitious and crafty Philip, Hammond explains, proceeded to exploit the conflict to his own advantage.

Philip took control in 359 not as king but as guardian of his nephew, Amyntas IV, a young boy. His country was on the verge of collapse, having lost 4,000 men in battle, while the victorious forces of Bardylis [king of the Illyrians] were in

Excerpted from *The Genius of Alexander the Great*, by N.G.L. Hammond. Copyright ©1997 by N.G.L. Hammond. Reprinted with the permission of the University of North Carolina Press.

occupation of towns in Pelagonia and Lyncus and threatened to invade Macedonia itself in 358. Philip put heart into his army by holding assembly after assembly, rearming and training his infantry, and inspiring them with his own indomitable spirit. In spring 358 he convinced the assembly of the King's Men that they should take the offensive. In a decisive battle with almost equal numbers he inflicted a crippling defeat on Bardylis, established the east bank of Lake Lychnitis (Ochrid) as his frontier, and confirmed a treaty of peace with Bardylis by marrying his daughter, Audata. His victory freed Pelagonia, Lyncus and the other tribal states of West Macedonia, then called 'Upper Macedonia', from raiding and occupation by the Dardanians. He now invited the peoples of these states to abolish their monarchies and to enter the Macedonian kingdom with equal rights to those of the Macedonians. The invitation was accepted. . . .

By this act, which Philip must have taken with the agreement of the Macedonian assembly, he doubled the resources and the manpower of the kingdom. It was important to raise the standard of life in Upper Macedonia to that of Lower Macedonia, and for that purpose he founded new towns there in which young men received educational and military training. As they graduated he recruited the best of them to enter the king's army and become members of the assembly as 'Macedones'. His innovations were so successful that the number of his Companion Cavalrymen rose from 600 in 358 to 2,800 in 336, and that of the Companion Infantrymen from 10,000 in 358 to 27,000 in 336. Alexander was to inherit the most formidable army in Europe.

Philip's Early Conquests

By a combination of diplomatic skill and military opportunism Philip defeated Illyrian tribes beyond his western frontier, forced the Paeonians to become his subjects, gained possession of Greek colonies on his coast, defended Amphipolis against the Athenians and Crenides—renamed Philippi—against the Thracians, and advanced his eastern frontier to the river Nestus (Mesta), all by late 354. He was fortunate in that Athens was distracted by the war against

her subject-states (357–355) and Thebes by the war against
Phocis, which became the Sacred War (355–346); and he
managed to make a treaty of alliance with his powerful
neighbour, the Chalcidian League of city-states [on the
three-fingered Chalcidic peninsula, just east of Macedonia],
on condition that neither party would enter into separate negotiations with Athens. During these eventful years he confirmed an alliance with the ruling house of Larissa in Thessaly by marrying a lady of that house, Philinna, and an
alliance with the Molossian royal house by marrying
Olympias in 357. . . . In that year, 357, he was elected king
in place of Amyntas IV.

The Sacred War was declared by a majority of the members of the Amphictyonic League, of which the Council laid
down rules of conduct in religious and other matters and in
particular administered the temple of Apollo at Delphi. That
majority was formed by the peoples of Thessaly, Central
Greece and Boeotia; but the minority included Athens,
Sparta, Achaea, and later Pherae in Thessaly, which all entered into alliance with Phocis. Other states showed sympathy with one side or the other. The Phocian occupiers of
Delphi survived by looting the treasures and hiring mercenary soldiers, and in 353 an able leader, Onomarchus,
launched an offensive against Thebes and sent 7,000 mercenaries to support Pherae against the other Thessalians. This
was Philip's opportunity; for the Thessalians asked him for
help and he enabled them to win a victory. But Onomarchus
came north and inflicted two defeats on Philip. He withdrew, as he said, 'like a ram, to butt the harder'. In 352 Philip
and his Thessalian allies won a decisive victory over Onomarchus' army of 500 cavalry and 20,000 infantry, to the
amazement of the city-states. Philip paraded his champi-
onship of Apollo. For his soldiers went into battle wearing
the laurel wreath associated with the god, and on his orders
3,000 prisoners were drowned as guilty of sacrilege. He also
championed the cause of liberty and federalism against the
dictators of Pherae, whom he now expelled together with
their mercenaries. His reward was election as President of
the Thessalian League, which placed its forces and its rev-

enues at his disposal. At this time he married Nicesipolis, a member of the leading family in Pherae.

Conclusion of the Sacred War

His chief fear was a coalition of Athens and the Chalcidian League; for the Athenian fleet could then blockade his coast and the armies of the two states could invade the coastal plain of Macedonia. In 349, when the Chalcidian League violated its treaty and entered into alliance with Athens, Philip in-vaded Chalcidice and despite the efforts of Athens captured Olynthus, the capital of the League, in 348. He held the Olynthians responsible for breaking the religious oaths which had bound them under the treaty. He razed the city and sold the population into slavery. He destroyed two other city-

---

Alexander Remembers His Father

Years after Philip's death, after his son Alexander had invaded and penetrated deep into Asia, some of the young conqueror's troops de-manded that the army turn back. According to the second-century A.D. Greek historian Arrian, Alexander shamed them by recalling what his father had done for them and for their country.

A horrified silence ensued, and Alexander stepped once again on to the rostrum and addressed his troops in these words: 'My countrymen, you are sick for home—so be it! I shall make no attempt to check your longing to return. Go whither you will; I shall not hinder you. But, if go you must, there is one thing I would have you understand—what I have done for you, and in what coin you will have repaid me.

'First I will speak of my father Philip, as it is my duty to do. Philip found you a tribe of impoverished vagabonds, most of you dressed in skins, feeding a few sheep on the hills and fight-ing, feebly enough, to keep them from your neighbours—Thracians and Triballians and Illyrians. He gave you cloaks to wear instead of skins; he brought you down from the hills into the plains; he taught you to fight on equal terms with the enemy on your borders, till you knew that your safety lay not,

states (Apollonia and Stagira) and incorporated the peoples of the Chalcidic peninsula . . . into the Macedonian kingdom.

Meanwhile the Phocians were running short of funds and also of mercenary soldiers, and the Thebans had been hammered into a condition of weakness. Who would administer the *coup de grâce* [deathblow]? Envoys from most of the city-states hastened to Pella, hoping to enlist Philip on their side in 346. At that time Alexander, as a boy of ten, will have watched with interest as his father found gracious words for all of them and committed himself to none. When the envoys were on their way home to their respective states, the Macedonian army reached Thermopylae, where the Phocian leader and his 8,000 mercenaries accepted the terms offered by Philip: to surrender their weapons and horses, and to go wherever they

---

as once, in your mountain strongholds, but in your own valour. He made you city-dwellers; he brought you law; he civilized you. He rescued you from subjection and slavery, and made you masters of the wild tribes who harried and plundered you; he annexed the greater part of Thrace, and by seizing the best places on the coast opened your country to trade, and enabled you to work your mines without fear of attack. Thessaly, so long your bugbear and your dread, he subjected to your rule, and by humbling the Phocians he made the narrow and difficult path into Greece a broad and easy road. The men of Athens and Thebes, who for years had kept watching for their moment to strike us down, he brought so low—and by this time I myself was working at my father's side that they who once exacted from us either our money or our obedience, now, in their turn, looked to us as the means of their salvation. Passing into the Peloponnese, he settled everything there to his satisfaction, and when he was made supreme commander of all the rest of Greece for the war against Persia, he claimed the glory of it not for himself alone, but for the Macedonian people.

Arrian, *Anabasis Alexandri*, published as *The Campaigns of Alexander.* Trans. Aubrey de Sélincourt. New York: Penguin Books, 1971, pp. 360–361.

wished. The Phocian people were now defenceless. . . .

Philip had acted as the champion of Apollo. It was for him a matter of religious conviction. He therefore entrusted the settlement to the Council of the Amphictyonic League, on which his allies in Thessaly and Central Greece had a majority of the votes, and they no doubt listened to his advice. The terms for the Phocians were mild by Greek standards (one Greek state proposed the execution of all the men): disarmament, division into village-settlements, payment of an indemnity to Apollo and expulsion from the Amphictyony. In their place the Macedonians were elected members. The two votes of Phocis on the Council were transferred to the Macedonian state. . . .

The Road to Chaeronea

Philip's aim was to bring the city-states into concord and set up a Treaty of Common Peace, of which Macedonia and they would be members. This . . . coincided with the tenor of a political pamphlet, entitled *Philip*, which [the noted orator] Isocrates published in 346 just before the capitulation of Phocis. He advised Philip as the ruler of the strongest state in Europe to bring the city-states into concord, lead them against Persia, liberate the Greeks in Asia, and found there new cities to absorb the surplus population of the Greek mainland. The price of concord was acceptance of the *status quo*. . . . Despite Philip's offers to set up a Common Peace, Athens, Sparta and Thebes went their own way in the name of 'freedom', and Philip realised in 341 that he might have to use force rather than persuasion if he wanted to exercise control.

Athens depended for her food-supply on imports of grain from South Russia, which had to pass through the Bosporus and the Hellespont. On the European side Byzantium was able to exact 'benevolences' [tolls] from shipping at the Bosporus, and Athens through her colonies on the Chersonese (the Gallipoli peninsula) could do likewise in the Hellespont. The Asian side was held by Persia, which had put down a series of revolts on the coast of the Mediterranean and could now muster a huge fleet. Philip approached this sensitive area through a conquest of the tribes of eastern Thrace. It was during the Thracian campaign in 340 that he appointed Alexander at the age of sixteen to act as his deputy in Macedonia. From then on Alexander was fully aware of Philip's plans.

Events moved rapidly. Philip laid siege to Perinthus and Byzantium, whereupon Athens declared war. He was thwarted by Persia and Athens acting in collusion. He summoned Alexander to join him . . . and extended his control of eastern Thrace to the Danube. During his return to Macedonia in summer 339 he had to fight his way through the land of the Triballi, a powerful tribe which captured some of his booty. In Greece another Sacred War had started, and the command of the Amphictyonic forces was offered to and accepted by Philip in the autumn. The sacrilegious state which he had to discipline was Amphissa. He took his Macedonian army and troops from some Amphictyonic states not towards Amphissa but through Phocis to the border of Boeotia, in order to threaten Thebes, which though his 'friend and ally' had been behaving in a hostile manner, and to act against Athens, with which he was still at war. The envoys which he sent to Thebes were outbid by the envoys of Athens. In violation of her treaty Thebes joined Athens and sided with Amphissa. Philip tried more than once to negotiate terms of peace, but in vain. The decisive battle was fought at Chaeronea in Boeotia in August 338. The troops of Boeotia, Athens, Megara, Corinth and Achaea numbered some 35,000; those of Macedonia and her allies somewhat less.

Alexander, in command of the Companion Cavalry, pitched his tent by the river Cephissus. When his father's tactics created a breach in the opposing phalanx Alexander charged through the gap, and it was he who led the attack on the Sacred Band of 300 Thebans [Thebes' crack military unit]. The Macedonian victory was total. Thebes was treated harshly as the violator of its oaths. Athens was treated generously. Alexander led a guard of honour which brought the ashes of the Athenian dead to Athens—a unique tribute to a defeated enemy—and the 2,000 Athenian prisoners were liberated without ransom. As Philip advanced into the Peloponnese, his enemies submitted and his allies rejoiced. Sparta alone was defiant. He ravaged her territory and he gave some frontier regions to his allies; but he did not attack the city. During his return northwards he left garrisons at Acrocorinth, Thebes and Ambracia. Meanwhile the Council or the Amphictyonic League reduced the restrictions on the Phocians, made the Amphissaeans live in villages and approved the acts of Philip.

Captain-General of the Greeks

The future of the city-states was in Philip's bands. He decided to create the 'Greek Community' (*to koinon ton Hellenon*), in which the states would swear to keep the peace among themselves, maintain existing constitutions, permit changes only by constitutional methods, and combine in action against any violator of the 'Common Peace', whether internal or external. His proposal, made in autumn 338, was accepted by the states in spring 337, and a 'Common Council' was established, of which the members represented one or more states in proportion to their military and naval strengths. The Council was a sovereign body: its decisions were sent to the states for implementation, not for discussion. The military forces and the naval forces at the disposal of the Common Council were defined: the former amounted to 15,000 cavalry and 200,000 infantry, and the number of warships, which is not stated in our sources, was later to be 160 triremes, manned by crews totalling some 30,000 men. Thus the Greek Community far outdid the Macedonian State in the size of the forces it could deploy. The Council had disciplinary, judicial and financial powers which were binding on the member-states. If we look for a modern analogy, we should look rather to the United States of America than to the European Community.

The next step was the creation of an offensive and defensive alliance between the Greek Community and the Macedonian State for all time. Because Macedonia was already at war with Persia, the Council declared war on Persia late in 337 and voted that the commander of the joint forces should be Philip. Within the Community his title was 'Hegemon' [supreme commander or captain-general], and the powers of his office were carefully defined. In the spring of 336 the vanguard [small, leading unit] of the joint forces crossed to Asia under the command of three Macedonian generals whom Philip appointed, and arrangements were made for the stipulated forces of the coalition to follow in the autumn with Philip as overall commander.

The brilliance of Philip's political initiative, power of persuasion and effective leadership is obvious. He brought into being the combination of a newly created Greek State, self-standing and self-governing, and a Macedonian State which was unrivalled in military power. If that combination should succeed in liberating the Greek cities in Asia and in acquiring extensive territory, it would provide a cure for many of the troubles of the Greek world. [The Greek historian] Theopompus, critical of Philip in many ways, entitled his history *Philippica* 'because Europe had never produced such a man altogether as Philip, son of Amyntas'.

Alexander's Conquests and Their Impact

Thomas R. Martin

This highly informative, concise overview of the exploits of Macedonia's Alexander III (later called "the Great") is by Thomas R. Martin, a professor of Classics at Holy Cross. Martin covers most of the familiar main events, such as the crossing of the Hellespont (in 334 B.C.), siege of Tyre, liberation of Egypt, and major victories in Persia. He also includes several anecdotes and details that shed light on Alexander's character, such as the fact that he kept a copy of Homer's *Iliad* (given to him by his tutor, Aristotle) with him always. As Martin points out, Alexander's most immediate legacy was the chaotic scramble to carve up his newly acquired empire in the years following his untimely passing.

A disgruntled Macedonian assassinated Philip in 336 B.C. Unconfirmed rumors circulated that the murder had been instigated by one of his several wives, Olympias, a princess from Epirus to the west of Macedonia and mother of Philip's son, Alexander (356–323 B.C.). Alexander promptly liquidated potential rivals for the throne and won recognition as king while barely twenty years old. In several lightning-fast campaigns, he subdued Macedonia's traditional enemies to the west and north. Next he compelled the city-states in southern Greece that had rebelled from the League of Corinth at the news of Philip's death to rejoin the alliance. (As in Philip's reign, Sparta remained outside the league.) To demonstrate the price of disloyalty, Alexander destroyed Thebes in 335 as punishment for its rebellion. This lesson in terror made it

---

clear that Alexander might claim to lead the Greek city-states by their consent (the kind of leader called a hegemon in Greek) but that the reality of his power rested on his superior force and his unwavering willingness to employ it.

Alexander Leads His Troops into Asia

With Greece cowed into peaceful if grudging allegiance, Alexander in 334 led a Macedonian and Greek army into Anatolia [Asia Minor] to fulfill his father's plan to avenge Greece by attacking Persia. Alexander's astounding success in the following years in conquering the entire Persian Empire while still in his twenties earned him the title "the Great" in later ages. In his own time, his greatness consisted of his ability to inspire his men to follow him into hostile, unknown regions where they were reluctant to go, beyond the borders of civilization as they knew it. Alexander inspired his troops with his reckless disregard for his own safety, often, for example, plunging into the enemy at the head of his men and sharing the danger of the common soldier. No one could miss him in his plumed helmet, vividly colored cloak, and armor polished to reflect the sun. So intent on conquering distant lands was Alexander that he had rejected advice to delay his departure from Macedonia until he had married and fathered an heir, to forestall instability in case of his death. He had further alarmed his principal adviser, an experienced older man, by giving away virtually all his land and property in order to strengthen the army, thereby creating new landowners who would furnish troops. "What," he was asked, "do you have left for yourself?" "My hopes," Alexander replied (Plutarch, *Alexander* 15). Those hopes centered on constructing a heroic image of himself as a warrior as glorious as the incomparable Achilles of Homer's *Iliad*. Alexander always kept a copy of the *Iliad* under his pillow, along with a dagger. Alexander's aspirations and his behavior represented the ultimate expression of the Homeric vision of the glorious conquering warrior.

Alexander cast a spear into the earth of Anatolia when he crossed the Hellespont strait from Europe to Asia, thereby claiming the Asian continent for himself in Homeric fashion as territory "won by the spear" (Diodorus, *Library of History* 17.17.2). The first battle of the campaign, at the River Granicus in western Anatolia, proved the worth of Alexander's Macedonian and Greek cavalry, which charged across the river and up the bank to rout the opposing Persians. Alexander visited Midas's old capital of Gordion in Phrygia, where an oracle had promised the lordship of Asia to whoever could loose a seemingly impenetrable knot of rope tying the yoke of an ancient chariot preserved in the city. The young Macedonian, so the story goes, cut the Gordion knot with his sword. In 333 B.C. the Persian king Darius finally faced Alexander in battle at Issus, near the southeastern corner of Anatolia. Alexander's army defeated its more numerous opponents with a characteristically bold strike of cavalry through the left side of the Persian lines followed by a flanking maneuver against the king's position in the center. Darius had to flee from the field to avoid capture, leaving behind his wives and daughters, who had accompanied his campaign in keeping with royal Persian tradition. Alexander's scrupulously chivalrous treatment of the Persian royal women after their capture at Issus reportedly boosted his reputation among the peoples of the king's empire.

The Defeat of Persia

When Tyre, a heavily fortified city on the coast of what is now Lebanon, refused to surrender to him in 332 B.C., Alexander employed the assault machines and catapults developed by his father to breach the walls of its formidable offshore fortress after a long siege. The capture of Tyre rang the death knell of the walled city-state as a settlement impregnable to siege warfare. Although successful sieges remained rare after Alexander because well-constructed city walls still presented formidable barriers to attackers, Alexander's success against Tyre increased the terror of a siege for a city's general population. No longer could the citizens of a city-state confidently assume that their defensive system could withstand the technology of their enemy's offensive weapons indefinitely. The now-present fear that a siege might actually breach a city's walls made it much harder psychologically for city-states to remain united in the face of threats from enemies like aggressive kings.

Alexander next took over Egypt, where hieroglyphic inscriptions seem to show that he probably presented himself as the successor to the Persian king as the land's ruler rather than as an Egyptian pharaoh. On the coast, to the west of the Nile river, Alexander in 331 founded a new city named Alexandria after himself, the first of the many cities he would later establish as far east as Afghanistan. During his time in Egypt, Alexander also paid a mysterious visit to the oracle of the god Ammon, whom the Greeks regarded as identical to Zeus, at the oasis of Siwah far out in the western Egyptian desert. Alexander told no one the details of his consultation of the oracle, but the news got out that he had been informed he was the son of the god and that he joyfully accepted the designation as true.

In 331 B.C., Alexander crushed the Persian king's main army at the battle of Gaugamela in northern Mesopotamia, near the border of modern Iraq and Iran. He subsequently proclaimed himself king of Asia in place of the Persian king. For the heterogeneous populations of the Persian Empire, the succession of a Macedonian to the Persian throne meant essentially no change in their lives. They continued to send the same taxes to a remote master, whom they rarely if ever saw. As in Egypt, Alexander left the local administrative system of the Persian Empire in place, even retaining some Persian governors. His long-term aim seems to have been to forge an administrative corps composed of Macedonians, Greeks, and Persians working together to rule the territory he conquered with his army.

To India and Back

Alexander next led his army farther east into territory hardly known to the Greeks. He pared his force to reduce the need for supplies, which were difficult to find in the arid country through which they were marching. Each hoplite in Greek armies customarily had a personal servant to carry his armor and pack. Alexander, imitating Philip, trained his men to carry their own equipment, thereby creating a leaner force by cutting the number of army servants dramatically. As with all ancient armies, however, a large number of noncombatants trailed after the fighting force: merchants who set up little markets at every stop, women whom soldiers had taken as mates along the way and their children, entertainers, and prostitutes. Although supplying these hangers-on was not Alexander's responsibility, their foraging for themselves made it harder for Alexander's quartermasters to find what they needed to supply the army proper.

An ancient army's demand for supplies usually left a trail of destruction and famine for local inhabitants in the wake of its march. Hostile armies simply took whatever they wanted. Friendly armies expected local people to sell or donate food to its supply officers and also to the merchants trailing along. These entrepreneurs would set up markets to resell locally obtained provisions to the soldiers. Since most farmers in antiquity had practically no surplus to sell, they found this expectation—which was in reality a requirement—a terrific hardship. The money the farmers received was of little use to them because there was nothing to buy with it in the countryside, where their neighbors had also had to participate in the forced marketing of their subsistence.

From the heartland of Persia, Alexander in 329 B.C. marched northeastward into the trackless steppes of Bactria (modern Afghanistan). When he proved unable to subdue completely the highly mobile locals, who avoided pitched battles in favor of the guerrilla tactics of attack and retreat, Alexander settled for an alliance sealed by his marriage to the Bactrian princess Roxane in 327. In this same period, Alexander completed the cold-blooded suppression of both real and imagined resistance to his plans among the leading men in his officer corps. As in past years, he used accusations of treachery or disloyalty as justification for the execution of those Macedonians he had come to distrust. These executions, like the destruction of Thebes in 335, demonstrated Alexander's appreciation of terror as a disincentive to rebellion.

From Bactria Alexander pushed on eastward to India. He probably intended to march all the way through to China in search of the edge of the farthest land on the earth, which

Aristotle, once Alexander's tutor, had taught was a sphere. Seventy days of marching through monsoon rains, however, finally shattered the nerves of Alexander's soldiers. In the spring of 326 B.C. they mutinied on the banks of the Hyphasis River (the modern Beas) in western India. Alexander was forced to agree to lead them in the direction of home. When his men had balked before, Alexander had always been able to shame them back into action by sulking in his tent like Achilles in the *Iliad*. This time the soldiers were beyond shame.

Alexander thereupon proceeded south down the Indus River. Along the way he took out his frustration at being stopped in his eastward march by slaughtering the Indian tribes who resisted him and by risking his life more flamboyantly then ever before. As a climax to his frustrated rage, he flung himself over the wall of an Indian town to face the enemy alone like a Homeric hero. His horrified officers were barely able to rescue him in time; even so, he received grievous wounds. At the mouth of the Indus on the Indian Ocean, Alexander turned a portion of his army west through the fierce desert of Gedrosia. Another portion took an easier route inland, while a third group sailed westward along the coast to explore for possible sites for new settlements and harbors. Alexander himself led the contingent that braved the desert, planning to surpass earlier Persian kings by marching through territory that they had found impassable. There a flash flood wiped out most of the noncombatants following the army. Many of the soldiers also died on the march through the desert, expiring from lack of water and the heat, which has been recorded at 127 degrees in the shade in that area. Alexander, as always, shared his men's hardships. In one legendary episode from this horrible ordeal, a few men were said to have brought him a helmet containing some water they had found. Alexander spilled the water out onto the sand rather than drink when his men could not. The remains of the army finally reached safety in the heartland of Persia in 324 B.C. Alexander promptly began plans for an invasion of the Arabian peninsula and, to follow that, all of North Africa west of Egypt.

Alexander a God?

By the time Alexander returned to Persia, he had dropped all pretense of ruling over the Greeks as anything other than an absolute monarch. Despite his earlier promise to respect the internal freedom of the Greek city-states, he now impinged on their autonomy by sending a peremptory decree ordering them to restore to citizenship the large number of exiles wandering homeless in the Greek world. The previous decades of war in Greece had created many of these unfortunate wanderers, and their status as stateless persons was creating unrest. Even more striking was Alexander's communication to the city-states that he wished to receive the honors due a god. Initially dumbfounded by this request, the leaders of most Greek states soon complied by sending honorary delegations to him as if he were a god. The Spartan Damis pithily expressed the only prudent position on Alexander's deification open to the cowed Greeks: "If Alexander wishes to be a god, we agree that he be called a god" (Plutarch, *Moralia* 219e).

Scholarly debate continues over Alexander's motive for desiring the Greeks to acknowledge him as a god, but few now accept a formerly popular theory that he sought divinity because he believed the city-states would then have to obey his orders as originating from a divinity, whose authority would supersede that of all earthly regimes. Personal rather than political motives best explain his request. He almost certainly had come to believe that he was the son of Zeus; after all, Greek mythology told many stories of Zeus producing children by mating with a human female. Most of those legendary offspring were mortal, but Alexander's conquest showed that he had surpassed them. His feats must be superhuman, he could well have believed, because they exceeded the bounds of human possibility. In other words, Alexander's accomplishments demonstrated that he had achieved godlike power and therefore must be a god himself. The divinity of Alexander, in ancient terms, emerged as a natural consequence of his power.

Alexander's overall aims can best be explained as interlinked goals: the conquest and administration of the known world and the exploration and possible colonization of new territory beyond. Conquest through military action was a time-honored pursuit for ambitious Macedonian leaders such as Alexander. He included non-Macedonians in his administration and army because he needed their expertise, not because he had any dream of promoting an abstract notion of what has sometimes been called "the brotherhood of man." Alexander's explorations benefited numerous scientific fields, from geography to botany, because he took along scientifically minded writers to collect and catalogue the new knowledge that they encountered. The far-flung new cities that he founded served as loyal outposts to keep the peace in conquered territory and provide warnings to headquarters in case of local uprisings. They also created new opportunities for trade in valuable goods such as spices that were not produced in the Mediterranean region.

No Ordinary Human Life

Alexander's plans to conquer Arabia and North Africa were extinguished by his premature death from a fever and heavy drinking on June 10, 323 B.C., in Babylon. He had already been suffering for months from depression brought on by the death of his best friend, Hephaistion. Close since their boyhoods, Alexander and Hephaistion were probably lovers. When Hephaistion died in a bout of excessive drinking, Alexander went wild with grief. The depth of his emotion was evident when he planned to build an elaborate temple to honor Hephaistion as a god. Meanwhile, Alexander threw himself into preparing for his Arabian campaign by exploring the marshy lowlands of southern Mesopotamia. Perhaps it was on one of these trips that he contracted the malaria-like fever that, exacerbated by a two-day drinking binge, killed him.

Like Pericles, Alexander had made no plans about what should happen if he should die unexpectedly. His wife Roxane was to give birth to their first child only some months after Alexander's death. When at Alexander's deathbed his commanders asked him to whom he bequeathed his kingdom, he replied, "To the most powerful [kratistos]" (Arrian, Anabasis of Alexander 7.26.3).

The Athenian orator Aeschines (c. 397–322 B.C.) well expressed the bewildered reaction of many people to the events of Alexander's lifetime: "What strange and unexpected event has not occurred in our time? The life we have lived is no ordinary human one, but we were born to be an object of wonder to posterity" (*Orations* 3.132). Alexander himself certainly attained legendary status in later times. Stories of fabulous exploits attributed to him became popular folk tales throughout the ancient world, even reaching distant regions where Alexander had never trod, such as deep into Africa. The popularity of the legend of Alexander as a symbol of the height of achievement for a masculine warrior-hero served as one of his most persistent legacies to later ages. That the worlds of Greece and the Near East had been brought into closer contact than ever before represented the other long-lasting effect of his astonishing career. Its immediate political and military consequences were the struggles among his generals that led to the creation of the kingdoms of the Hellenistic world.

Chapter 2

The Hellenistic Greeks in Collision

Turning | Points

IN WORLD HISTORY

The Long Wars of Alexander's Successors

Hermann Bengtson

After Alexander's death in 323 B.C., the eastern Mediterranean and Near Eastern spheres erupted in long, repeti-
tive, chaotic, and bloody conflicts among his former generals (the *Diadochoi*) and their sons. In the following
summary of this complex and at times confusing period of
Greek history, the distinguished German historian Hermann Bengtson ably sorts out the key events and leading
personalities.

Alexander's death in Babylon (10 June, 323 B.C.) left the empire without a direct heir. It consequently fell to the Macedonian military assembly, that is, to the Macedonians who
found themselves in Babylon, the capital of the realm, to decide the fate of the empire. A bitter dispute over the succession between the companions and the infantry of the phalanx
was finally settled by the mediation of the astute Greek
Eumenes, the former Chief Secretary. In a compromise solu-
tion, Arrhidaeus, the feeble-minded half-brother of Alexander, favoured by the phalanx, was to become king under the
name of Philip (III), along with the yet unborn child of the
Bactrian princess Roxane, should it be a boy. No decision was
taken to establish the position of a regular "Imperial Administrator." Perdiccas, as Chiliarch ("Grand Vizier"), was invested
with the superintendence of the Asiatic empire. Antipater remained *strategos* of Europe, while Craterus, as "protector of
the royal interest," was placed in charge of the imperial forces
in Asia, which Philip Arrhidaeus was incapable of leading.
Since Craterus, who had proven to be an outstanding general

Excerpted from *History of Greece: From the Beginnings to the Byzantine Era*, by Hermann Bengtson, trans. Edmund F. Bloedow. Copyright ©1988 by the University of
Ottawa Press. Reprinted with the permission of the University of Ottawa Press.

in India . . . was not present in Babylon (he happened to be on his way to Macedonia with the veterans of Alexander's army), Perdiccas became the actual regent of the Asiatic empire of Alexander. He had unlimited control over the vast resources of Asia, and under his leadership, a new division of the satrapies [Persian provinces] was arranged. Egypt fell to Ptolemy, son of Lagus; Paphlagonia and Cappadocia, districts still to be conquered, were promised to Eumenes; Pamphylia, Lycia and Greater Phrygia to Antigonus Monophthalmus (the "One Eyed"); and Hellespontine Phrygia to Leonnatus. On European soil, Lysimachus gained possession of Thrace, nominally under the supervision of Antipater the *strategos* of Europe. In contrast, almost all the satraps [rulers] of Iranian blood lost their territories. . . .

The first two decades after the death of the youthful ruler were years of bitter struggle between the idea of the unity of the empire, championed by Perdiccas, then Eumenes and finally and most energetically Antigonus, and the idea of particularistic states, which was most vigorously pursued by the satraps of Egypt and Thrace, Ptolemy and Lysimachus. . . .

The Greek problem played an important role in the policies of the successors—the *diadochoi*. Whoever controlled Hellas had in his possession the heart and nerve centre of the world. Thus the various rulers repeatedly attempted to renew the Corinthian League of Philip II and Alexander, to establish the hegemony of an external power over the Hellenes, with liberty and autonomy promised to the Greeks. But with continual changes in the power situation the notion of liberty lost more and more of its actual meaning, so that the "liberty of the Hellenes" was just propaganda of diadochian politics.

The Demise of Perdiccas and Craterus

The transformation of the universal empire into a group of self-interested states went through four different stages. The breaks fall in the years 321, 317/6, 311 and 306/5 B.C., each of which marks an important advance in the divisive idea over that of the unity of the empire. In 321 Perdiccas was murdered; in 317 Philip III Arrhidaeus and Eurydice met their doom; in 317/6 came the death of Eumenes, who up to then had championed the royal interests most decisively and most disinterestedly; in 311 a peace was concluded and practically signified the partitioning of the empire among the various rulers; with the adoption of the royal title in 306, at first by Antigonus and Demetrius, then also by Ptolemy, Lysimachus and Cassander, the idea of the unity of the empire was abandoned. On the battlefield of Ipsus in 301 B.C. it was buried once and for all.

While Asia remained quiet, apart from the revolt of the military colonists which had already broken out previously in Bactria, in Greece Alexander's death precipitated a great deal of unrest. . . . Antipater the *strategos* of Europe was no match for the Greek forces, which were strengthened by the Aetolians, who had gone over to the Greek camp. The Greeks shut Antipater and his army up within the stronghold of Lamia (so-called Lamian or Hellenic War). . . . The decisive turn in events occurred in the summer of 322 B.C., at sea. At Amorgos the Athenian fleet was forced to strike the flag [surrender] before the Macedonian admiral Cleitus. For the Athenians Amorgos signified the loss of maritime supremacy, and with it, the leading position in Greece—and that for all time. When Antipater, reinforced by the arrival of Craterus, ultimately emerged as victor on land at Crannon (in Thessaly), the pro-Macedonians in Athens, led by Phocion and Demades, gained the upper hand over the radicals. Antipater insisted on unconditional surrender. . . . A final settlement of the situation in Greece was not achieved, for Antipater and Craterus had to abandon their campaign against the Aetolians, as events in Asia were casting their shadow as far as Greece.

In Asia the departure of Craterus for Europe had given free rein to the ambitions of Perdiccas. With undisputed supreme power over the Asiatic part of the empire Perdiccas planned a marriage alliance with Cleopatra, the sister of Alexander, in order to bind himself to the royal dynasty and the dead king, whose name still continued to hold an indescribable fascination for the Macedonians. He set the enterprise in motion when Antigonus the satrap of Greater Phrygia fled to Europe. Soon a large coalition emerged against Perdiccas, a league of almost all the leading successors, with the exception of Eumenes. Perdiccas, forced into a war on two fronts, in Asia Minor and against Egypt, did the worst thing possible in his position. He took the offensive against the land of the Nile, which was superbly fortified by the desert strip on its eastern frontier. The campaign ended in his defeat, and he died in his own tent under the blows of an assassin (321 B.C.). Ptolemy, the victor, did not, however, accept the position of administrator of the empire offered to him, but contented himself with the satrapy of Egypt. . . . In Asia Minor, however, Eumenes, as Perdiccas' general, emerged victorious over Craterus and Antigonus. Craterus, the idol of the Macedonian army, had fallen in battle (321 B.C.).

The reorganisation of the supreme power of the empire in 321 B.C. . . . brought the aged Antipater as majordomo of the kings to the head of the entire empire. . . . The military assembly condemned the Greek Eumenes to death, commissioning his inveterate foe Antigonus to carry out his execution. Antipater's departure from the soil of Asia Minor in the same year, accompanied by both puppet kings, appeared to indicate a decisive shift in the centre of gravity front east to west, from Asia to Europe. In Antipater the empire did indeed have an administrator, but on the other hand no energetic central power, since Asia had been delivered up to the personal ambitions of Antigonus.

Shifting Alliances

Antipater's death (summer 319 B.C.) marked a further step along the road. In appointing the aged veteran Polyperchon to become his successor as "administrator of the empire and *strategos* of Europe"—without the concurrence of the Macedonian military assembly, which alone had the authority to do so—Antipater did not make a fortunate move. In particular Cassander, son of Antipater, opposed the arrangement of his father with the utmost resolution, and in East and West the centrifugal elements moved into the foreground. Cassander, Antigonus, Ptolemy and Lysimachus united against Polyperchon, the inadequate representative of the supreme power. Polyperchon set his hopes on the Greeks of the motherland. With the aid of a decree issued by King Philip Arrhidaeus he once more sought to revive the Corinthian League of Philip and Alexander. To begin with he would proclaim in Hellas a general peace, which the alliances of the various states were to join along with Macedonia.

The naval war, however, brought about a fundamental transformation of the situation. Cleitus, the victor of Amorgos, was, after initial successes, decisively defeated by Antigonus at the Bosporus (autumn 318 B.C.). Athens, where the rule of Polypercon rested on a weak footing, went over to the side of Cassander (spring 317 B.C.). As caretaker for Cassander, Demetrius of Phalerum seized the reins of power in Athens. . . . At this juncture Alexander's mother, Olympias, returned from Epirus to Macedonia, an event which culminated in a dreadful catastrophe. Philip Arrhidaeus and Eurydice fell victim to her revenge, but Olympias herself was besieged in Pydna by Cassander. She died in the following year (316 B.C.), slain by the swords of the Macedonians. The house of the Argeads focussed on one individual, the seven-year-old boy, Alexander (IV), whom Cassander held, together with Roxane, in safe keeping at Amphipolis. . . .

The remaining successors now viewed the "One Eyed" as their chief enemy, and never acknowledged his leading position. Seleucus, the satrap of Babylonia, fled to Egypt. Ptolemy, Lysimachus and Cassander formed a new coalition aimed against the ruler in Asia. Antigonus parried this thrust by proclaiming from Tyre in 315 B.C. that he had consummated the takeover as administrator of the empire, using, undoubtedly, a decree of the Macedonian military assembly. . . .

Although Antigonus had the advantage of the home bases, he did not succeed in exploiting this advantage. In particular, the defeat of his son Demetrius by Ptolemy in the battle of Gaza (312 B.C.) was a serious reverse for the aspiring Antigonus. After this battle the Babylonian satrap Seleucus returned to his old province, where fighting continued until 309/8 B.C. with oscillating results.

With the Peace of 311 B.C., concluded between Antigonus on the one side and Ptolemy, Lysimachus and Cassander on the other (Seleucus was not included in the Peace), the struggle for Alexander's empire saw a temporary conclusion. For Antigonus the result was disappointing. Instead of recognition as "Administrator of the Empire" he was only conceded a kind of superintendent right over Asia. His opponents were confirmed in the possession of their territories, Ptolemy as ruler of Egypt and dependencies, Lysimachus as master of Thrace. Cassander was the only one who found himself in an essentially worsened position. He was to exercise the sovereignty over Macedonia only so long as the young Alexander IV remained a minor. . . . In 310/9 B.C. Cassander had him and his mother Roxane put to death. . . .

Early Hellenistic Kingdoms Emerge

The peace treaty of 311 B.C. and the obliteration of the Macedonian royal house formed the conditions for the emergence of five large territorial states. The most important was the Asiatic realm of Antigonus . . . derived from the *"strategia* of Asia" created in 321 B.C. It embraced the regions from the Hellespont to the Euphrates. . . . Until its fall at the battle of Ipsus (301 B.C.) the empire was continuously on the defensive, so that the organisational reform inaugurated by Antigonus was repeatedly interrupted and impeded. The loss of Babylonia (312 B.C.) and the regions between the Tigris and the Indus—conquered by Seleucus in the closing decades of the fourth century—shook the empire. But Antigonus, as lord of Asia Minor and Syria, still controlled the important trade routes from Upper Asia to the Mediterranean, and thereby substantially tapped the revenues from world trade. The state founded by Antigonus was a reflection of Alexander's global empire, both politically and economically overshadowing all other kingdoms of its time.

The vulnerable empire of Antigonus contrasted with the smaller and more compact domain of the Lagid Ptolemy, composed of Egypt, Cyrenaica, South Syria (temporarily) and the island of Cyprus. Cyprus, greatly coveted for its wealth in copper and timber, after 306 B.C. was in the possession of Antigonus, and later of Demetrius (until 295 B.C.). Attempts on the part of Ptolemy to gain a solid foothold on the south coast of Anatolia and above all in Greece were in the long run without important success. Apart from Antigonus, it was Cassander who exerted a decisive influence on Greece. His garrisons were to be found in many regions throughout Hellas and in Epirus (until 307 B.C.). He was especially active in the Peloponnesus, where since 308 B.C. the aged Polyperchon appeared as his deputy (*strategos*). Cassander's confederate Lysimachus held the key to the straits, so important for the subsistence of the Greek motherland. His Thracian empire, extending from the Aegean Sea to the mouth of the Danube, also included the Greek cities on the west coast of the Black Sea. Following in the footsteps of King Philip II, Lysimachus achieved much of an exemplary and enduring character in spreading Greek culture and civilisation in the Balkan countries. His sharp sword maintained a guard against the barbarians surging down from the north.

While the realms of Antigonus, Ptolemy, Cassander and Lysimachus were oriented towards the Mediterranean, the efforts of Seleucus took him in the opposite direction. Beginning with a military campaign from Babylon in 308 B.C. he conquered the entire Iranian East, and halted only at the portals of India. . . .

Antigonus was apparently absorbed in indecisive battles with Seleucus in Babylonia until 309/8 B.C. By 307 B.C. Antigonus had mobilised enough to assume the offensive against Ptolemy and Cassander, the masters of Greece. His first objective was Athens, which had been under the sovereignty of the Macedonian ruler since 317 B.C. When the fleet of [his son] Demetrius Poliorcetes forced an entry into Piraeus the Athenians openly sided with the party of the Antigonid. The regent of Athens, Demetrius of Phalerum, had no alternative but to capitulate. . . . In exuberant enthusiasm at having regained their "liberty" the Athenians conferred a number of unusual honours on Antigonus and Demetrius Poliorcetes. Both rulers were celebrated as "Saviour Gods," and gilded statues were erected in their honour. . . .

The second blow of Antigonus struck the Egyptian satrap, Ptolemy. In the great naval battle of Salamis (on Cyprus) Demetrius emerged as decisive victor (306 B.C.). For two decades after this control over the Aegean and the eastern Mediterranean was in the hands of Antigonus and the "sea king" Demetrius. As did Alexander after Gaugamela, Antigonus after the naval victory decorated himself with the royal title and conferred it on his son as co-regent. Antigonus regarded himself as the successor to Alexander and as master of the entire former empire of the Macedonian conqueror, with all other rulers his subordinates. The latter were, however, by no means prepared to acknowledge the superiority of the "One Eyed." After Antigonus' attack on Egypt by sea and by land had proved abortive, Ptolemy I also adopted the royal title (305 B.C.). The other successors—Cassander, Lysimachus, Seleucus—followed suit. . . . The royal title had now become the expression of sovereign rule over a territorial realm and thus the dismemberment of Alexander's empire into five individual kingdoms was formally acknowledged.

Ipsus: Victory of a New Idea

Antigonus continued the struggle against Ptolemy with an attack on the island of Rhodes, which was on friendly terms with the Egyptian ruler (305 B.C.). With the latest siege machines, which included a "helepolis" [siege tower] nine storeys high with catapult cannons, Demetrius rammed the walls of the city for a whole year, but without success. A peace treaty was then concluded in 304 B.C. through the mediation of Greek states. The Rhodians retained unlimited possession of their freedom and autonomy. The feat of surviving the siege marked the beginning of a great rise to power for the city. Within a short time Rhodes became the leading commercial power and the great clearing-house of the eastern Mediterranean.

On Greek soil, developments were much more promising for Antigonus and Demetrius. Here Cassander had indeed made progress, chiefly in central Greece. . . . Demetrius, however, succeeded in forcing him into substantial retreat. The military and political progress of Antigonus' highly-talented son was ultimately crowned by the renewal of the Panhellenic Corinthian League. . . . All Hellenic states (with the exception of Sparta, Messenia and Thessaly) sent their representatives to the constituent session of the new Hellenic Alliance, and elected Antigonus and Demetrius as its protectors. As with the League of Philip and Alexander, this present federation was concluded in perpetuity. . . .

The opponents answered this with a new alliance against Antigonus. The plan of the members of the coalition provided for a combined attack by Cassander, Lysimachus, Ptolemy and Seleucus. Although seriously threatened by an offensive thrust of Demetrius against Thessaly, Cassander nevertheless placed a considerable part of his troops at the disposal of Lysimachus for the assault on Asia Minor. Cassander had correctly judged the situation. Demetrius was recalled to Asia Minor by his father.

Antigonus' position was greatly weakened at its most sensitive point, in western Anatolia, when two senior provincial governors . . . went over to the camp of Lysimachus. With the object of splitting the forces of the great coalition, Antigonus sent a flying corps to Babylonia, to force Seleucus to rush back from Asia Minor to Babylonia. This move on the part of Antigonus had no success. Much more effective, the forces of Lysimachus and Seleucus effected a union in the spring of 301 B.C. in northern Phrygia. Lysimachus, the most competent general of the coalition, had until then kept Antigonus saddled down with delaying tactics, although the latter was superior to him in strength. The decision came in the summer of 301 B.C. at Ipsus, in the vicinity of Synnada. In numbers the armies which faced each other were almost equal. The members of the coalition, slightly weaker in infantry, possessed an indisputable superiority in elephants. The 480 elephants which Seleucus . . . had put into the field were opposed by only seventy-five of Antigonus. In the battle an essential factor was the conduct of Demetrius, who permitted himself to be lured off the battlefield while pursuing the enemy cavalry. Antigonus fell in battle, eighty years of age, his army routed.

From the booty Lysimachus received Asia Minor as far as the Taurus. From then on he ruled over a powerful empire on both sides of the straits and controlled communications between Europe and Asia. Seleucus obtained the remainder of Antigonus' realm, in the main only Syria. In Asia Minor Cassander did not receive anything, although it is possible that he was granted a free hand in Greece. . . . Ptolemy, who had kept in the background during the struggle against Antigonus, was ordered to hand over South Syria to Seleucus. He did not, however, and South Syria (Coele Syria) hereafter was the bone of contention between the Seleucids and the Ptolemies for 150 years.

The battle of Ipsus buried the idea of the single, undivided empire of Alexander, and established the system of Hellenistic states. Although the various states would still experience many changes, the system resting on a balance of power remained. It was the hallmark of Hellenistic history until the Romans plunged into the intricate works and knocked one Hellenistic state after another from the political scene. Ipsus was the victory of a new idea, the concept that a particular territory belongs to the individual who acquires it by force of arms and can guarantee it his protection. . . . The new monarchies rested not on birth and not on legitimacy, but on the practical ability of the ruler to conduct the army and the affairs of state. . . .

The Tumultuous Exploits of Demetrius

The political situation in the two decades following the battle of Ipsus (301 B.C.) was controlled by a system of states comprised of four empires. Outside this system, represented by the territorial states of Seleucus, Lysimachus, Ptolemy and by Macedonia, was the restless figure of Demetrius Poliorcetes. His domain was not the land, but the sea, over which he had control with his great fleet. He was the first of the successors who allowed his plans to range westwards, to Italy and Sicily, and in this he was the forerunner of Pyrrhus. . . . There arose the vision of a great Mediterranean empire ruled by Macedonians and Greeks, but within a short time this idea sank into oblivion. In general, the inconstant nature of Demetrius was the animating force in the history of the first fifteen years after Ipsus (301–286 B.C.). At one point the strivings of almost all the kings intersected in the attempt to gain control of the Macedonian monarchy. After the death of the energetic and resolute Cassander (298 B.C.) and after the elimination of his sons, practically all the successors in turn had themselves proclaimed "King of the Macedonians" by the military assembly. Demetrius, Pyrrhus, Lysimachus, Seleucus and Ptolemy Ceraunus all took that title—evidence not only for the great material importance of the country which had been the cradle of all their states, but no less also for the indescribable fascination which the Macedonian kingship held. . . .

The opposition between Seleucus and Ptolemy contributed essentially to the general situation. During the decisive struggle against Antigonus . . . Ptolemy had occupied South Syria (Coele Syria), and did not return it even after Ipsus. In order to strengthen his position the Lagid established dynastic relations with Lysimachus and later also with the house of Cassander. . . .

Due to the dominions of Demetrius on the Phoenician coast, the empire of Seleucus was greatly confined and robbed of its most important access to the sea. . . . The death of Cassander prompted Demetrius to exert his efforts in a new direction. He resumed the struggle for Greece (296 B.C.). After an initial assault on Athens failed, he blockaded the city by sea and by land in 295 B.C. This time the Athenians resisted to the utmost. The Athenian "tyrant" Lachares had the temple treasures melted down; even the golden robe of Pallas Athena which had survived the Peloponnesian War was not spared. When Ptolemy's attempt to send a naval relieving force miscarried, Athens was forced to capitulate. . . . Demetrius stationed garrisons [nearby and] . . . the city became part of his empire.

Demetrius had meanwhile suffered serious territorial losses in Asia. Seleucus had taken possession of Cilicia, Lysimachus of numerous Greek cities in Asia Minor, and Ptolemy of important Cyprus. The most vital naval bases were thereby lost. At this juncture the struggle for the inheritance of Cassander presented Demetrius with the desired opportunity to intervene in the throne disturbances in Macedonia. Antipater and Alexander, the sons of Cassander, had divided the country between them. Alexander called in Demetrius and the Epirote king, Pyrrhus. Demetrius was the more unscrupulous; he had Alexander murdered, whereupon the Macedonian military assembly proclaimed Demetrius king of the Macedonians (294 B.C.).

Demetrius, as master of Macedonia and Thessaly, large parts of central Greece and the Peloponnesus . . . was at that time . . . the most powerful figure in Europe. His resources and the number of his forces very considerably surpassed those of Philip II and Alexander (before his departure for Asia). . . . Demetrius did not understand how to exploit his great advantages, for his great deficiency was political adaptability. . . . He was indeed a great general but no statesman. For Macedonia his rule was a disaster, and . . . the country never had a worse king than Demetrius. . . .

The dream of the unification of Alexander's empire still continued to occupy the mind of Demetrius. In the midst of his preparations he was surprised by an attack from his opponents. From east and west, at first Lysimachus, and then Pyrrhus also invaded Macedonia. Defection from the unpopular Demetrius rapidly spread throughout the country. His rule collapsed, and Pyrrhus and Lysimachus divided the land between them (summer 287 B.C.). . . .

Abandoned by his followers, Demetrius fell into the hands of Seleucus (286 B.C.), and died in 283 B.C. in royal confinement, in the vicinity of Apameia on the Orontes. With him disappeared the individual who had been the moving force of the period. He kept the world in suspense for fifteen years after the downfall of the empire of Antigonus, . . . moved by a restless mind which did not capitulate in the face of even the greatest difficulties—most often created by himself. . . .

The Emergence of Stable Empires

Now tensions in the family of the Hellespontine king, Lysimachus, still prevented the world from finding rest. Lysimachus had forced his rival, Pyrrhus, out of western Macedonia (286 B.C.?). He also conquered Paeonia and extended his sphere of influence through Thessaly deep into Hellas. As administrator of a great empire Lysimachus achieved exemplary results, chiefly in the field of finance. His coins were famous and still struck long after his death in Greek cities, valued for commercial reasons, primarily trade with the Balkan peoples. The Greek cities of his empire found Lysimachus a hard master. . . . Arsinoe, the daughter of Ptolemy and third wife of Lysimachus, was able to prejudice him against his own son . . . Agathocles, who had just distinguished himself as an outstanding *strategos* against Demetrius. Lysimachus had him executed (283 B.C.). The followers of Agathocles now took up relations with Seleucus. Defection from Lysimachus spread in Asia Minor. . . . The issue was decided at Curupedion (north of Magnesia [in western Asia Minor]). . . . Seleucus emerged as victor, and Lysimachus fell in battle (February 281 B.C.). Seleucus could not remain inactive at the Hellespont, for the European dominions of Lysimachus required a new master. What is more, Seleucus regarded himself as legitimate "king of the Macedonians," perhaps on the basis of a proclamation by his army after the victory at Curupedion. At that moment, as Seleucus set foot on European soil, he was snatched away by the murderous dagger of Ptolemy Ceraunus . . . (the "Thunderbolt"), eldest son of Ptolemy I. . . . The army now proclaimed Ptolemy Ceraunus king of the Macedonians. . . .

The death of Ptolemy I (283 B.C.) preceded that of Lysimachus and Seleucus. As early as 285 B.C. he had appointed Ptolemy the son of Berenice as viceroy. Thus the change of sovereigns in Egypt transpired without friction. The Hellenistic system, however, which had experienced two decades of fighting and disturbances since the battle of Ipsus, had stood the crucial test. The idea of a universal empire, a dream that Seleucus had been the last to entertain, had become a thing of the past. From unsettled states with continuously oscillating frontiers, stable empires had emerged: Egypt, with its dependencies, under the Ptolemies; Asia under the Seleucids; while Macedonia alone . . . had still to wait for a few years to become consolidated. With Ptolemy II and Antiochus I a new generation took over the destinies of the Hellenistic world. The great Alexander, whose example had again and again spurred the successors on in the struggle for the universal empire, they knew only from the accounts related by their fathers. His image grew gradually dimmer. The goal was not the struggle for the empire of Alexander, but maintenance of the separate kingdoms which had been won by the sword. As a result of almost endless wars the requirements of peace-time had not received due attention. The problems of population, the economy, the formation of an efficient bureaucracy, the creation of a monarchical constitution and of an official ruler cult—all this and much more claimed the total energies of the new rulers. Problems which the fathers had had to postpone, the sons attempted to solve by their own methods.

Hellenistic Armies and Warfare

Peter Connolly

Knowledge of the weapons, armor, and battlefield formations and tactics of the Hellenistic period greatly illuminates the battles and wars fought by both Alexander's immediate successors and the Greek monarchs who succeeded them. This informative overview of Hellenistic warfare is by the noted ancient military historian (and foremost artistic interpreter of the ancient world) Peter Connolly. He begins by introducing the main sources for the armies of the period—the second-century B.C. Greek historian Polybius, the first-century B.C. Greek writer Asclepiodotus, and the first-century A.D. Greek biographer Plutarch. Connolly then goes on to describe the makeup and weapons of the Macedonian phalanx (composed of pikemen, as opposed to the traditional Greek phalanx, made up of spearmen called hoplites) and how the formation moved and attacked.

Most of our knowledge of the phalanx and of Hellenistic warfare in general comes from the later Hellenistic period (c. 220–168 BC). Our principal source is Polybius, the most reliable of all the ancient historians on military matters. He gives many descriptions of battles in which the Macedonian type of phalanx was used, and at one point even describes the basic structure and function of the phalanx. However, he never goes further. He wrote a separate treatise on this subject which is no longer extant, and probably for this reason did not elaborate on the subject in his history. Arrian in his *Ars Tactica* confirms the existence of this work but gives no details. It is unfortunate that Polybius never mentions the title of even one of the subordinate officers of the phalanx, which would give us a foothold when examining the writings of the later tacticians.

The Hypothetical Phalanx

By the 1st century BC Hellenistic warfare was virtually dead and the study of Macedonian tactics had become a branch of philosophy. From this period comes the work of Asclepiodotus. In his treatise he gives an account of the structure, drill and tactics of an idealised phalanx. He gives a complete breakdown of a phalanx of 16,384 men, which is composed of 1,024 files, each of 16 men. The figure of 1,024 is arrived at because it is the tenth power of two. Such a phalanx as this probably never existed. Only at the battle of Pydna [fought between the Romans and Macedonians in 168 B.C.] is a 16,000 phalanx attested. Within this framework Asclepiodotus can project a mathematical formula for the phalanx. As the files are coupled in twos, fours, eights and so on, he can record the name of every unit and officer. Arrian in his *Ars Tactica* gives an almost identical account drawn either from Asclepiodotus or from a common source.

The basic unit of Asclepiodotus' phalanx is the *syntagma* (meaning literally that which is put together). It consists of 256 men (16 files of 16) plus a rear guard officer (*ouragos*), adjutant (*hyperetes*), herald (*stratokeryx*), signaller (*semeiophoros*) and a trumpeter (*salpingktes*). These were all supernumeraries [extra personnel] and were not part of the phalanx. The *syntagma* was commanded by a *syntamatarch*. It was divided into two *taxeis* commanded by a *taxiarch*. Following the usual Greek practice the *syntagmatarch* would command the right half of the unit and his subordinate, the *taxiarch*, would command the left. Each *taxis* was in turn divided into two *tetrarchies* commanded by *tetrarchs*. Each *tetrarchy* was divided into two *dilochiai* or double files each commanded by a *dilochites*, and each *dilochia* was subdivided into two *lochoi* or files commanded by *lochagoi*. . . .

Asclepiodotus couples two *syntagmata* into a *pentekosiarchy* commanded by a *pentekosiarch*, which he similarly doubles to form a *chiliarchy* commanded by a *chiliarch*. Two *chiliarchies* formed a *merachy* under a *merarch*. Asclepiodotus adds that this 2,048-strong unit had formerly been called a wing (*keras*) or a complement (*telos*). Consequently two of these would have made up a phalanx in an earlier period. This is reflected in the name for a double *merarchy*—a *phalangarchy* commanded by a *phalangarch* (who was originally a general—*strategos*). A double *phalangarchy* formed a wing (*keras*) commanded by a *kerarch*, and two wings formed a phalanx commanded by a *strategos*.

It seems worth recording all this to save the reader having to refer to the original work, but there probably never was such a phalanx as this. Most of the divisions and officers above the *syntagma* are probably hypothetical, arrived at by collecting all the names that could be found and making up those that could not, to build up a rigid mathematical pattern.

A More Realistic Breakdown for the Phalanx

In 1934 and 1935 a fragmentary list of Macedonian military regulations which had been found at Amphipolis was published. This inscription, which dates to the reign of Philip V (221–178 BC), lists, among other things, a series of fines to be imposed for loss of equipment and disciplinary matters such as sleeping when on guard. It also mentions several lower officers and units. The *syntagma* is never mentioned, nor is it mentioned by Polybius. The Greek historian, however, regularly mentions a unit called a *speira*. He also uses this word for the Roman *maniple*, which was the smallest tactical unit of the legion, just as the *syntagma* is the smallest tactical unit of Asclepiodotus' phalanx. The *speira*, or its commander the *speirarch*, is also mentioned several times on the Amphipolis inscription. The term *syntagma* is never used in relation to the armies of the Greek peninsula but it is mentioned in documents relating to the Hellenistic armies outside Europe. Similarly, the *speira* is never mentioned outside Europe. It therefore seems reasonable to conclude that the *speira* was the Greek version of the *syntagma*.

The Amphipolis inscription regularly mentions *tetrarchs* with *speirarchs* in such a way as to suggest that the former were the immediate subordinates of the latter. A *speira* was composed of four *tetrarchies* which were each made up of four *lochoi*. . . . One must therefore hold in doubt the intermediate officers—the *taxiarch* and the *dilochites*—mentioned by Asclepiodotus.

It would seem that the structure of the Macedonian phalanx above the *speira* was also organised on a four-fold basis, i.e. four *speirai* formed a battalion (possibly called a *chiliarchy*), and four battalions formed a *strategia* commanded by a *strategos*. . . .

The only trouble with a basic *strategia* of around 4,000 men is that we are beginning to get back to the problems posed by Asclepiodotus' formula, i.e. how do you divide into two wings a phalanx of 10,000, which was the basic strength of the phalanx of both Antigonus Doson and Philip V?

Two units appear tantalisingly in the ancient authors but, like the silver shields of Alexander's army, they are never clearly identified. Again one gets the feeling that everybody knew what they were and therefore there was no point in wasting time identifying them. The first is the brazen shields, and the other the white shields. Polybius mentions the brazen shields in his account of the battle of Sellasia (222 BC) where they appear to be part of the 10,000-strong phalanx, but he does not give their strength. Three years later they again appear, also apparently as part of the 10,000-strong phalanx. Philip takes 3,000 of them (implying that the unit was larger than this) on his winter expedition to the Peloponnesus. Plutarch mentions them again at the battle of Pydna in 168 BC, but he too adds no explanation.

The white shields turn up in Plutarch's account of the battle of Sellasia and again in his account of the battle of Pydna. On both occasions they seem to be part of the phalanx. I would therefore tentatively suggest that Philip's phalanx was made up of two 5,000-strong *strategiai* called the white and brazen shields, each consisting of five *chiliarchies*.

The Pike

The Macedonian phalangite [phalanx member] was armed with a long pike (*sarissa*) which Polybius says in his day measured 14 cubits (c. 6.3m). This length is not quite so outrageous as some commentators would suggest. In the Middle Ages the Swiss used pikes 5.5m long, and pikes up to 5.75m in length are preserved in the New Armouries of the Tower of London.

Polybius states that the *sarissa* was weighted at the butt end (presumably this means that it had a heavy shoe). He then goes on to explain how it was held. The front hand (left) grasps the *sarissa* about 4 cubits (c. 1.8m) from the butt, with the right hand about 75cm further back. This meant that 10 cubits (c. 4.5m) of the pike projected beyond the body. In the file each man was 3ft (c. 90cm) from the man in front; therefore in a charge the pikes of the first five ranks would project beyond the front rank with, as Polybius says, 2 cubits between each line of points.

The rear 11 ranks did not level their spears but kept them slanting up in the air to break the force of missiles, whilst at the same time using their weight to add to the force of the charge. The phalanx could be drawn up either in open order with two paces per file, in close order with one pace per file, or in locked shields formation with only half a pace per man. Alexander's phalanx formed up with locked shields against Porus' elephants in India.

The pikes were carried in the upright position but on the order to attack were levelled and the phalanx charged.

A massive spear butt weighing 1.07kg and a small spear head weighing 0.097kg were found among the weapons in the tomb of Philip II at Vergina in Greece. Fitted with a 5.9m haft tapering from 17mm at the point to 40mm in diameter at the grip produced a pike with a point of balance at almost exactly the point where Polybius says the front hand should be.

The Macedonian hoplite also carried a sword which he would only use if his pike broke. The hoplite sword remained in use, but the most popular sword of the period was the *kopis*, a single-edged weapon with a curved blade; an example 72cm long is in the Athens Archaeological Museum.

The Shield

The phalangite was armed with a small, round shield (*aspis*) which Asclepiodotus describes as made of bronze, not too concave and about 8 palms (c. 60cm) in diameter. Like everything else to do with the Macedonian phalanx, the shield has caused much confusion.

Fragments of a Macedonian shield were found at Pergamum in Turkey. These consisted only of the bronze sheath (65–67cm in diameter) and small fragments of parchment that had been used as padding between the wood and bronze. Nothing remained of the grip. The sheath was attached to the wooden core by four rectangular tongues and a little over 100 darts cut along the edge of the metal which were folded over on to the inside.

Plutarch, describing the Macedonians at the battle of Pydna (168 BC), says that their shields were hung on their left shoulders, and when they advanced they brought them round to the front. This has led some commentators to suggest that the shield had no grip. Representations of the Macedonian shield show that it was rimless, i.e. that it did not have the broad rim on the inside edge that was so characteristic of the Argive [earlier standard hoplite] shield. This type of shield was adopted as it was impossible to hold a two-handed spear whilst using an Argive shield, as the left forearm was held against the inside of the shield by the armband and the hand could not reach the pike. This is obviously why Asclepiodotus says that the shield must not be too curved.

The Aemilius Paullus victory monument at Delphi shows the inside of such a rimless shield. It has an Argive-style armband and handgrip. A few years ago the author made a copy of this shield with a bronze facing similar to the one found at Pergamum. The shield weighed about 5kg. Experiments showed that it could be handled very efficiently using only the armband and controlling the angle with the neck strap. When an Argive shield is being carried, the inside of the rim fits comfortably over the left shoulder taking the weight off the arm. It was the absence of this ridge on the Macedonian type that made a carrying strap necessary. This strap would also have taken much of the weight of the great pike. When used outside the phalanx without a pike, the handgrip would be used. . . .

Breastplate and Helmet

The Amphipolis inscription lists a scale of fines imposed on Macedonian phalangites for loss of pieces of their equipment. The cuirass [body armour] for the ordinary rank and file is called a *cotthybos*, whereas for the front rankers or officers it is referred to as a *thorax* or *hemi-thorax*. The *cotthybos* has been plausibly identified with the linen cuirass, whilst the *thorax* and *hemi-thorax* were probably metal plated. This difference is amplified when one reads that the officers were fined twice as much as the rank and file.

The implication of this is that the front rank was more heavily armed than the succeeding ranks, and it is possible that the rear ranks wore no body armour at all. The Amphipolis relief mentions greaves, helmets and cuirasses, but this does not necessarily imply that all the ranks wore them. It certainly seems unlikely, for example, that the men behind the front five ranks would need greaves.

The sculptures and paintings of the period, both Greek and Etruscan, show the wide variety of armour in use at this time. Besides the basic linen cuirass typical of the classical era, quilted cuirasses also appear on later Etruscan sculptures. On these sculptures one also finds varieties of plated linen cuirass, covered with either scales or overlapping rectangular plates. . . .

The victory frieze from the temple of Athena at Pergamum in western Turkey shows a full-length muscled cuirass, a shorter cuirass which could be the *hemi-thorax* of the Amphipolis inscription, and part of a decorated linen type cuirass. This, of course, could have been made of iron like the cuirass from Vergina. This frieze also shows a Celtic mail shirt. Polybius, in his description of the Roman army of this period, says that the wealthier Romans wore mail. As he does not explain what mail is, one must assume that the Greeks of his day also wore it.

The Thracian helmet continued to be popular and is shown on the Pergamum reliefs. Several types of high-crowned helmets are also shown. These may have been developed as a defence against the slashing swords of the Celts. This type of helmet allowed for a great deal of padding between the top of the head and the helmet. At this period, which coincides with the most aggressive period of the Celtic invasions, there was a general tendency to adopt high-crowned helmets.

The Composition of the Army

At a glance the composition of the later Hellenistic armies does not seem to have changed much since Alexander's day. The Macedonian army of Antigonus Doson and Philip V still had *hypaspists* [a later name for traditional Greek hoplites, fighting with shields and six-foot spears], peltasts [javelin throwers], slingers and archers supporting the phalanx. However, these do not always seem to perform the same tasks as in the earlier period. The *hypaspists* now seem to refer to a body of staff officers (who undertook special tasks) and the *agema*, the king's bodyguard. The Amphipolis code says that their tents are to be erected immediately after those of the king and his immediate entourage.

The peltasts of Philip's army appear to have completely changed. At Cynoscephalae they formed up alongside the phalanx and even doubled their depth. . . . These peltasts were in fact *hypaspists*. Whether they were armed with pike or spear is impossible to say as the sources are contradictory. . . .

The most noticeable change since the time of Alexander was the switch of priority from cavalry to infantry. In Alexander's army the proportion of cavalry to infantry was about 1:6, whereas in the later Macedonian army it was around 1:20. One should not make too much of this—at the battle of Chaeronea in 338 the proportion was 1:15. The reason for the high proportion of cavalry in Alexander's army was that mobility was the key to the conquest of Persia. It was well known that Greek infantry was superior to anything Persia could produce, but the phalanx could only defeat what it could catch. It was Philip's phalanx that won the battle of Chaeronea, and yet the massive build-up of the Macedonian cavalry must be credited to Philip. There could only be one reason for this—the planned invasion of Persia with its vast cavalry resources. Although cavalry continued to play an important part in Asia for about 100 years, after the death of

Alexander in Europe it quickly reverted to its subsidiary position as phalanx battled with phalanx. Epirus and all the old city states had adopted the Macedonian phalanx and, since the result of the battle depended on this, it tended to become heavier and consequently less manoeuvrable. . . .

After the death of Alexander, the veteran silver shields regiment had come under the control of Eumenes, on whose death they passed to Antigonus. Here we lose track of them. If they were a permanent veteran unit and constantly receiving recruits from the veterans of other units, they could have survived. If not, they must have died out. A hundred years later Antiochus, the successor of Seleucus who had deposed Antigonus, had 10,000 soldiers 'armed in the Macedonian fashion', most of whom were armed with silver shields. These are distinct from his 20,000-strong phalanx and one is tempted to suggest that these were *hypaspists*. Certainly Antiochus has *hypaspists* in his army, as well as an *agema* which is mentioned at the siege of Sardis.

The Army on the Move

On the march in hostile territory the army was led by a regular vanguard of light-armed troops. Philip used his mercenaries for this job. They were accompanied by pioneers whose job was to clear the road. Behind these came the phalanx, with light-armed troops in parallel columns on either side to ward off attacks. If an attack was threatened from one flank, the light armed would cover this side only. Similarly, the rear guard was also made up of light-armed troops. Philip used his Cretans, whom Polybius describes as the most effective skirmishers, as his rearguard. The baggage train was placed at the point farthest from any expected danger. If the threat was from the front, the baggage would be at the back, and when retreating it would be at the front. If an attack was expected from one flank, the baggage train would be placed alongside the phalanx on the other flank.

When looking for a camping site, ground was chosen which offered the best natural defences. Polybius criticised the Greeks for their lack of energy when camping, comparing them unfavourably with the Romans. In light of this it seems unlikely that the Romans got their ideas of camping from Pyrrhus when they captured his camp at Beneventum. . . . When necessary the Macedonians did entrench, especially if they intended to stay at the same site for some time. Like the Romans, they constructed a ditch and rampart with a palisade along the top. The palisade stakes were cut branches with stout shoots all round the main stem. Polybius is very critical of these, as he says that two or three attackers could together get hold of one stake and rip it out. When they had removed it, there was a gap left wide enough for them to break through.

The Macedonians may not have camped as well as the Romans, but they did post pickets [guards] along the approaches to the camp—a thing that the Romans do not seem to have done. It was the responsibility of the *tetrarchies* to provide these pickets and of the *tetrarchs* to inspect them. This duty was probably done on a rota as it was in the Roman army. The Amphipolis code stresses that, at night, inspections should be made without a light so as not to give advance warning to the guard.

Preparing for Battle

The line-up for battle was still basically the same as in the previous period, with the phalanx in the centre flanked by the peltasts, the light armed and the cavalry. The difference now was that the key to the battle was in the centre and not on the wings.

At the battle of Raphia in 217 the young Antiochus III of Syria, trying no doubt to emulate Alexander, charged the Egyptian cavalry and drove them from the field. He pursued them so far, however, that by the time he returned the battle was over and he had lost. Ptolemy, who appeared to be losing the battle, took over the phalanx who, encouraged by his presence, drove the Syrian phalanx from the field. By the time that Antiochus, confident that he had won the battle, returned, Ptolemy was in possession of the battlefield and Antiochus' infantry was scattered across the country in flight. Ptolemy stripped the enemy dead and collected and buried his own, whilst Antiochus was humiliated by being forced to retrieve his own dead under a flag of truce.

On rare occasions the phalanx was broken up into companies with other troops interspersed between them. Pyrrhus did this in Italy and Antigonus Doson did it with his silver shields at Sellasia.

Before battle commenced the general would ride along in front of his troops with his officers and friends reminding the soldiers of their past achievements and exhorting them to fight bravely, pointing out the advantages of victory, usually concentrating on the booty to be won. In the case of Ptolemy and Antiochus, both of whom had only recently come to the throne and therefore could hardly boast of their past accomplishments, they relied more on their promises for the future.

The signal for battle, possibly a flag, was raised and the soldiers shouted their war cry several times. At Gabiene in 316 BC, where two Macedonian armies faced each other, they raised their war cries alternately several times.

Whilst waiting for the order to prepare for battle, each phalangite stood with his pike resting on the ground and held upright with his right hand. His shield hung by its strap around his neck and over the back of his left shoulder. On the order to prepare for battle, he would swing the shield round to the front and pass his left forearm through the band. He would then raise his left hand across his chest and grasp the pike level with his head. On the order 'level pikes', his right hand would slip down until the arm was straight, then he would lower his pike until it was parallel to the ground at waist level. The order to charge was given on the trumpet. If, however, the ground was very broken and the army split up as it was at Sellasia, the signal to charge was given with flags—a white one for the infantry and a red one for the cavalry—and would be relayed by the trumpeter attached to each *speira*. The battle was normally started on the wings.

Advancing on the Enemy

When advancing in battle order, the phalanx had to be drawn up in open order and double depth. This was achieved by the alternate *lochoi* falling back and coming into line behind the file on their right. On coming into range of the enemy, the alternate *lochoi* moved up again to form close order. This was done because of the difficulty of advancing through open country in close order with no room to manoeuvre around natural obstacles.

If there was no room to deploy the whole army before reaching the battlefield, Polybius suggests that the advance should be made in either double or quadruple phalanx, and that the rear phalanxes should deploy on either wing when they reached the open ground. When the route to the battlefield was restricted, the phalanx could form up and then turn into column of march so that all the officers were on one side of the column and all the *ouragoi* on the other. Asclepiodotus mentions this formation and Polybius is certainly describing it at the third battle of Mantinea in 207 BC, and again at the battle of Cynoscephalae ten years later. At Mantinea the Spartan tyrant Machanidas wheeled his column to the right to form up in battle order, and at Cynoscephalae Philip wheeled his to the left to form up his right wing. . . .

If the enemy appeared in the rear the phalanx had to turn about. This, however, would leave the *ouragoi* in the front rank and the officers at the back. This was rectified by countermarching. Any one of three methods could be used to do this. The file leaders could stand still while the rest of the file formed up in front of them, and then the whole file turned about face. This was the Macedonian method. Asclepiodotus is not very happy about this as it appears to be a retreat. He prefers the method used by the Spartans where the rear tankers stood fast and the rest of the file formed up behind them and then faced about. This appears to be an advance. There was a third possibility, the Cretan or Persian countermarch, where the file leader and the *ouragos* changed places and the intervening ranks did likewise. This involves neither an advance nor a retreat. Whichever method is used, the problem with countermarching is that the commanders finish up on the left of their units and not the right. This could be rectified by countermarching the ranks of each unit. Of course it was possible to countermarch the whole phalanx or wing in this way, but to do so in the face of the enemy would be suicidal and could only be considered as a parade ground manoeuvre. Anyway, there was no great disadvantage in having the chain of command from the left. Normally, if it was considered necessary, each *speira* would countermarch its ranks. . . .

Polybius lists the advantages and disadvantages of the phalanx to explain to his readers why the Macedonians lost the battle of Cynoscephalae. Under ideal circumstances nothing could withstand the charge of the phalanx. But the phalanx can only operate really efficiently over even ground with no ditches, clefts, clumps of trees, ridges or water courses which break up the formation and so destroy its strength. At Pydna the flexible Roman maniples forced their way into the gaps in the phalanx and broke it up. Once this had happened the phalanx was defenceless as the *sarissa* was obviously useless for close combat and, encumbered by their long pikes, the Macedonians were unable to turn and face an attack from any other direction than the front. To signal that they wished to surrender or desert the phalangites customarily raised their *sarissae* into the upright position.

After the Fighting

When the battle was over the troops were recalled by trumpet. The victor stripped the enemy dead and buried his own. The captured armour was hung up in the temple porticos. In thanks for the victory shields were usually inscribed and dedicated in a shrine. Polybius tells the amusing story of the dedication of the shields after the siege of Medion by the Aetolians. The siege was almost over but, as the elections were due, the Aetolian general was frightened he might be replaced before he had captured the town and so lose the credit for it. (This is a very common feature in both Greek and Roman warfare.) In order to appease the current general, but at the same time not detract from whoever might succeed him, a compromise was reached and it was determined to inscribe the shields as being won 'by the Aetolian general and the candidates for the next year's office'. Embarrassingly for the Aetolians, the siege was raised and the Medionians parodied the Aetolian resolution in amusing fashion by using exactly the same wording for their shields, changing only the 'by' of the inscription to 'from'.

Egypt and Alexandria Under the Ptolemies

Frank J. Frost

The Ptolemaic Kingdom, established by Alexander's general Ptolemy, was the longest-lived of the Hellenistic states, retaining a certain degree of independence until the death of its last ruler, Cleopatra VII, in 30 B.C. In this lucid, well-informed tract, University of California at Santa Barbara scholar Frank J. Frost describes the effective exploitation of Egypt by Ptolemy and his successors. In addition to the crucial areas of farming, the economy, and education and learning, Frost covers the uniqueness and importance of the city of Alexandria, which became a model for the other large cosmopolitan urban centers that sprang up in Hellenistic times.

For over 3,000 years, the inhabitants of the Nile Valley had lived in very much the same way, their lives dictated by one overwhelming factor, the Nile River. Each year, about the middle of July, the Nile began to rise. As it receded, it left behind a thick new layer of rich muck. The peasants of the Nile Valley needed only to trample in seed grain; the sun shone without interruption, irrigation was easy, and two or three harvests could be won from the constantly refreshed soil with a minimum of effort.

From the earliest times, powerful individuals had recognized that the land along the banks of the Nile was too valuable to be entrusted haphazardly to anyone who chose to farm it. All the land of Egypt, therefore, and the bodies of its inhabitants as well, were held to be the property of the god-king, the Pharaoh. Temporary title to some land was as-

Excerpted from *Greek Society*, by Frank J. Frost. Copyright ©1980 by D.C. Heath and Company. Reprinted with the permission of the Houghton Mifflin Company.

signed by the royal household to priests and nobles; the lands of all were worked by the Egyptian peasantry whose status was half serf–half tenant.

Every year, peasants sowed new crops, tended them to the extent necessary, and at harvest time, turned over the required quota to their landlord, whether a noble, a high priest, or Pharaoh himself. All details of acreage under cultivation, irrigation systems, planting, and harvest were under the supervision of a tightly organized bureaucracy that was able to calculate to a handful the amount of grain every plot ought to produce. Not only grain, but livestock as well were owed to the ultimate landlord, the Pharaoh.

The rigidly authoritarian social structure of Egypt was made possible by the world-renowned docility of the Egyptian peasant who took it for granted that Pharaoh was the son of God and held it to be only natural for Pharaoh to own the Nile Valley and to do with its inhabitants as he wished. We know that Egyptian peasants complained from time to time about unjust exactments or unrealistic quotas, or grumbled about haughty and arbitrary tax collectors; but the system itself was never questioned and seemed to all Egyptians of whatever station to be as permanent and unchanging as the Nile itself.

Such a rich land and such remarkably placid and hard-working inhabitants could not fail to attract attention from neighbors, particularly when the vigor of native Pharaohs began to flag. After 945 B.C., Libyans, Ethiopians, and Assyrians in succession became masters of the land. A native dynasty undertook a revival from 663 to 525, but in that year, the Persian Empire swallowed Egypt with minimal difficulty and exercised more or less effective control until the triumphant entry of Alexander the Great in 332.

Alexander and Ptolemy

The foreign masters of Egypt never considered tampering with the Egyptian economy or the well-established bureaucracy that made that economy work. All that was necessary to grasp the reins and enjoy the fruits of Egypt was to come to a satisfactory accommodation with the Egyptian priesthoods and to put one's own officials in charge of the tax-collecting apparatus. As long as the gods of Egypt were served, as long as priests and nobles were allowed to retain nominal honors, incomes, and lands, whoever was master of the Nile Valley could enjoy the enormous revenues of what had once been the royal lands of Egypt.

In his invasion of Egypt, as in so many other ventures, Alexander planned to outstrip his predecessors in every way. The first absolute necessity was to reach an accord with the gods who ruled the Nile Valley. The most recent Persian conquerors had plundered the Egyptian temples in an excess of monotheistic zeal. Alexander, with the usual Greek assumption that gods were universal, entered fully and sincerely into Egyptian religious life, restored the power of the priesthoods, and subsequently was recognized by the priests—and therefore by all Egypt—as the legitimate successor to the Pharaohs. . . .

The second necessity was to build an administrative headquarters where Alexander's deputies could rule Egypt while living in as Greek a setting as possible. For this purpose, the city of Alexandria was laid out along the sands of the Mediterranean on the western edge of the Nile Delta. It was to the infant capital of Alexandria that Ptolemy came in 322 to bury his friend and commander in a spot where his magnificent tomb would serve to enhance the legitimacy of Macedonian rule. Immediately, Ptolemy showed that he had fully understood Alexander's genius for organizing and consolidating new conquests. Egypt would give its new ruler obedience and wealth; it was up to Ptolemy to use these gifts constructively.

Throughout the Greek world the word went out: Ptolemy needed Greeks of every sort—clerks, accountants, masons, engineers, artists, doctors, actors, scholars, and of course, able-bodied men to serve in his army. Ptolemy intended that the Egyptian economic system should continue as before, staffed at the lowest bureaucratic levels by Egyptians, but that at a certain point, every channel of authority, every chain of command should become Greek, or Macedonian, and continue to the upper levels where an entirely Graeco-

Macedonian elite would exist and operate in an artificially created Greek world, a thin veneer riding upon and wholly insulated from the great mass of Egyptian peasants.

Exploiting Egypt's Farmlands

The Ptolemies, just like previous conquerors, intended that the land of the Nile should become a gigantic revenue-producing machine; but no earlier rulers had labored so fanatically and incessantly to make the machine so ruthlessly efficient. Through the centuries of Ptolemaic rule, an army of bureaucrats worked to record every transaction, every impost, every grain of wheat due to the crown, every fraction of the more than 200 taxes that could be levied on the foreign and native population. In the course of time, file cabinets had to be emptied to make room for more records; the used papyri were dumped in rubbish heaps out in the desert, soon to be covered and preserved by the shifting sands. Thousands of fragments from old Ptolemaic wastebaskets have been recovered, and these have made it possible for modern scholars to reconstruct a detailed picture of an ancient economy in operation.

Most of the Egyptian farmland was owned outright by the crown, and the rest of it was tightly controlled. The royal land was tilled by royal peasants. Each planting season they were issued seed grain to plant, and each harvest they were expected to turn over a certain percentage of the crop to the rent collectors. On the village level, these financial officials were themselves Egyptians who could read and write Greek. A number of villages formed a larger district, called *topos*; these in turn were divided among the major provinces of Egypt, called *nomoi*. In general, all officials above the village level were Greek or Macedonian.

The land of Egypt not directly owned by the crown was parceled out to worthy recipients on a more or less permanent leasehold system. The various Egyptian priesthoods were allowed to retain the use of wide temple lands because it was considered an absolute necessity to keep the native religious establishment complaisant; nevertheless, temple lands were taxed like any others. The Ptolemies also let out choice real estate to the high Greek and Macedonian officials as a form of incentive above and beyond mere salary. Finally, thousands of small tracts were awarded to mercenary soldiers who were thus lured into Ptolemaic service (the idea of arming native Egyptians was long resisted; when finally tried, it proved a mistake). Veterans were allowed to farm this land tax-free as long as one member of the family in each generation served in the army.

The millions of bushels of grain—primarily wheat and barley—harvested each year were Egypt's greatest export and financial resource. Grain harvesting along the Nile was supervised so efficiently that even after being taxed several times on its way down the Nile, after being assessed for warehouse charges, after being charged export duty, Egyptian wheat was still cheap enough to drive Sicilian or Black Sea wheat off the market in the cities of Italy and Greece.

But grain was only the largest item of the Nile Valley's agricultural bounty. Orchard crops, flax, and papyrus were also grown under royal supervision, while the Ptolemies vastly increased production of livestock, particularly sheep and pigs. Probably the second greatest revenue-producing export of Egypt was papyrus. The pith of this splendid reed was the universal writing material of the entire ancient world, and virtually every scrap was produced in Egypt where its manufacture was a royal monopoly.

Local Industries and Trade

This brings up another aspect of Ptolemaic enterprise. The Egyptians had been skillful and conscientious craftsmen for thousands of years. Taking this quality to be no less a valuable resource than the soil of the Nile, the Ptolemies converted all the most successful industries of Egypt into royal monopolies whose revenues, after wages and other overhead, went directly into the treasury. Among these industries was the production of beer—the Egyptian national drink from time immemorial. Every drop of the millions of gallons of this beverage consumed every year was supposed to be brewed in royal breweries. Even home production for home consumption was theoretically forbidden, although we may suppose this law received no more compliance than it deserved. Other rewarding monopolies were producing sesame and cottonseed oil for cooking, salt manufacture, linen weaving, operating public baths, and refining various highly prized scents and perfumes such as myrrh and frankincense.

A third rigorously exploited source of revenue was from trade—primarily foreign trade. Egypt produced for export a surplus of grain, papyrus, linen, ivory, cosmetics, various kinds of cut stone, drugs and cosmetics, and a wide variety of manufactured articles famed all over the Mediterranean world for the beauty and precision of Egyptian craftsmanship. Every item exported by the entrepreneurs of Alexandria and Naucratis was taxed up to a dozen or so times: compulsory warehouse charges, export duty, lading charges, and so forth until the price was possibly doubled or trebled.

The same was true of imports. Vital necessities to Egypt were timber in a treeless land; various metals, of which iron and copper were the most important; horses; and to some extent, slaves. The large Greek community was also responsible for a number of imports, insisting as it did on an abundant supply of wine instead of the local beer, and olive oil instead of the ubiquitous Egyptian vegetable seed oil. Neither vines nor olive trees ever did well in Egyptian soil. The Ptolemies were fully in accord with such parochial tastes for they enabled the tax collectors to saddle these imports with as much as a 300 percent duty.

The sort of economy the rulers enjoyed is called by modern economists a command economy, meaning that every phase of the economy is under state control, from production quotas to artificially rigged wage and price controls. Such systems have, in the past, been referred to less accurately as "state socialism," which obscures the meaning by introducing a concept of political ideology. None of the Ptolemies ever displayed the slightest interest in political ideology; their economic system was entirely a pragmatic one, devised to exact the greatest amount of revenue possible from the Nile Valley.

Command economies have had little success in the modern world, whether based on political ideology or not; there are generally far too many unpredictable factors involved in any aspect of a complex modern economy to make it subject to rigid state control of any kind. But the Ptolemaic command economy worked for two important reasons. First one could predict that every year the Nile would overflow its banks and deposit new soil, which would once more bear one or two or even three bumper crops. Second, the economy was based on the existence of several million Egyptian peasants who were in effect slaves, who would work every year just as hard in a docile and uncomplaining fashion as they had worked for thousands of years, and who never dreamed that any other existence was possible or even preferable. Some of the later Ptolemies, forced to the wall by the expenses of foreign war, made the mistake of pressing the peasantry too hard, which led to native revolt; but for the most part, the Egyptian peasantry was as predictable as a finely tuned machine.

Education and Learning Were Subsidized by the State

If the Ptolemies brought to the Greek world the concept of a controlled economy, they also vastly increased the Greek notion of the responsibilities the state owed to its citizens. The idea of the welfare state was probably a direct result of the fact that the first Ptolemy had to recruit his entire government and army from elsewhere. The Greeks who responded were promised various benefits, and after a while, these began to be taken for granted. One of the most notable innovations of the Hellenistic world was the idea that the state ought to provide a free education for the young. At first this extended only to the construction of buildings by the municipality, but soon the teacher's stipend was being paid as well. The government also spent a great deal of money on internal improvements like roads, canals, irrigation systems, and reclamation of land from desert or marsh. Much of this sort of public work was directly subsidized by tolls or imposts on those benefited or was accomplished in part by a corvée [arrangement in which workers provided free labor instead of paying taxes]. . . .

By far the most startling new institution created by the Ptolemies was the Museum of Alexandria and its adjunct the Library, which were totally unique in that they were wholly subsidized by the state. The Macedonian kings in the past, perhaps smarting under the usual Greek notion that Macedonians were unlettered barbarians, had for centuries adorned their courts with the most fashionable Greek poets, philosophers, and actors and rewarded them with royal honoraria. But Ptolemy's creations went far beyond anything envisioned by previous Macedonian patrons of the arts.

The Museum was actually part of the palace complex. Here lived and worked world-famous scholars invited to carry on their research, to engage in learned discourse, and in general to make Alexandria the new capital of Greek scholarship. The Museum was not a university in the modern sense, for the resident scholars gave no regular courses of instruction, but they did attract disciples from all over the Greek world who worked under them and sometimes succeeded them after their death or retirement. The primary duty of the Alexandrian scholars was to continue to produce works of literature or scholarly research in order to keep their names renowned all over the world and thus increase the fame of the Museum—in short, the theoretical duty of university professors today. . . . Fine work was produced during the last three centuries B.C., particularly in the fields of science and literary criticism.

The Library of Alexandria was an essential part of the Museum, designed to be the world's first complete collection of published works and to serve the needs both of the Museum fellows and of numerous visiting scholars, artists, and literati who converged on Alexandria. Begun perhaps in the 280s, by the first century B.C. the Library contained over 700,000 works and remained the largest and most impressive library in the ancient world even in Roman times.

Alexandria: The World City

From the beginning, Alexandria was a work of mortals rather than gods. The streets were laid out on a grid plan and temples were situated in the most practical place, just like the market, theater, and gymnasium. The most famous structures of Alexandria—the Museum and Library and the Lighthouse—were secular. . . . The enormous Pharos could be seen from far out at sea. This lighthouse, with its beacon four hundred feet above the ground, warned mariners of the coastal shallows. Even the most famous religious structure, the Sarapeion, housed a man-made cult created for the Alexandrian Greeks by theological pedants [scholars], as if urban planners had been set loose in the City of God. The god Sarapis combined Hellenic and Egyptian attributes intended to appeal to Alexandrians and other Greeks as well, and his temple, the Sarapeion, was listed as one of the wonders of the world.

Alexandria was planned as an administrative center from which Greeks could rule Egypt. It was always more European than Egyptian—in Africa, but not of it. Here was fresh water, limestone for building, and a continual cool breeze blowing from the Mediterranean creating a climate more like the Aegean than the rest of the Nile Valley. It became, as planned, the bureaucratic nerve center of the Ptolemaic Empire, but it was much more. It was the first Greek megalopolis—a world-city where anyone could live without the bothersome formalities of citizenship: political loyalty, military obligations, traditional social status. Here anyone could rise to wealth and fame, or seek out utter anonymity with no questions asked. Here opportunity and oblivion walked hand in hand, available to all.

Alexandria was also the first city where anyone could become a Greek, regardless of ethnic origin. From its very start, the city attracted residents from all over the eastern Mediterranean: Phoenicians, Jews, Babylonians, Arabs, Syrians. The more pious Jews founded a quarter and stayed in it, keeping their faith and their customs, but the young and adventurous joined youths from a hundred other races in taking Greek names and mastering the Greek language, for this way lay advancement. By the time of Cleopatra, it would have been impossible to unravel the ethnic background of an average Alexandrian—even if anyone had cared.

The city of the Ptolemies was only the first of the many

Hellenistic Greek megalopoleis that sprang up throughout the former empire of Alexander in outright imitation of the conqueror's creation. Seleucus built Antioch on the Orontes River in northern Syria and Seleuceia on the Tigris, a day's journey away from old Babylon. When Seleuceia did not seem to be filling up satisfactorily, the king forcibly removed part of Babylon's population to his new city. By mid-third century, Pergamon in Phrygia had become the capital of an Anatolian empire and had a museum and library that nearly rivaled those of Alexandria. Even the cities of old Greece were copying the style of the super-cities and opening their gates (and sometimes even their citizenship rolls) to newcomers. The great mercantile centers like Corinth, Rhodes, and Smyrna were first but were soon joined by some of the formerly most exclusive and chauvinistic cities, including Athens and even Sparta where money itself had once been illegal.

The promise of the Hellenistic super-cities was irresistible to idealists. The megalopolis offered to Greeks and Hellenized Orientals opportunities that had never existed in the tribal community or the city-state, where social mobility depended on the correct ancestry or the proper credentials of citizenship. Many of the ministers and commanders of the Ptolemies and Seleucids had risen from obscure origins and their cities served as magnets attracting those who sought similar eminence. . . .

A "Tyranny of Talent"

In the Hellenistic megalopolis, all people were liberated individuals—organisms competing for the free energy of the system in the classical Darwinian sense. For every clever young person who rose to the top of this "tyranny of talent," there were perhaps dozens who were unable to compete and thus sank into crushing poverty in the permanent slums that became as characteristic a part of the new cities as their libraries and museums. If rulers gave food to the poor and free education to the young, these were merely public services performed as impersonally as collecting the garbage. These services gave the recipients no true sense of belonging to a community but were designed primarily to maintain good order in the city and provide a minimum of training for future potential civil servants.

It is no surprise that Hellenistic cities were the birthplaces of a number of associations that offered the poor, the hopeless, and the alienated an opportunity to rejoin a community in at least a symbolic sense. Guilds of artisans appeared, although the purposes of these were patently more social than economic. The proliferation of burial associations must be interpreted as a yearning for the old tribal tradition that assured all members of proper burial rites and a certain amount of care for widows and dependents. Of great importance were the mystery religions that grew up in Hellenistic cities and soon numbered their adherents in the millions. For those who needed spiritual consolation, these new cults offered the advantages of older, more traditional societies. The communion of initiates with a god or cult figure gave the lonely city dweller a consciousness of belonging to a community once more, whether it was the Solar City or the family of fellow Christians.

For adventurous soldiers, politicians, bureaucrats, entrepreneurs—and even criminals—Alexandria offered a playing field for competitive energies. By coming to the megapolis, these immigrants demonstrated that they had outgrown their dependence on a sense of kinship and community with fellow citizens. They were the spiritual ancestors of generations of gifted individualists ever after, from the Greeks who pulled the strings behind scenes in the Roman Empire, to the energetic expatriate Greek entrepreneurs scattered throughout the world today.

The Macedonian and Seleucid Kingdoms

Michael Grant

In this excerpt from his wide-ranging study of Hellenistic civilization, Michael Grant, of the University of Edinburgh, describes the large realms ruled by the Antigonid and Seleucid monarchs in the third and second centuries B.C. Grant explains how a ravaged countryside, small population, and the excessive ambition of its rulers were weaknesses that Macedonia was ultimately unable to overcome. He then examines the Seleucid Empire's strengths, primarily its energetic program of colonization and exploitation of local trade routes; and its weaknesses, including the difficulty of holding together so vast a realm and its failure to achieve a true fusion of its Greek and Asian elements.

The ancient kingdom of Macedonia was centred upon the lower plain of the country, which is drained by the rivers Haliacmon and Axius and their tributaries and ringed around by mountains. The national rulers had from an early date regarded themselves as Hellenic, but their subjects, who were of very mixed race, tended to see the Greeks as foreigners, an attitude that was generally reciprocated. Nevertheless a form of the Greek language was spoken in Macedonia, and Hellenization began to make headway from the early fifth century onwards—when King Alexander I (*c.* 495–450) was recognized as a Greek by the presidents of the Olympic Games. Yet even in Hellenistic times the distinction between Greeks and Macedonians remained a feature of the political scene in Europe, though it tended to become partly effaced among settlers overseas.

Excerpted from *From Alexander to Cleopatra*, by Michael Grant. Copyright ©1982 by Michael Grant Publications, Ltd. Reprinted with the permission of Scribner, a division of Simon & Schuster.

Macedonia Before the Hellenistic Age

The continued existence of kingship in Macedonia . . . before the Hellenistic period struck Greeks as foreign or anachronistic [a throwback to the dim past]. And indeed the Macedonian monarchs retained some of the characteristics of a chieftain of the Heroic Age. They were on frank and familiar social terms with the nobles, who ranked as their kinsmen and provided their Companions. Yet the king continued to personify the state, and exercised supremacy in every aspect of public life. The army, it is true, retained certain traditional, limited powers, including the right to appoint the monarch by acclamation; but in the classical epoch it had already ceased, once the royal appointment had been made, to go on playing a leading part as an assembly of free men in arms, as has sometimes been supposed.

The country's greatest asset was its peasantry, which had to be tough because the Macedonians' tribal neighbours were warlike and threatening; it combined independent-mindedness with staunch reliability and loyalty. The country was also rich in timber, grain and wine. Its original royal residence at inland Aegae (now identified with Vergina, where sensational archaeological discoveries dating from *c.* 340 have recently brought the number of tombs found there up to eight) was known as the Garden of Midas—proverbial for his wealth—because of its vines, orchards and roses. But when urbanization began to take place it was Pella, fifteen miles from the sea but linked to it by a river and lake (now silted up), which became the country's capital and largest city.

This perhaps occurred in the reign of Archelaus (413–399), who built straight roads and well-fortified strongholds and developed his heavy cavalry. But the decisive figure in the rise of the country was Philip II (359–336), who vastly increased its power and strength in every field. He seized and exploited the enormous riches of Mount Pangaeum's gold and silver mines—the major source of supply of these metals in Greek lands—using this wealth to create and pay for a first-class, up-to-date infantry army. He transformed the adjacent highlanders, it was said, from shepherds wearing skins into civilized citizens. And finally he crushed the

Greek city-states at Chaeronea (338), compelling them to form the Federal League of Corinth under his own leadership.

Philip had set the stage for the conquering expedition of his son Alexander III the Great—an enterprise he would have conducted himself, had he not been murdered at the age of forty-six. . . . Philip's exploits continued to arouse violent controversy among the Greeks: yet all had to agree that it was he, quite as much as his son Alexander, who created the new epoch, the Hellenistic age, that was to follow.

The Successors Ravage the Country

Alexander worked to transform the army from a predominantly Macedonian institution into a cosmopolitan force owing loyalty only to himself. But the wars between his successors tossed the land of Macedonia, and its army, disastrously from hand to hand, and left the country ravaged, mutilated and partitioned. By unprecedentedly sweeping amalgamations of small communities, Cassander founded the new cities of Cassandrea (316, on the site of old Potidaea), and Thessalonica (the modern Salonica), which was made out of twenty-six former communities in 316/315 and replaced Pella as Macedonia's principal port; though Cassander rebuilt Pella as well. . . . Then Demetrius I Poliorcetes (the Besieger) founded Demetrias on the Gulf of Pagasae in Thessaly (c. 293), once again by merging numerous small local towns. . . . Yet none of these new foundations regarded themselves as integral parts of the Macedonian kingdom.

Indeed, the fortunes of the kingdom still remained highly uncertain, until Antigonus II Gonatas (284–239) revived them. In the earlier 280s, restricted and harassed by his neighbour Pyrrhus I of Epirus, he had just managed to hold on to the strategic [military garrisons]. But then in 278/7, near Lysimachia in Thrace, he scored his resounding success against the invading Celts (Gauls), whose threat to Macedonia and Greece was thus averted, so that Antigonus II had played a major part in saving Hellenism from the barbarians.

Thus began a new and tenacious line of Macedonian kings, devoting close personal attention to government, and drawing the bulk of their revenue from their own personal estates, without the need to impose oppressive taxation. They were still the national rulers of a free Macedonian people. But the day of Philip II's professional long-term force was over: the Macedonian part of the army had once again become a levy of farmers, called up only when they were needed. By this time, however, these potential Macedonian warriors only numbered 30,000 at most, since wars and emigrations had eaten their numbers away. The bulk of the armed forces consisted, instead, of mercenary soldiers— Greeks and Illyrian and northern tribesmen, many of whom had been settled on Macedonian soil to replace gaps in the peasantry. These were the men the monarchs employed to garrison the strongpoints of Greece.

Macedonia's Rulers Overreach Themselves

Meanwhile the Hellenization of Macedonia itself continued. In the third century the national dialect was largely replaced by the current, uniform Greek speech (*koine*), and the native pantheon [collection of gods] gave way to the Olympian deities. Prosperity continued under Philip V (221–179) and Perseus (179–168), who developed Demetrias as a flourishing cosmopolitan port, now revealed by excavations. Grain was stored in Macedonian warehouses against the hour of need. And that hour was soon at hand, because both monarchs in turn overreached themselves and became disastrously embroiled with Rome, the latter with terminal results for his kingdom: after Perseus' defeat at Pydna in 168 it was converted into four weak republics, which were in their turn abolished to form a Roman province in 148.

The Macedonians had been defeated because Rome's armies and generals had achieved overall superiority: the Greek phalanx of the time was no match for the more flexible Roman legionary tactics. But Macedonia also succumbed to Rome because there were so few Macedonians. There had never been more than four million, and now there were less— too few to stand up successfully to the manpower of Italy. . . .

The Seleucids in their great early days . . . ruled over an empire of a million and a half square miles, extending from the Aegean Sea as far as Afghanistan and Turkestan, and containing perhaps thirty million people (compared with less than seven million in Egypt, and four million in Macedonia). The unique size of these enormous dominions enabled the Seleucids to claim that they themselves, rather than the Ptolemies or Antigonids, were in a very special sense the heirs of Alexander the Great, who had ruled the world. The overworked Seleucid monarchs, able to appeal to no unifying principle except their own persons and troops— a standing army of not more than 70,000, supplemented by mercenaries—had to devote their major energies just to holding on to this cumbersome realm.

And indeed it displayed numerous factors positively encouraging disunity. This was evident from the co-existence of two capitals, two new cities in different countries: Antioch in Syria, and Seleucia on the Tigris in Babylonia. There was also, inside each separate territory of the empire, a sharp distinction between the central, directly controlled region or regions and the less accessible outlying districts. Moreover, in the latter, as in lands under even looser, indirect control outside the royal frontiers, the local rulers were often not Seleucid governors (though even they were relatively autonomous) but partially independent kings or dynasts or tribal chiefs, or the priestly rulers of ancient temple states. The dynasts of these temple states, great and small—especially in Asia Minor and Syria—operated antique feudal systems that the monarchs habitually tried to restrict, annexing and secularizing as much of their land as they could, but never terminating their existence altogether.

This was a situation with which the now vanished . . . Persian rulers had been familiar. But unlike the Persian empire, the Seleucid dominions also contained very numerous self-administering settlements or colonies containing Greek or Hellenized populations. Greek colonization had been in abeyance for two or three centuries until Philip II, in Thrace, and his son Alexander III the Great, much more comprehensively, revived the programme, seeing it as a fundamental feature of the new historical epoch that they were bringing into existence. Twenty such cities founded by

Alexander . . . have been located with some probability. . . .

Alexander does not seem to have been deliberately acting as an apostle of Hellenism, for the purpose of his settlements (other than Alexandria in Egypt) was primarily military. Their sites were chosen—often in places where towns existed already—with a view to guarding strategic points, such as passes or fords, or supervising tracts of the surrounding recently conquered territories (with an eye on trade). The new communities were equipped with the fortifications needed to ensure their defence. The new settlers at these various Alexandrias were mostly conscripted ex-mercenaries capable of fighting again if they had to—men performing the function of a trained reserve to be called up in emergencies. About the constitutional status of the new settlements we know little. Most of them probably lacked the formal organization of a city (*polis*) and remained under the authority of the royal governors; though promotion to city status, it was envisaged, could come later, if the foundations proved successful. For a colony to have a fairly advanced urban organization from the beginning, like Alexandria in Egypt, was probably exceptional. . . .

Apart from the famous Egyptian foundation, most of Alexander's colonies failed to take root.

Massive Drives to Found New Colonies

Yet his pioneer example had fired his successors, and especially the Seleucids, to make further attempts to people the enormous spaces they controlled, either by resuscitating Alexander's vanished settlements or by creating new ones on their own account. Like Alexander's colonies, most of the Seleucid foundations started as military settlements initially lacking full urban organization. Whether veterans or still, in a sense, active soldiers, the first settlers of these Seleucid foundations once again performed the duties of a trained reserve, ready to defend their fortified posts at any time.

The most remarkable work in this field was done by the first two Seleucid monarchs, Seleucus I Nicator (312–281) and Antiochus I Soter (281–261). Not every city that bears a Seleucid name was a Seleucid colony, since some ancient urban foundations merely took on Seleucid names without any influx of new settlers. . . . Yet the king's achievement is remarkable enough if, as seems likely, he founded . . . sixteen colonies named Antiochia (after his father, a Macedonian called Antiochus), five Laodiceas (after his mother Laodice), four Apameas (after his Iranian wife Apama), one Stratonicea (after his Macedonian wife Stratonice, whom he married after Apama's death), and nine settlements named Seleucia after himself. His son Antiochus I Soter, too, although otherwise a shadowy figure, somehow made the time—amid the unending troubles of his unwieldy empire—to establish something like twenty more foundations, though some of these may have been the work of Antiochus II Theos (261–246). Later, Antiochus IV Epiphanes . . . renewed the process, as well as transforming many oriental towns into cities of the Greek type by the donation of new civic charters.

The seventy-odd colonies were spread throughout the Seleucid empire. Many of them were in Syria-Cilicia, Asia Minor and Mesopotamia, countries in which the Greek city-organization thus established was to continue onwards into Roman and Byzantine times. But there was also a far-reaching, if less long-lived, horseshoe of foundations around the fertile fringes of the Iranian plateau—and in lands even farther east as well. Two settlements in this distant region that could belong to early Seleucid times have now been unearthed. One is at Aï Khanum, on the bank of the river Oxus in Bactria (Afghanistan). . . . It is a purely Greek city, with a gymnasium, a walled sanctuary, a peristyle courtyard, statues by Greek sculptors, and an inscription telling how a certain Clearchus went to Delphi to copy out the moral maxims of the oracular shrine. The existing remains date from about 300 BC, and the colony may well have been a foundation of Seleucus I Nicator. . . . A second colony of comparable date and Greek character, again with a walled sanctuary, has come to light at Kandahar in a more southerly region of Afghanistan. . . . This, too, is likely to be a very early Seleucid colony, though, once again, Alexander could have been the original founder. . . . These Seleucid attempts to colonize vast tracts of the continent of Asia were planned with systematic determination, and carried out with speed, energy and skill. It was one of the most remarkable enterprises of ancient times, exceeding even the great archaic age of Greek colonization in the size of the territory it covered. Indeed, only the Spaniards, in Mexico and Peru, have equalled it: like Spanish America, the Seleucid east was open to all who were adventurous enough to take their chance.

Why Seleucid Cities Tended to Be Loyal

The new colonies brought in relatively few Macedonian settlers, but attracted many Greeks, mainly from the poorer regions of the homeland, who wanted to escape poverty and unemployment at home. Like Alexander, as we have seen, the first intention of the Seleucids was that their colonies should serve a military purpose. But traces have also been found of certain settlements that seem to have possessed a civilian character from the outset. This was a sign that various non-military aims quite soon supplemented the original military purpose. Above all, the Seleucids were clearly interested in the unification of their heterogeneous territories. These lands were to be, as far as possible, a union of cities. As in Alexander's day, the settlements were intended, at a later age, to develop into fully-fledged cities of the usual Greek pattern: and in fact many Seleucid colonies (unlike Alexander's) were allowed the necessary time to reach the second phase, and duly did so. That is to say, they became equipped with the normal institutions of Greek cities—a code of law of their own, the traditional civic governing bodies and magistrates (state officials), a council, usually an assembly, and temples and gymnasia.

All this meant that the Seleucid empire—to a far greater extent than rival monarchies—became an aggregate of Greek cities, linked one with the other. And it also meant something else. For the founders of new cities were traditionally accorded divine honours, and so the Seleucid colonies established cults of their monarchs: this was a potent bond, especially as no formal constitutional link between kings and cities had been devised. The only link that existed, other than these royal cults, consisted of such individual privileges as the rulers may have conferred and felt obliged to respect. These privileges were substantial, including liberal grants of municipal autonomy—often a virtue of necessity on the part of the monarchs in times of stress when the collaboration of the local communities was urgently needed. The Seleucids were strongly on the side of the cities against the native feudal landowners, whom (like the temple states) they tried to cut down to size. In consequence, the cities were loyal, like Rome's later colonies in Italy.

Economic and agricultural considerations were not usually paramount in Seleucid plans, but some of the colonies, notably Seleucia on the Tigris, became large-scale trading centres. Moreover, the strips of cultivable territory granted to the new foundations were sometimes of remarkably large dimensions, comparable only to those of Athens and Sparta in the homeland. These pieces of land allotted to the new settlements had formerly belonged to the monarchy. Their cession to the cities meant gain as well as loss for the royal exchequer, since the recipients had to pay taxes on the land that they thus acquired. The existence of the cities was a financial help to the central authority in another way as well, since their ability to govern themselves made it possible for the rulers to cut down their own administrative staffs.

The new colonial enterprises also brought the local native populations into the picture. In the first place, a number of Asians (notably Persians) were included among the colonists—and indeed at the civilian colonies natives often constituted the bulk of the settlers. Furthermore, it was the people of local origin who provided the labour force working the land for the Greek and Macedonian colonists. . . . Conversely, too, Greeks were sometimes introduced into pre-existing native villages or cities; or when amalgamations (synoecisms) of two, or several, such communities took place, a further Greek ingredient was added. Besides, settlers, being short of women of their own race, often took local women as their wives.

Attempts at Racial and Cultural Co-existence

These developments meant that a considerable number of local inhabitants were included within the orbit of the new foundations, so that some formula of racial co-existence . . . had to be worked out. . . . The more thoughtful of the Seleucid rulers and administrators must have hoped that the natives involved with the new cities would at least become sufficiently assimilated to ensure effective collaboration— and to increase the empire's reservoir of utilizable manpower. The earlier Seleucid colonies, therefore, although they did not usually confer citizenship upon Asians, were at least prepared to concede them certain lesser rights; and it was with the same intention of gaining their cooperative services that Antiochus IV Epiphanes was so ready to grant Greek civic charters to whole native communities.

In some countries such policies enjoyed a measure of success; for example, the more cultured classes in Syria and certain regions of Asia Minor were happy enough to become partially Hellenized. Elsewhere, however, further east, this scarcely happened. True, the Asians in those lands sometimes accepted the Greek forms, or even became wholly or partly 'culture-Greeks', speaking the universal Greek dialect, the *koine*. But they rarely took on the Greek spirit. And so they outstayed their visitors—and the success of the Seleucid colonizing effort had, after all, only been limited.

The fault also lay to a large extent with the Greek (and Macedonian) settlers, who, despite the inevitable links that have been mentioned, for the most part still passionately practised linguistic and cultural *apartheid* [overt segregation]. Moreover, since they let the natives till the land, that meant they did not go on it themselves; thus the ancient antagonism between town-dwellers and peasants remained undiminished, and became an antagonism between Greeks and natives. Besides, the settlers were not numerous enough: the immigration of useful elements into Asia gradually waned and ceased in the second century BC, when Greece no longer had a surplus population (of any value) to send. Besides, by that time, after a last brave effort by Antiochus IV Epiphanes, the Seleucid rulers were too critically beset by their enemies to have funds or time for major colonial programmes. Their most dangerous threat came from the Romans, who, indeed, finally suppressed their kingdom. And yet, by a curious paradox, it was also the Romans who saved and perpetuated the Seleucid colonies in Asia Minor and Syria.

Every King a Tycoon

The Seleucids had taken what measures they could to whip up the resources needed for the prosecution of these extremely costly colonizing efforts. Seleucid taxation was organized on a highly systematic basis, from which no section of the community escaped. It included a uniform land tax, which became fixed at the high rate of one third of every crop. Much of the empire's cultivable soil, however, remained directly under the kings themselves, whose henchmen organized its cultivation on old-fashioned lines, employing peasants on a hereditary basis.

But although agriculture was important to the Seleucids, it was not as important as international trade, which they elevated to unprecedented dimensions. Every Seleucid king was a tycoon on an enormous scale, making millions from the great trade routes from the Mediterranean to central Asia, India and Arabia: routes which passed through their empire and were served by a network of good roads. Trading was also facilitated by the creation of an impressive unified coinage, which the rulers issued themselves and made the basic currency of the whole of their huge territories, speeding up the process, begun by the Persians, of transforming an economy of kind on to a monetary basis. Even if, therefore, they were occasionally hard pressed by the ambitious dimensions of their policies, the Seleucid kings remained immensely rich; and they were surrounded by an increasingly elaborate hierarchy of court officials, including for example Hermias—minister of Antiochus III the Great—who could pay an army out of his own personal resources.

Experiment in Federalism: The Aetolian and Achaean Leagues

F.W. Walbank

Because of the seemingly ingrained spirit of disunity among the Greeks, the concept of *sympoliteia*, the joining of two or more communities into a single state, never became popular on a large scale in Greece. The most conspicuous attempts at such unity rose to prominence in the Hellenistic Age. These were two small federations of cities, the Aetolian League, located in central Greece, and the Achaean League, in the Peloponnesus. University of Liverpool scholar F.W. Walbank here describes these alliances, citing their strengths and weaknesses, and suggests that they might have been more successful had they had more time to grow and develop.

The Aetolian federation is . . . an example of an important form of *sympoliteia* which grew in strength and influence in Greece proper during the third and second centuries. Federalism, that is, the merging of a group of cities in a larger organization to which they have surrendered some (but not all) of their independent rights, in order to strengthen themselves, was a reasonable and, one might think, obvious development in a world in which large territorial monarchies dwarfed individual cities and the disadvantages of the old city-state exclusiveness had already begun to be apparent. In fact however it was primarily in those areas of Greece where the city-state had not hitherto found strong roots or developed a history of traditional independence and even hegemony that the more important federal states arose. The two most influential were in Aetolia and Achaea. . . .

The Aetolian League

The Aetolian League had a primary assembly consisting of all men of military age, meeting twice a year, in spring and autumn. Its chief magistrate, elected annually, was the General and there was also a council *(boule* or *synedrion)* which seems to have seen to government between the meetings of the assembly but not to have been associated with the latter's decisions in the normal Greek fashion. This council, composed of city representatives elected in proportion to populations, amounted to several hundred men. Day-to-day business was conducted by a small committee of the council, the *apokletoi*, something over thirty in number, who met under the presidency of the General, but vital issues of foreign policy were decided by the assembly.

The Aetolians were at pains to exploit the great prestige which they had won by saving Delphi from the Gauls in 279 and subsequently they extended their federation across central Greece. As they took over more and more peoples they were able to exercise their votes in the Amphictyonic Council [group of representatives from several nearby states] controlling Delphi, a fact which enables the stages of their expansion to be followed and dated. The citizens of these peoples and cities were either incorporated in Aetolia as full members or they received a grant of *isopoliteia* [citizenship rights in the League]. *Isopoliteia* was also used to attach more distant states such as Chios [an Ionian island], Vaxos in Crete, or Lysimacheia, Cius and Calchedon [Greek cities lying beyond the Hellespont]. By expansion of this kind the Aetolians became a power of some account, which the king of Macedonia had to take seriously. They later became allies of Rome against Philip V, with dire consequences for Greece.

The Achaean League

Still more important for the history of Macedonia and mainland Greece was the Achaean League. From early times the cities of the Achaean people on the northern coast of the Peloponnese had enjoyed some kind of federal association, but under Alexander and his successors this had fallen apart. In 280 the cities of Dyme, Patrae, Tritaea and Pharae came

together in a new federation which was later joined by
Aegium, Bura, Ceryneia, Leontium, Aegira, Pallene and
perhaps later Olenus (though by the time Polybius was writing in the second century Olenus, like Helice, no longer existed). In 251 a young Sicyonian named Aratus expelled the
local tyrant and brought Dorian Sicyon into the Achaean
League, and in 243 he seized Corinth from Antigonus Gonatas. Between 243 and 228, thanks to Aratus' successful
policy of aggression against them, most of the Isthmus
states, Arcadia and Argos became federal members. But the
rise of Cleomenes III at Sparta threatened the League with
disruption and in the winter of 225/4 the decision was taken
to call in the help of Antigonus III. . . . The outcome was
that from 224 until 199 Achaea, after rising to power largely
through a policy of opposition to Macedonia, was now tied
closely to the king as a member of an alliance of federal
states established by Antigonus and for some time operative
under his successor Philip V. Membership of this wider organization brought Achaea into collision with Rome in the
First Macedonian War (215–205) and when the Second
Macedonian War broke out in 200, Achaea perforce
switched its allegiance to Rome. As a Roman 'ally' it was
permitted to expand to take in the whole of the Peloponnese
but Sparta was never reconciled to League membership and
it was finally a quarrel with Sparta which in 147/6 led to a
Roman ultimatum, a short and ruinous war and the dissolu-
tion of the League. The history of Achaea illustrates both
the advantages that federation could bring and the limitations felt by a federation even as strong as Achaea in confrontation with the Macedonian monarchy and even more
with Rome.

League Structure and Administration

The historian Polybius, born at Megalopolis in Arcadia [in
the central Peloponnesus], grew up a citizen of Achaea and
played an active role as a statesman in its service. His account of the merits of this federal state, though prejudiced in
its favour, illustrates the ideals which to some extent actu-
ated those who administered it.

In the past many have tried to unite the Peloponnesians in a single policy of common interest, but no one was able to achieve this since each was striving, not in the cause of general freedom, but for his own power. But in my own time this object has been so much advanced and so far attained that they not only constitute an alliance and friendly community, but they have the same laws, weights, measures and coinage, as well as the same magistrates, council-members and judges, and almost the whole Peloponnese only falls short of being one city through the fact that its inhabitants do not possess one single walled refuge (ii, 37, 9–11).

There is some exaggeration here. The separate cities kept their own laws in addition to those of the federation and the coins were those of the separate cities until the early-second century, when from about 190 federal coins were first issued. The League did however possess a single general (after 255), ten *damiurgoi* [administrators], and various other magistrates such as the cavalry-commander, secretary, sub-general and admiral.

There was also an assembly, the role and composition of which has been the subject of long controversy. The evidence is not entirely clear but in the present writer's opinion, throughout the third and second centuries down to 146 a primary assembly open to all male adult citizens met four times a year at meetings known as *synodoi* to transact normal business. At those meetings the council (*boule*) which was open to men aged thirty and over, and the magistrates, were also present. But, at any rate in the second century, the laws laid down that questions of war or alliance and the receipt of messages from the Roman senate had to be dealt with at a special assembly, which usually but not invariably was also open to attendance by the whole adult male population, but at which voting was probably by cities. This rule, designed to ensure that certain business was reserved to specially convened meetings, was probably introduced once the appearance of the Romans on the scene made foreign policy a more delicate matter, and provides a good example of how the presence of the Romans changed both the principles and the practice of government within the Greek states.

For rather more than a hundred years the Achaean League played an important role in Greek politics. Polybius asks himself the reason for its success and answers the question in idealistic terms.

> It is clear that we should not say that it is the result of chance, for that is a poor explanation. We must rather look for a reason, for every event, probable or improbable, must have a reason; and here it is more or less as follows. One could not find a political system and principle more favourable to equality, free speech and in short genuine democracy than that existing among the Achaeans. This system has found many of the Peloponnesians ready to join it voluntarily and many have been won over by persuasion and argument; while those who at the appropriate moment were compelled by force to join rapidly changed their attitude and became reconciled, since by reserving no privileges to the original members and putting all new adherents on the same footing, the League quickly reached the goal it had set itself, being aided by two powerful factors, equality and humanity. This then we must consider to be the initiator and cause of the present prosperity of the Peloponnese (ii, 38, 5–9).

The Weakness of Federalism

The sanguine [confident] and optimistic tone of this passage—clearly written before the disasters of 146 [when Rome eradicated the League and destroyed Corinth]—ignores the very real weaknesses of the League. Politically it may have been democratic, in as much as vital decisions were taken by an assembly open to all adult males. But its officers seem to have come from a fairly small group of families based on a few cities; and its collapse before the assault of Cleomenes, which forced Aratus to reintroduce the Macedonians into the Peloponnese, reflects a fundamental weakness for which Plutarch alleges these causes:

> There had been agitation among the Achaeans and their cities were eager for revolt, the common people hoping for land distribution and the cancellation of debts, and the leading men in many places being dissatisfied with Aratus, and

some of them being angry with him for bringing the Macedonians into the Peloponnese (*Cleomenes*, 17, 5). . . .

The opposition of the upper class to his Macedonian policy suggests that many would have preferred to go with Sparta. One can hardly therefore resist the conclusion that the Achaean League had not won the allegiance of the cities it had incorporated by force to the extent that Polybius asserts.

Nevertheless, despite these weaknesses, in a world of monarchies the federal states of Achaea and Aetolia exemplify the continuing ability of the Greeks to respond to a new political challenge with new solutions. One is bound to ask whether, given another century without Rome, federalism might not have developed fresh and fruitful aspects, for despite the use of force (and that Polybius admits) these federations grow out of an internal response of the Greeks themselves and are in consequence quite different in character from the leagues imposed upon Greece by Philip II, Antigonus I and Demetrius Poliorcetes, and Antigonus Doson. Federalism offered the possibility of transcending the limitations of size and relative weakness of the separate city-state. But time ran out.

Chapter 3

Hellenistic Society and Culture

Turning | Points

IN WORLD HISTORY

Hellenistic Social and Economic Conditions

George W. Botsford and Charles A. Robinson Jr.

The spread of Hellenism (Greek culture and ideals) throughout the East in the wake of Alexander's conquests created the so-called *oikoumene*, or "inhabited world." The major social and commercial aspects of that world are explored in this essay by George W. Botsford, former professor of history at Columbia University, and Charles A. Robinson Jr., former professor of Classics at Brown University. They describe the new emphasis on the individual (as opposed to the community, as in prior ages) and experiments with new ideas and religions; they also discuss the Hellenistic world's widespread and prosperous trade network, which stimulated the growth of numerous large cosmopolitan cities and commercial centers, such as Alexandria, Antioch, Byzantium, Rhodes, and Delos.

Perhaps the most striking fact about the Hellenistic Age is the unity of the large world which had been opened by Alexander's expedition. In spite of the warfare of the various states, trade between East and West was now easier. New lands— Egypt, India, Bactria-Sogdiana, Iran, China, Arabia, Central Africa, Western Africa, Western Europe—now came, in one way or another, within the orbit of the Greeks. Alexander gave a new impetus to the economy, and indeed to every aspect of the life, of the ancient world. With the political domination of new lands, with the diffusion of Hellenism and city life came new opportunities and new markets. The Greeks were responsible for the spectacular growth of the wealth and population of Asia and Egypt and were quick to take advan-

Excerpted from *Hellenic History*, by George W. Botsford and Charles A. Robinson Jr. (New York: MacMillan Company, 1922).

tage of it. The sense of unity was heightened by the breaking down of barriers between cities; in fact, . . . many cities ceased to exist as separate political entities. The new order of the day was the large state; people were conscious of the *oikoumene*, the inhabited world, and some individuals were actually thinking about the brotherhood of man.

A Single Culture-sphere

The large state had been bought at a price, for it meant the triumph of monarchism, which was anathema to [hated by] most Greeks. In Greece proper, to be sure, many cities retained their liberty. . . . But for the new large states, such as that of the Seleucids, monarchism was especially suited. It was almost necessary in states of wide areas, with slow communications and different populations. The problem was further aggravated by the crowds of Greeks, who settled in Asia and Egypt and stood apart from the natives. The kings did all they could to attract Greeks, for they were necessary for the development and the defense of the state. Consequently, we find concessions to the Greek love of autonomy—a new type of democracy and without much real meaning, but the Successors did grant a large measure of self-government to the Greeks in their new cities. The status of the new foundations varied, but as a rule they had their own Assembly and Council and owned much land. The new cities were nominally the allies of the king, but in reality the king owned all the land round about and subjected the population to taxation and conscription; in Egypt Ptolemy owned the entire valley of the Nile, which made possible a despotic control of the individual's life.

The Successors of Alexander took as their model the old Macedonian monarchy, with a certain outward simplicity to the court-life, but actually they were autocratic rulers, who made the laws and appointed the officials, and upon their death were defied, if this had not already been done during their life. Deification was unknown to Macedonia, however, where all of life was far simpler and more democratic, but it was developed by the Ptolemies into an official imperial cult.

The native peasants formed the mass of the population in

the new Hellenistic kingdoms. They lived in villages, without much self-government, and interference with their ancestral ways was rare. Hellenism touched them little, as events proved, but the ambitious native would learn Greek and Greek ways and try for a minor post in the bureaucracy. It was inevitable that there should be some fusion between Greek and Oriental, but this had always been the case. The Greek never had any racial prejudice, of a physical sort, although he disliked the confusion which resulted, for example, from a mixture of customs, and considered his own political institutions and his culture superior. In the Hellenistic Age culture, and not race, became the important thing, but it must be emphasized that, so far as actual race mixture in Asia was concerned, there was no great increase during the Hellenistic Age. The Hellenistic world did, however, constitute a single culture-sphere.

Individualism and Experimentation

In this vast new world man emerged as an individual. He could live anywhere; in fact, the Cynics [a group of philosophers who advocated the use of self-control to attain virtue] said, "make the world your city." This meant that a substitute had to be found for the city-state of old, with all its obligations and privileges; clubs and associations might be a poor substitute, but they satisfied man's longing in part. The clubs were generally of a social and religious nature and were usually small, though the associations of Dionysiac artists were as large as they were popular. Similarly, we can understand the growth of astrology, mystery cults, and other strange religions. The Hellenistic Age was a period of experiment, novelties, and individualism. A feature of the time . . . was the growth of arbitration between cities, a disinterested city being invited to appoint a commission for the task. In like manner the disputes between individuals were often settled by judicial commissions from another city, but the irregularity of their visits made them a not wholly satisfactory substitute for the old-time juries and their political activities. The desire for arbitration was promoted by trade and by the consciousness of a common nationality and led in time to a certain standardization of laws and customs. The solidarity and friendliness of the Hellenistic Age is illustrated, for example, by the way in which kings and cities rushed aid to Rhodes at the time of her disastrous earthquake in 225 B.C. It is also illustrated by the numerous grants of citizenship by one city to individuals in another city and indeed to entire cities (isopolity).

The provision of a steady and adequate supply of grain was a pressing problem for most Greek cities, the possibility of hunger being the chief cause, no doubt, for the marked limitation of the size of families (by infanticide). Some cities had regular grain funds and regulated the wheat trade by law, but in time of famine it was often necessary to appeal to the rich. The rich could generally be counted upon in any crisis, though their gifts would be intended for the entire population and not for the poor as such. Another pressing problem for most Greek cities was the perpetually bad state of finances. The Greeks raised much of their revenue by indirect taxation, but they had no reserves and no budget. The cities, however, did take a greater interest in education, which was centered in the gymnasia under the charge of officials called gymnasiarchs; a settlement without its gymnasium could not hope to be regarded as a city. Emancipation was possible for women, since girls as well as boys now received an education. At nineteen a boy went on to the ephebate, a system that was universal, though no longer compulsory. The training was athletic and intellectual, the military features having been dropped, and at the end of the year the youth who desired a higher education sought his own teacher.

Economic Conditions and Trade

The Hellenistic Age was also a period of contradictions. In the midst of all the festivals and luxury, with a spirit of *homonoia*, Concord, abroad, the condition of the laboring man was very low. Alexander's capture of the Persian hoard [treasury] had put an enormous amount of money into circulation, so that the value of the drachma grew less. Prices inevitably rose (wheat doubling in price) and though these later fell, the wages of the worker rarely rose above the fourth-century level. This led, of course, to social unrest, and the familiar cry for the cancellation of debts and the re-distribution of property was heard. . . .

Agriculture, of course, was the basis of the Hellenistic world. It will be recalled that in Greece property was private and belonged to the individual, but in the East, owing to the divine or semi-divine position of the ruler, the king theoreti-cally owned the land, except for the land of the new Greek cities. Consequently, the Greeks found themselves competing in the East with royal and temple estates, worked by slaves, but nevertheless their initiative and ability won them a liveli-hood. Technical works were written on agriculture, and in Egypt especially experimentation was carried on. Vine-growing was introduced to western Asia, while the Greeks for their part had to learn methods of irrigation. Many sections of the world were famous for their special products. Fertile Asia Minor was famous for its olives, wine, sheep, and grain; Syria and Mesopotamia for their barley, wheat, and vegeta-bles. Because of the annual overflow of the Nile, Egypt was extraordinarily fertile and produced large quantities of grain, flax, vegetables, papyrus, sesame and other plants. From the Black Sea came salt fish, from Athens oil and honey, from Bithynia cheese, from Pontus fruits and, later, medical drugs. The nuts of Babylonia, the prunes of Damascus, the raisins of Berytus were prized and show that relatively small products competed in the international markets, while of greater im-portance were the timber of Macedon, the cedars of Lebanon, and the pitch of Mt. Ida in the Troad.

All these products, and many more, were exchanged, as well as used locally; indeed, it was commerce that tied the Hellenistic world together. Each king tried to attract trade to his own state, the Seleucids looking especially toward India and the Far East, the Ptolemies toward India, Arabia, Nubia, and Central Africa, while both states competed with Mace-don in the Aegean. Ships sailed the Mediterranean and other seas, going as far as Arabia . . . and to the cinnamon country of East Africa. The rivers of Europe, Asia, and Africa were laden with traffic. Everything was done to make travel safe;

desert routes were policed and provided with wells; harbors were improved; breakwaters built. The excellent road system of the Persian Empire was expanded, and great caravans wound their way across Central Asia. Men traveled from the Adriatic and the Balkans to Ethiopia, from Arabia and India to the Jaxartes and southern Russia. There were three main routes connecting the East with the Mediterranean. The northern one, from Bactra across the Caspian to the Black Sea, was little used. The central route was the most important. It ran by sea from India to the Persian Gulf and up the Tigris to Seleuceia, the commercial capital of Asia. Cross-continental caravans also ended their journey at Seleuceia. Thence the goods were sent overland to Antioch [in Syria] and Ephesus [in western Asia Minor]. The southern route also came from India by sea, but it rounded Arabia and continued up the Red Sea. Much traffic eventually reached Petra in this manner, but the Ptolemies, who were most interested in the traffic, developed Berenice as a port on the Red Sea; goods were sent thence across the desert to Coptos on the Nile. There was a lively traffic, of course, between the various ports of the Mediterranean, and as Italy increased in importance, we note the rise of two new ports, Puteoli, near Naples and Pompeii, and Ostia, at the mouth of the Tiber. The boats were generally small, of about 250 tons. . . .

Agricultural produce, timber, wool, raw materials, and manufactured articles were sought and traded. Gold came from Nubia [in Africa], Spain, and India; silver from Spain and Mt. Pangaeus [in northern Greece]; . . . copper came from Cyprus; tin from Cornwall and Brittany [in what are now England and France]; iron from various sections, but especially from . . . northern Armenia. . . . Ebony from India, ivory from India and Africa, gems from India and Arabia constituted a luxury trade, though in this category first place was held by the trade in spices, the cinnamon of India, and especially the frankincense of Arabia, which was used by every religion. The greatest trade was in grain. Though most sections produced enough grain for their ordinary needs, certain places, such as Athens, Corinth, Delos, and Ionia, were compelled to import. . . .

Many Prosperous Cities

Certain cities grew rich on trade. Athens and Piraeus declined in importance, but not Corinth, which was famous for its bronzes and had a great transit trade. New importance attached to Ephesus, the terminus for trade from the East . . . ; to Seleuceia on the Tigris; to Alexandria, Tyre and Sidon, Antioch, Seleuceia in Pieria, Byzantium, and Tanais. The wealth of these cities was in large part, and in certain instances exclusively, due to the transit trade. Rhodes and Delos are special cases in point. Rhodes is famous for its prestige in antiquity, for its love of learning, the beauty of its city, the great docks, the temples, and its Colossus [giant statue]—Apollo as the Sun-god astride the harbor. It was also a great commercial city, with a busy carrying-trade, the meeting point of East and West. The chief trade was in grain, and we can form an idea of the importance of the total trade when we consider that the customs revenue of Rhodes in 170 B.C. was a million drachmas as against the 200,000 drachmas of Athens in 401 B.C. (the rate of duty in each case being 2%). Rhodes had a cosmopolitan population, with many merchants and bankers. It was the policy of the state to suppress piracy, to enforce the freedom of the seas, and to maintain the independence of the Greek cities. The Rhodian sea-law was so famous that it was eventually adopted by the Mediterranean states.

To destroy the dominance of Rhodes, Rome declared Delos a free port in 167 B.C. Delos had always been something of a banking center, since the sanctity of the island made it a safe place for deposits, but after 167 B.C. its importance greatly increased. The island became an Athenian cleruchy [colony] in name, with Athenian magistrates in charge, but actually the merchants and bankers were in control. The merchants had their own associations, the Italians, with their large meeting-hall, being particularly well organized. Delos owed much of its prosperity to the slave trade, it being able, so it was said, to handle 10,000 slaves in a day. . . .

The prevalence of slavery probably prevented the invention of machinery in antiquity, and consequently industry did not develop as rapidly as trade and commerce. Old

Greece maintained its prosperity as compared with its own past . . . but it did not share the great increase in prosperity of the rest of the world. In fact, during the Hellenistic Age the center of industry shifted eastward to Asia Minor, Rhodes, and Egypt. Alexandria was easily the busiest industrial center, with factories for paper, textiles, oil, perfumery, beer, linen-weaving, metal work, and so on. Alexandria, like Sidon, was famous for its glass, and, like Pergamum, had factories in which the workers were slaves and serfs. Pergamum had a monopoly of parchment, and its textiles, particularly its gold-woven cloth, enjoyed a great reputation. The demand for textiles was large; indeed, Greek textiles have been found in Mongolia. Miletus [in Ionia] was the center of the wool industry, as Alexandria was of the linen. Cos spun silk from the thread of the wild silkworm of Asia Minor, though beginning in the first century Chinese silk was imported. In the West Tarentum [in southern Italy] was noted for its textiles and its pottery, but fine ceramics were driven from the market by the demand for silver plate; ordinary pots came from Samos, Rhodes, and other places.

Money and Banking

The spread of the Greek language and the gradual development of common principles and of a common law greatly helped trade. Trade was also promoted by the growth of a money economy, which was rare in the Near East before Alexander. There had always been moneychangers, but now the world saw regular banks—private, city, and state—which received money on deposit and made loans. Commerce, of course, needed credit, and the business in mercantile loans, as well as the investment business, was large. Cheques and letters of credit were in use. We have already said that Alexander's capture of the Persian bullion put an enormous amount of money into circulation, and the fact that there were fewer mints during the Hellenistic Age and that two main currencies became widely adopted served further to break down the barriers to trade. The Alexander-drachma was based on the Attic [i.e., Athenian] and was in use in Macedonia, Athens, Asia Minor, and the Seleucid Empire generally. The Ptolemies adopted the Phoenician standard, which was used at Carthage, Syracuse, and Massilia.

It is clear that the upper and middle classes were well off during the Hellenistic Age and that their higher standard of living stimulated trade. Wealth, however, was unevenly distributed, and the lot of the worker, as already stated, was bad, though nothing could equal the condition of the convicts in the mines and quarries. The free craftsman generally followed in his father's steps and was the victim of extreme specialization; for example, the stone mason did not sharpen his own tools. The free craftsman, too, had to compete with the serf and slave workshops of kings and priests in Egypt and Asia. There was a slow development of trade guilds, particularly in Egypt, but strikes were rare, passive resistance being adopted instead. As wages failed to rise, however, or actually fell, unemployment and social unrest followed. Some people began to advocate communism, especially as developed by the Stoics [a group of philosophers who advocated calm acceptance of divine will and the natural order of things]. . . . By the third century Delos and other cities were issuing free corn . . . and by the second century revolts of slaves had broken out in Sicily, Greece, and Pergamum. In the midst of the great trade in slaves it is refreshing to note that Delphi steadily preached the necessity of manumission [freeing slaves]; it became common for a slave to purchase his freedom, generally by a "sale" to a god, and thereupon he acquired the status, essentially, of a metic [resident foreigner].

Literature, Science, and Philosophy Flourish in Hellenistic Times

Chester G. Starr

In retrospect, it seems somewhat ironic that the age which witnessed the last gasps of ancient Greek power and independence was also a period of fertile experimentation and production by writers and thinkers. In this concise, lucid essay, the late University of Michigan scholar Chester G. Starr summarizes these writers and thinkers and their influence, including the popular playwright Menander, the so-called Alexandrian scholars and scientists, and philosophers like Epicurus (Epicureanism) and Zeno (Stoicism).

Hellenistic Literature and Scholarship

The political and social developments after Alexander had a great effect on the ancient world itself. Achievements in the arts, literature, and science were in a sense even more important, for they have influenced Western civilization ever since—more directly than has any other phase of Greek culture.

The most appealing among the many authors of the period is undoubtedly Menander, who wrote over 100 comedies at Athens. These comedies were not like those of Aristophanes a century earlier, which had attacked political figures; Menander's stories largely revolve about lovers. Parents in Menander do not understand their children, who have to plot to get their own way. Cunning slaves, prostitutes, and other figures who cross the stage suggest the breaking down of old social standards. Menander showed good and bad with sympathetic understanding and quick wit; he is the source of many famous lines, such as "Whom the gods love die young." Even Saint Paul quotes him: "Evil companionships corrupt good morals."

In the Hellenistic age poetry revived after the lull in the 4th century. Some poets wrote learned epics; others turned remedies for snakebites into verse, celebrated the pleasures of countryside, or composed witty epigrams. This poetry is often called "Alexandrian" inasmuch as it was centered on that city; in general it is marked by learned mythological references and a high polish. Frequently the meaning of the poets is as deliberately obscure as in modern verse. [The seventeenth-century English epic poet John] Milton drew heavily on Alexandrian styles as have others down to the present day.

The poetry of earlier times had been designed for presentation to groups; Hellenistic verse was largely intended to be *read* by individuals. This was true of the abundant prose too. Romantic accounts of Alexander flourished alongside tales of imaginary heroes and heroines. Scientific and philosophic treatises were turned out by the hundreds. Particularly notable were the learned commentaries on Homer and other earlier authors along with critical editions of the great Greek authors and studies in grammar. These works mostly written at Alexandria from the 3d century B.C. on, began a tradition of scholarly criticism on which Christian thinkers later leaned very heavily in studying the Bible. This tradition survived across the Middle Ages and served as a model for modern historical study and literary criticism.

Hellenistic Science

The field in which Hellenistic civilization broke the freshest ground was that of science. Aristotle had established the scientific approach in the time of Alexander, and across the next few generations there came the greatest explosion of scientific interest the world saw before the 16th century after Christ. This interest was centered in Alexandria, where the Ptolemies supported the creation of the greatest library of the ancient world as well as a research institute called the Museum.

In medicine Herophilus was the first to study anatomy by dissecting corpses. He traced much of the nervous system, and his contemporary Erasistratus did the same for the veins and arteries. Erasistratus came close to discovering the theory of the circulation of the blood, which William Harvey was not to propose until the 16th century. In the biological field on the whole, however, the most important practical advances came in the improvement of plants and animals for farming purposes through the deliberate selection of better specimens.

Developments in the physical sciences and in mathematics were even more notable. The astronomer Aristarchus advanced the guess that the earth revolved around the sun, but he postulated movement of the planets on circular orbits at regular speeds. This theory conflicts with observable evidence, and as the greatest astronomer of ancient times (Hipparchus) said, "We must abide by the facts of observation." So Hipparchus and others perfected a mathematical scheme of the heavenly system which put the earth at the center of the universe but came closer to agreeing with the known evidence. In the 16th century [the Polish astronomer Nicolaus] Copernicus ran across a reference to Aristarchus and was led to his own theories [about the sun-centered solar system].

Hipparchus also invented trigonometry, partly in order to improve geographical measurements. The Greeks not only knew that the earth was round but had a method of measuring its size; they were only 200 miles off from the correct figure. The most-lasting single achievement of Hellenistic mathematics, though, was the composition of the most famous textbook ever written, in which Euclid summed up and systematized earlier Greek geometrical reasoning. The more original mathematician Archimedes of Syracuse became a legendary hero for devising skillful machines to withstand the Roman siege of his native town in 212 B.C.

The Weaknesses of Ancient Science

Despite his own practical work Archimedes said he "looked upon the work of an engineer and everything that ministers to the needs of life as ignoble and vulgar." This expresses one defect of Hellenistic science: it was not intended to lead to practically useful results. Another problem was the limited range of ancient technology. Hero of Alexandria made a

Menander's Cantankerous Old Man

In this excerpt from Menander's Dyskolos *(Bad-tempered man), a servant named Pyrrhias runs up to two fellows, Chaireas and Sostratos. The latter is in love with the daughter of a cantankerous old farmer, Knemon, with whom Pyrrhias has just had a disquieting run-in. (In the end, Knemon is pressured into attending the wedding of his daughter and Sostratos, but remains a disagreeable old sot.)*

(At this moment the servant Pyrrhias rushes, blindly onto the stage.)

Pyrrhias Let me get past, look out, get out of the way, everybody—he's insane, the chap who's chasing me, he's off his rocker.

Sostratos What's the matter, boy?

Pyrrhias He's throwing lumps of earth at me, and stones. I'm all in.

Sostratos Throwing? Where, you fool? . . . What are you talking about?

Pyrrhias Please, let's get away from here.

Sostratos Where to?

Pyrrhias As far away from that door there *(he points to Knemon's door)* as we possibly can. He's a son of grief, a madman, a raving lunatic, that fellow you sent me to see, who lives there. Herakles! It's awful. I've broken practically all my toes with tripping over these rocks.

Sostratos (to Chaireas) This fellow's acting as if he's drunk, it's plain to see.

Pyrrhias (thinking that the last remark was a reference to Knemon, not to himself) Yes, he's quite out of his mind. But

simple steam engine, but this and other inventions could not be put into general use because iron-workers could not provide adequate materials. Further, observations were hampered by the lack of instruments: there were no microscopes, thermometers, or even accurate yardsticks.

Perhaps most important of all as a check to scientific study was the generally held view that the natural world, no less than

Sostratos, I'll be murdered. We've got to be careful. But I can't get my breath to speak. It's sticking in my throat . . . Well, I knocked at the door of that house. A miserable old hag came out. I said I was looking for the owner. She pointed him out to me from here, where I'm standing now as I tell you this. He was mucking about, gathering pears on the hilltop. . . .

I climbed onto his land and started walking up to him. Now I wanted to make the right impression on him from a long way off, you know, I wanted to look like a friendly sort of chap. So I gave him a shout and said, "I've come to see you, sir," I said, "there's a matter I want to see you about, it concerns you." But he came back at me right away, with "You damnable blackguard you, why the hell are you trespassing on my land?", and he picked up a lump of earth and threw it right into my face.

Chaireas Good heavens! . . . This farmer sounds absolutely insane.

Pyrrhias Well, in the end I ran for it, and he's chased me nearly a couple of miles, first around the hill, and then down here into the wood, slinging sods and rocks at me, and his pears too, he hadn't anything else. It's a barbarous sort of business, he's a perfectly murderous old man. I do beg you, get out of here.

Sostratos That's cowardice.

Pyrrhias But you don't realize what sort of trouble this is. He'll eat us alive!

Quoted in Kenneth J. Atchity, ed., *The Classical Greek Reader*. New York: Oxford University Press, 1996, pp. 232–233.

mankind, was fundamentally alive and was divinely governed. To understand its character one could better turn to philosophy and to religion than to science, which was little more than a hobby. In the disasters of life, prayer or resignation to the will of God were the principal props for man. Before the end of the Hellenistic period scientific advances had almost stopped; but the achievements of the scientists down to this time had created the picture of the world and man which Western scholars accepted until Copernicus, Galileo, and Harvey.

Hellenistic Philosophers

The writings of Hellenistic philosophers were as dry as those of the scientists. Most of them have disappeared, but the ideas they proposed have had tremendous effects ever since they were written. Essentially these philosophers were seeking to give guidance to individual men so they could live with serenity in an unstable world.

Two schools of thought came down from the past. Plato's Academy continued to flourish, but it had now become a conservative center for men who felt it was impossible to reach ultimate decisions. An Academic of the Hellenistic world simply balanced possible alternatives and skeptically did whatever seemed best at the moment. Aristotle's Lyceum also survived, largely as a focus for scholarly and literary activity. Out of these schools and the work of other early Greek philosophers, however, more vigorous approaches emerged.

One was that of the Cynics, who disdained the conventions of the day and urged that men live simply and in accordance with the ways of nature. The Cynic Diogenes was said to have spent most of his time in a tub; when Alexander the Great came to visit him and asked if he wanted anything, Diogenes replied, "Yes, please don't block my sunshine." Cynics often gave "sermons" or short, practical speeches to the men in the streets and harbors of the Hellenistic cities.

Another school of thought was that founded by Epicurus, who was a contemporary of Menander at Athens. Epicurus took over the atomic theory of [the earlier Greek thinker] Democritus and used it to demonstrate that the gods had no effect in the world; man's soul was an accidental grouping of atoms which dissolved on his death. So the Epicurean objective was to enjoy *this* life with the least amount of pain, and virtue was meaningless except if it might aid that enjoyment. Epicureans accordingly gained a bad name as atheists and pleasure-seekers, but in strict Epicurean theory a man would lead a very simple, secluded life so as to avoid pain and distress. Falling in love and having children were two sure ways to such distress. No other ancient philosophy was as rationally derived from a few simple premises as Epicureanism.

More generally influential was the Stoic philosophy, which eventually became the principal philosophy of Greece and then of Rome. Saint Paul learned about Stoicism in his home town of Tarsus. This philosophy was begun by a gaunt merchant from Cyprus named Zeno, who came to Athens on business just before 300. In Athens, Zeno became interested in the problems which philosophers debated and remained there for the rest of his life, arguing with them in short, clipped paradoxes in the Stoa of the Athenian marketplace. Later Stoics developed and altered his terse opinions, so Stoicism cannot be summed up as easily as the sharp, clear doctrine advanced by Epicurus.

In general, however, the Stoics created a view based on the theory of the 5th-century thinker Heraclitus that the supreme power of Zeus was divine reason or fire (*logos*), a spark of which resided in each human being. The world was directed by a rational plan, and it was the duty of each man to live so as to improve his soul (divine spark) and to understand the divine will which governed all. What happened to his body was incidental (hence our meaning of "stoic"); his mind was free and must accept the cardinal virtues of temperance, judgment, bravery, and justice. Moreover, all men were basically equal brethren, living in the great city which we call the world under the rule of Zeus.

Stoicism and Christianity

In its practical advice Stoicism was markedly like Christianity, but the theories behind the advice were quite different. Stoics eventually accepted astrology as revealing the divine will; they had, moreover, no concept that a human being had an individual eternal existence. When a man died, his divine spark or soul went back into the divine "logos." Some Stoics argued indeed that at the end of a very long era the whole world "burned up" and started over on exactly the same course; thousands of years from now, in this theory, we shall all be here again, doing exactly the same things.

Most people found it very hard in practice to live up to

another part of Stoic theory. This was the doctrine that one must eliminate all emotional responses lest they affect one's internal tranquility. An ideal wise man was pitiless though he would work unflinchingly for his fellow men and do his duty by family and state. As Christian preachers later pointed out, true Christians on the other hand must love their neighbors; and as was observed, Christ Himself had emotions.

New Directions in Art and Architecture

William R. Biers

In this essay, William R. Biers, a professor in the Department of Art History and Archaeology at the University of Missouri, Columbia, begins with a brief synopsis of the new directions art took in the Hellenistic era. He then focuses on one artistic form, public architecture. First, he examines the structure and decoration of various new temples, which, as in prior ages, remained important fixtures of Greek cities. (Mentioned frequently are the three orders, or styles, of temple architecture, determined largely by the columns. The Doric order features simple, unadorned column capitals (tops); Ionic capitals have scroll-like decorations; and Corinthian capitals are covered by ornate masonry leaves.) Biers then describes secular architecture, including Hellenistic builders' frequent use of the stoa (a long building with one open side lined by columns); and the great altar and adjacent complex of public buildings at Pergamum (or Pergamon), one of the supreme architectural achievements of ancient times.

The Hellenistic world was more "modern" than any up to that time. The tremendous increase in population, the rise of urban centers, the emphasis on manufacturing and commerce, the growth of foreign and ecstatic religions, growing separation of rich and poor, bureaucracy, scientific investigation, reverence for the past, taxes—all these characteristics of the Hellenistic age are familiar to us today. . . .

The new world created by Alexander demanded a new art. Various factors combined to form this art, including the

Excerpted from *The Archaeology of Greece: An Introduction*, by William R. Biers. Copyright ©1996 by Cornell University. Reprinted with the permission of the Cornell University Press.

changing way in which people thought of themselves and their relationships with others. Also important was the increased contact between the Greeks and other lands and peoples. The artistic needs of the Hellenistic kingdoms were different from those of the earlier city-states. Artistic creations still had to be dedicated to the gods—the traditional gods as well as new ones—and monuments still had to be erected for the dead, but a growing wealthy class in the great cities now wanted art for decoration to an extent not known before. Houses were decorated with mosaics and gardens with statuary, and the rich collector became a force in the art world. Individual tastes can be detected in some Hellenistic works, especially in sculpture. The occasional artistic tour de force is to be found in this period also. But Rome, the biggest collector of them all, dominated the latter part of the period, and the Romans' appetite for old works stimulated artists and sculptors to produce works with the Classical and Archaic qualities they prized.

The variety of art in the Hellenistic age is staggering, stretching in time over almost three hundred years and in space from India to Egypt. It is a tremendously rich and vibrant field, but one that is exceedingly difficult to understand fully and impossible to condense into a few short pages. In order to appreciate the range of Hellenistic art, one must look beyond mainland Greece, for in this period Greece was fast becoming a provincial backwater.

The period may be divided artistically into three phases. The second century—perhaps the most original period . . . is bracketed by two periods with roots in the past, the earlier a continuation of fourth-century styles and the later incorporating some characteristics of the past in contemporary artistic expressions.

In the history of Greek art we have seen a relatively constant development toward the realistic representation of nature. In the Hellenistic period this development reached a certain climax, then occasionally lapsed into stale repetition or exaggeration. For the first time all classes of society and all gradations of physical condition were realistically shown, and often caricatured. Technically, Greek art had never reached such heights as those attained by Hellenistic practitioners. It was this art that had such influence on the Romans, and through them on the Italian Renaissance.

Temple Architecture

The conquests of Alexander and the subsequent founding of new cities spawned much new building. It is in the East, where opportunity and funds were abundant, that most new examples are to be found. Architects of the Hellenistic age had freedom to experiment. The Ionic order reigned supreme in its homeland and was developed to a height of elaboration. The Doric order continued to be used for traditional temples and utilitarian secular constructions, but in the second century it fell into neglect. The Corinthian order was slow to develop. It was first used as an exterior free-standing order only in the third century, and was left for the Romans to explore fully. . . .

The traditional Doric temple of Athena Polias Nikephoros (Bringer of Victory) was one of the earliest buildings erected on the hill at Pergamon during the reign of the city's founder, Philetairos (282–263). Later, in the first half of the second century, its terrace was surrounded by a colonnade [row of columns]. A short building (21.77 by 12.27 meters), the temple continued the fourth-century tendency toward slimness and lightness: the height of its widely spaced columns, six on each end and ten on each flank, was seven times their lower diameter. The wide spacing of the columns allowed three metopes [panels bearing sculptures or paintings] between each pair of columns instead of the canonical two, a fashion begun in the fifth century. The columns . . . were never finished, not even when the later stoa was built. This lack of interest in completing the columns has been interpreted as a loss of interest in the order itself. . . .

The temple of Artemis Leucophryene (white-browed) at Magnesia [in western Asia Minor] . . . demonstrates the new freedom to experiment with plans. It was built by one of the most famous architects of the age, Hermogenes of Priene. He was renowned as a theoretician and is said to have devised a new system of proportional relationships for the

Ionic order that was based, at least in part, on the relationship between the height and diameter of columns to the distance between them. . . . Set on a high podium of seven steps, the marble temple measured 57.90 by 31.61 meters on the stylobate [floor] with eight columns across each end and fifteen on each flank. The Ionic columns were evenly arranged, except at the central space at both ends, where they were more widely spaced. . . . On the exterior a sculptured frieze ran above the epistyle [beam lying atop the columns], but no sculpture adorned the pediments. Instead there were apparently openings or windows at each corner. . . .

Probably the Hellenistic temple most often cited is the temple of Apollo at Didyma, near Miletos [on Asia Minor's western coast]. Work began about 300 on a great new temple in the tradition of the huge religious buildings of archaic Ionia. The temple is one of the largest (109.38 by 51.14 meters) and most grandiose ever built. Work continued on it until the second century of the Christian era but it was never finished. Raised on a high podium, the cella was surrounded by some 120 columns, 19.70 meters high, standing in two rows. . . . Ten columns stood on each end and twenty-one along each flank. The cella [main interior room] itself was open to the sky along most of its length, providing a setting for a small . . . free-standing Ionic shrine for the cult statue of Apollo. Apollo spoke through an oracle, and the whole ornate pile was designed to surround this open court, which was originally planted with trees and contained an oracular spring and a shrine that was considered to be the original home of the oracle. . . . Opposite the little temple, a massive staircase of twenty-four steps led up between two semi-detached Corinthian columns to a rectangular room whose ceiling was supported by two free-standing Corinthian columns. It was probably from the threshold of this room . . . that the oracle spoke. Small doors on either side of the pronaos led to sloping barrel-vaulted passageways that led down to the courtyard, while staircases from the rectangular room led to the roof, perhaps for ritual purposes. The building was loaded with ornament, much of it dating from the last years of the building's construction. The ornamentation and the interest shown by the architects in working with space are characteristics of Hellenistic architecture. Interesting evidence for construction methods has been revealed by the discovery that working drawings of architectural details were inscribed on the walls of the temple to guide the construction workers.

Another colossal temple, this time in Athens, was worked on in the Hellenistic age. The sons of [the tyrant] Peisistratos had begun a large temple to the east of the Acropolis in the sixth century in emulation of the great buildings being erected by tyrants in Asia Minor and Samos. It was originally to have been built in the Doric order but was never completed. One of the Hellenistic kings, Antiochos IV, engaged a Roman architect, Cossutius, to rebuild it in 174 in the more modern Corinthian order. Some of its columns still stand today. The great building, 108.00 by 41.12 meters, with three rows of eight columns on each end and two rows of twenty along each flank, is notable for the Corinthian capitals designed for it. Coming out of the Greek tradition, they may have had a strong effect on the Roman Corinthian order, for after the sack of Athens in 86, some were removed to Rome by the Roman general Sulla. In these capitals the bell is almost covered by acanthus leaves. Work on the temple stopped with the death of the king, and it was completed only under the Roman emperor Hadrian in the first half of the second century of the Christian era.

Hellenistic Stoas

In the course of the second century considerable changes were made in the plan of the Athenian agora [marketplace]. . . . The changes essentially took the form of the addition of long stoas. To the south a subsidiary square, called the South Square, was created by the construction of two long stoas to the north and south and a short building connecting them to the east. This complex is associated with the law courts by the excavators. The east side of the Agora square was closed by the erection of the Stoa of Attalos, a two-story building given to Athens by King Attalos II of Pergamon (159–138), who had studied in the city in his youth. The building was

destroyed in a barbarian raid in A.D. 267 and then incorporated in a late fortification wall. So much of the fabric was
preserved that it was possible to rebuild the building with a
high degree of accuracy. The reconstruction was carried out
between A.D. 1953 and 1956 by the American School of
Classical Studies at Athens to serve as a museum and work-
rooms for the Agora excavations. Thus a complete reconstruction of an ancient building containing much of the
original material can be seen today standing where it stood
over two thousand years before.

The Stoa of Attalos is a fine example of an advanced form
of Hellenistic stoa, measuring 116.50 by 20.5 meters and
utilizing Pentelic marble for facade and columns. Stoas were
designed to provide protection from the sun and cold winds,
as informal gathering places, and as shopping centers. The
colonnade on each floor was backed by a series of shops. The
Doric order was used on the ground floor on the outside,
with Ionic columns on the inside. The upper story had piers
with Ionic half-columns on each end and marble balustrades
[railings] between them. The interior order was the new
Pergamene order, which had capitals in the form of curving
petals supporting the abacus [flat slab at top of column]. . . .

Thus in the second century the Athenian agora took on a
more ordered look, with stoas defining the south and east
boundaries. This use of the stoa to surround or define a space
reflects the contemporary interest in space and planning.

A New Concern for Organization and Visual Harmony

Stoas played a great part in the unified complexes that are
found where new Hellenistic cities or sanctuaries were laid
out. A concern for the relationship of buildings in structural
settings together with an interest in visual effects developed
in the Hellenistic period and led to the orchestrated architecture of Roman times. This new tendency to place buildings in architectural settings can be seen in the Asklepieion
on Kos, built in the third and second centuries. Here the
most important building, the temple, was placed at the highest point, at the head of a flight of stairs, and framed on three

sides by stoas. below it stretched two large terraces, more or less formally laid out and serving to emphasize the temple above them. Although cult requirements dictated the placement of some of the buildings and although the lowest terrace was not exactly in line with the temple, the builders clearly took care to relate elements of the sanctuary to one another, rather than simply adding new structures wherever space was available.

A similar concern is evident in the plan of the great city of Pergamon, whose principal portion was built on a steep hill. A series of large terraces connected by a broad street ascends the hill, on the slope of which is a great theater. Below lie an agora, gymnasium, and two sanctuaries. The major monuments of the city are on the fortified hill, however, including three terraces that are arranged around the top of the hill and placed so as to give unobstructed views out over the valley. The Pergamene kings considered themselves to be the standard-bearers and protectors of Hellenic civilization, and this concept was clearly expressed in the great monument that occupied the lowest of the three terraces. The Pergamon Altar bore a relief of the battle of gods and giants as a victory monument to the Pergamenes' defeat of the Gauls, which they equated with the Athenians' defeat of the Persians. The altar was linked visually with the temple of Athena on the next highest terrace by the alignment of its first step with the flank of the temple. To the north of the two-story stoa that surrounded the court of the temple stood a great library, where the Pergamene rulers kept what they considered to be their written heritage and works of art. Another terrace, farther to the north, is now adorned with the remains of a temple built by the Roman emperor Trajan. It is uncertain what was there in Hellenistic times. Opposite, on the east side of the hill, was the modest palace of the kings of Pergamon and some barracks. Pergamon was thus a carefully planned citadel and a grandiose monument to the power and culture of the age.

The Drive for Greater Realism in Art and Science

Michael Grant

One of the hallmarks of the Greek lands during the Hellenistic Age was a newfound preoccupation with the reality of the natural world, which generated more realistic depictions of men and women than had been seen in prior ages. This was accompanied by an emphasis on the individual and his or her feelings, needs, and desires. The following insightful essay, by Michael Grant, the popular author of numerous widely read books about ancient Greece and Rome, examines this emphasis on realism and individuality. Grant begins by showing how the new spirit expanded educational opportunities and scientific inquiry, then explores the emphasis on the individual in literature (including the genres of biography, autobiography, and love poetry), sculpture, and painting (including realistic portrait busts).

A common form of education is one of the phenomena of the Hellenistic epoch. It was dominated by the rhetorical type of instruction advocated by the Athenian Isocrates (*d.*338), who had become the chief creator of rhetoric [the art of persuasive speaking] as a distinct science. For him, education above all meant developing the ability to *speak*, which distinguishes human beings from animals—and was, in any case, the favourite occupation of the Greeks. Yet he was also at pains to propose a broader and more liberal programme than the mere rules and techniques of the professional rhetorician. In fact, he wanted to reduce theory to a minimum; whereas Aristotle on the other hand, although he

Excerpted from *The Founders of the Western World: A History of Greece and Rome*, by Michael Grant. Copyright ©1991 by Michael Grant Publications, Ltd. Reprinted with the permission of Scribner, a division of Simon & Schuster.

saw the dangers of the rhetorical art, elaborated it by introducing a variety of new definitions. And it was under the influence of Aristotle's *Rhetoric* that Greek education assumed its typical Hellenistic form, characterized by a multitude of rhetorical textbooks.

In most parts of the Greek world the primary stages of teaching were left to private enterprise, although some cities appointed official supervisors of primary education *(paidonomoi)*. Children were usually taught reading, writing, gymnastics and music, and sometimes painting, too. In secondary schools, physical and musical training proceeded further, and a certain amount of mathematics and science was taught as well. But literary subjects also played an extremely prominent part: Homer, Euripides and others were studied with care and in detail.

Athens, where this type of work was especially well developed, also became the model for the form of training known as the ephebate, organized in *c.*335 and 322, and copied at numerous other centres. It started as a sort of upper-class militia for eighteen-year-olds, but came to concentrate on character development and instruction in social behaviour. The ephebes congregated, and were taught, in their city's gymnasium, which increasingly superseded family life as the principal training ground of the young, and became, indeed, the focus and hallmark of Hellenism.

Directors of gymnasia, the gymnasiarchs, were appointed by their governments. But the extent of civic intervention varied widely from place to place. Rhodes and Miletus were among cities which believed that education should be the business of the state, as Plato and Aristotle had urged. Royal Pergamum had no less than five gymnasia. Like Rhodes and Athens, too, Pergamum was a place which provided a higher education, in rhetoric and philosophy. And in Alexandria was another centre where one could learn a variety of subjects at this more elevated level.

Knowledge from Rational Methods

Aristotle's share of responsibility for the rhetorical, word-orientated bias of Hellenistic education was counterbalanced by the stimulus that he also offered to Greek science. The scientific developments that continued to occur after his lifetime formed part of a new, general drive towards seeing things as they are: a drive, that is to say, towards greater reality and realism, accompanied by a conscious or unconscious jettisoning of some of the more idealistic, unreal conceptions that had characterized the classical past.

At the outset of this Hellenistic epoch, Aristotle's successor Theophrastus of Eresus on the island of Lesbos (*d*.288), while understandably dubious about the purposefulness *(telos)* of the universe envisaged by his master, nevertheless inherited his flair for classification, undertaking for botany what Aristotle had achieved for human beings and animals. After Theophrastus, the Greek study of biology did not advance much further. Other scientific studies, however, liberated at last from *a priori* speculations [i.e., assumptions rather than direct investigation], showed greater progress than in any comparable period until the birth of modern science.

The same applied to mathematics, and one of the first men of learning to reside at Alexandria (*c*.300), where the Ptolemies lavishly stimulated such studies, was the mathematician Euclid. His summing up of the current condition of his subject was the culmination of all that had gone before, for the benefit of the future. His *Elements* demonstrated how knowledge can be attained by rational methods alone: and no book except the Bible has enjoyed such a long subsequent reign. Another Alexandrian, Ctesibius, who flourished in the 270s, was a versatile mechanical inventor. Then Strato of Lampsacus (*d.c.*269) confirmed the growing opinion that science had a right to exist independently of philosophy, and converted the Lyceum—of which he succeeded Theophrastus as head—from the latter to the former.

Archimedes of Syracuse (*d*.212) was a legendary mathematical genius who expanded the frontiers of knowledge. In solid geometry, he broke entirely new ground. He also prepared the way for the integral calculus, devised a new system for expressing large numbers, virtually invented hydrostatics, and excelled as an engineer. The polymath Eratosthenes of Cyrene (*c*.275–194), who lived at Athens and Alexandria, was the author of a *Geographica*, which was inspired by the conquests of Alexander the Great, and contributed to an accurate delineation of the surface of the earth. Greek mathematical geography was largely based on astronomy, which fascinated Hellenistic scholars. Aristarchus of Samos, a pupil of Strato, discovered that the earth revolves round the sun. Hipparchus of Nicaea (*c.*190—after 126) regarded this as unproven, but nevertheless transformed observational techniques, gaining recognition as the outstanding astronomer of antiquity.

Medicine, too, benefited from notable improvements. Most of the Hippocratic Corpus [writings of the famed Greek physician Hippocrates and his followers] was of Hellenistic date, and the various advances that its contents registered meant that the Greeks could now increasingly employ methods based not only on theory but on accumulated case studies as well. The dissections conducted by Herophilus of Calchedon, in the first half of the third century, enhanced knowledge of the brain, eye, duodenum, liver and reproductive organs. His younger colleague Erasistratus, who like him worked at Alexandria, made discoveries relating to digestion and the vascular (circulatory) system. Herophilus has been called the founder of anatomy, and Erasistratus of physiology. Moreover, Erasistratus also turned his attention to the nervous system, and led the way towards psychiatry. . . .

More Realistic Literary Characters

The impulse towards finding out about reality which had set science and medicine, for a time, on such a prominent course was paralleled in literature, and particularly in writings related to the operations of the human personality.

The thoughts of the Greeks had already been working in that direction when Euripides produced his harrowingly true-to-life personality studies, and when Aristotle amassed evidence about differing patterns of human behaviour. Then his pupil Theophrastus wrote his *Characters*, thirty satirical, razor-sharp sketches of persons suffering from various psychological flaws. One of his pupils was the Athenian practitioner of the New Comedy, Menander (*c*.342–292), who was also keenly interested in human emotions, at a down-to-earth level. Substantial passages or fragments of ten of his more than a hundred plays are now available, including a more or less complete text of the *Epitrepontes* (Arbitrators). These works show that Menander prefers to avoid the politics dear to the Old Comedy of [the fifth-century B.C. Athenian playwright] Aristophanes, whose stock figures he replaces by more three-dimensional people. . . .

In the next generation, the literary mimes of Theocritus (*c*.300–260?)—who came from Syracuse, but lived at Cos and then worked mainly at Alexandria—introduced a new sort of realism. Mimetic dances had been popular since early times, and mime had now become the most favoured Greek theatrical form. For it was a popular medium among people who wanted a humorous, but direct and unencumbered, picture of the world around them. Theocritus, famous for his pastoral idylls, . . . endowed this sort of composition with a new life, adapting the mime-form to elegant allusive verse, and employing his strong sense of the ridiculous to make fun of a vast section of contemporary life—the sort of men and women whom the poet's own fastidious circle despised. He brings to life their platitudinous [trite] sentiments with an unerring light touch, and the joke is enhanced by the inappropriately unnatural literary diction that he puts into the mouths of these trivial low-brow characters.

Not long afterwards Herodas, perhaps from Cos, evolved another type of literary mime, the *mimiambus*, comprising brief, pithy, versified sketches of relentless pungency [sharpness]. Once again part of the joke lies in the piquant [charming] contrast between his treatment of his themes, which is naturalistic and realistic, and the artificial, elevated, erudite style in which it is . . . framed.

Lifelike Sculptures and Paintings

The visual art of the Hellenistic period, while following on with direct continuity from the achievements of the previous epoch, nevertheless also rivalled contemporary literature in its increasedly determined move towards various forms of realism. The figure of the Apoxyomenus (Man Scraping Himself), made in the later years of the fourth century by Lysippus of Sicyon, shows not only a new and more natural, or at least more fashionable, set of anatomical proportions (smaller head, more slender body), but also a new sense of spiral movement, and a new three-dimensional method of composition. The Tyche (Fortune) of Antioch by his pupil Eutychides developed this three-dimensional concept further, presenting a cunning structure of lines and folds set obliquely in different planes.

The climax of these techniques, however, was to be seen in the no longer surviving bronze Helios or sun-god (Colossus) of Rhodes by another of Lysippus's pupils, the Rhodian Chares (292–280), and in the still extant [surviving] Victory (Nike) of Samothrace, by an unknown sculptor of early second-century BC. Originally tinted, the Victory is seen alighting exultantly upon a ship's prow—and a calculated counter-twist of her swirling, windswept robes shows how she is leaning forward to meet the rush of the wind.

Yet, somewhat paradoxically, this very time when drapery was receiving such sensitive attention also witnessed an intensification of the interest in the naked feminine form. . . . Thus the bodily planes of the Venus of Milo (Melos), of the second-century date, move and turn in multiple, contrasting directions, which reveal how, although classical purity and austerity have not been abandoned, they are modified by novel ideas and methods that have been mobilized to exploit the Hellenistic taste for realistic interpretation.

And meanwhile another sort of sculptural realism was developing too, with theatrical emphasis upon the emotions, which the sculptors of the time, echoing Aristotle, regarded as an essential element in human character. Major achievements in this field took place at Pergamum, the only royal capital where sculptors undertook extensive and important work with the backing of ample official patronage. Thus the bronze groups of statuary dedicated by the Pergamene king Attalus I Soter to the goddess Athena (c.200), in order to celebrate his victories over the Celtic Gauls (Galatians) who had invaded Asia Minor, was one of the most ambitious

Example A

sculptural complexes ever attempted. The bronze originals have vanished, but a marble copy of the centrepiece still survives. It is the 'Ludovisi Group', consisting of the figure of a defeated, desperate Gaul stabbing himself to avoid capture while supporting the body of his wife whom he has just killed. Her limp, inanimate form contrasts with the tension of the man's contorted pose, as he plunges the dagger into his own neck. This central composition was originally surrounded by a series of half-recumbent figures, of which one, the 'Dying Gaul', is preserved, in the form of a fine copy, perhaps of the first century BC. . . .

For the 'Dying Gaul' once again combines the traditional simplifying pattern of Greek classicism with the emotional impact, and freshly direct observation of nature, which were features of contemporary Hellenistic art. There is emphasis upon the vanquished in this monument: they appear not as embodiments of evil, but in all the defiant agony of their defeat. And their portrayal is realistic. The same taste for realism, too, inspired other sculptors belonging to what has been called the 'miserabilistic' school, who depict hunchback dwarfs, and battered fishermen, and maudlin female alcoholics. And yet another facet of realism can be seen in the intimate, amusing terracotta statuettes which take their name from Tanagra in Boeotia, although they were first produced at Taras (Taranto, c.350) and then at Athens.

Wall-painting evidently reflected similar tendencies, represented above all by Apelles of Colophon in Ionia, who enjoyed the patronage of Alexander the Great and Ptolemy I Soter. His exploitation of illusionistic *trompe l'oeil* [a highly realistic painting style] and foreshortening effects was especially notable, and the men and women whom he painted were shown exhibiting a whole range of different emotions. He specialized in easel-paintings, none of which have survived.

But his style may well be reflected in some of the large pebble-mosaics of the period. One such mosaic at Pella, the capital of Macedonia, is a picture of a stag-hunt signed by Gnosis (c.320–300), whose foreshortened figures and shaded, wind-blown draperies convey an illusion of depth and of real life, as it appears to the eye.

Biography and Portraiture

This realism was a keynote of contemporary art, because it mirrored what Hellenistic man was thinking and feeling. And, by the same token, he was individualistic. Despite all the troubles of the time, he was liberated from many earlier conventions and restraints, and more and more conscious of his own capacities and needs and rights. City-state life had weakened, and the royal centres were too remote to occupy its place. To fill the vacuum, people belonged to clubs, lived in better houses, read more—and read about other individuals.

Theophrastus's *Characters* had described what individuals were like, without naming anybody in particular. But people also wanted to read about real, important, picturesque men—in an age which indulged, freely, in personality cult. They were catered for by Aristoxenus of Taras (*b.*375/360), who did much to develop, out of earlier precedents, the art of biography—including lives not only of men of action, but of philosophers as well. In the third century, Satyrus of Callatis Pontica (Mangalia) composed further biographies, writing attractively but inserting much legendary material. But the *Lives of Philosophers* by Antigonus of Carystus (*c.*240) showed an unprecedentedly high standard of accurate description. So biography, by now, had been launched; and autobiography, too, was foreshadowed by the *Memoirs* of the Achaean League statesman Aratus of Sicyon (271–213).

Sculptural portraiture, the visual counterpart of the biographer's art, was likewise virtually an original creation of the Hellenistic world. Men who sought to depict Alexander the Great set the tone. The king's own favourite sculptor, as far as portraits of himself were concerned, was Lysippus of Sicyon, who alone, Alexander believed, could truly capture the leonine aspect of his appearance. Such portraits, like other forms of art, retained a delicate balance between the old idealism and the new realistic trends: as Lysippus himself remarked, 'While others made men as they were, I make them as they appeared to be'—or as they wanted to be, for heads of early Hellenistic monarchs tend not only to reproduce their actual features, but also to hint at the providential foresight and care for his subjects that a king ought to display, and wished to seem to be displaying.

Realistic Depictions of Love

So realism, of a sort, was a characteristic of 'Hellenistic man'. But this was also an age when Greek women came to the fore. As we saw, Hellenistic sculptors, for the first time, were exploring the naked bodies of women: and this was only one aspect of a whole phenomenon of female emergence that was typical of the age.

The tendency was stimulated by the careers of queens of terrifying ability and force, enjoying unlimited freedom of action and power: women such as Arsinoe II Philadelphus, sister and wife of Ptolemy II of Egypt. The reverence accorded to these Ptolemaic queens was related to the worship of the mother-goddess Isis, with whom, indeed, it seemed natural that such formidable human women should be identified.

But, in addition, the prestige and activities of such personages could not fail to contribute to the emancipation of women in general—which in consequence proceeded on a substantial scale, though sometimes patchily. Liberation had at least gone far enough for two ladies whom Theocritus brings to the festival of Adonis to grumble about their husbands in a highly unsubservient fashion. . . . The development of private houses made women's lives more agreeable, and eminent women of the time included a portrait-painter, an architect, harpists and at least three poets.

And male poets, too, wrote elegies and epigrams reflecting a new kind of literary interest in the analysis of heterosexual love. The best epigrams of Asclepiades of Samos (c.290), for example, deal with this kind of erotic theme, employing his original, dramatic talent to explore the neurotic obsessions which accompanied it. But love, to him, meant sex more than romance. The women he wrote about were mostly attractive prostitutes (hetairai), and he commented on them in satirical and scandalous language—himself being weary of living, to use his own words, at the age of scarcely twenty-two. Theocritus, too, agrees with him in failing to envisage love as an ennobling or purifying passion, but stresses it for a different reason: because he knows all about the misery of amorous frustration, the agony of the heart.

In the next generation Apollonius Rhodius, librarian at Alexandria from *c.260* to *c.247*, by depicting Medea's passion for Jason in his poem the *Argonautica*, became the first poet to use love, romantic love, as the central theme of a whole epic. And meanwhile the same passion, too, of a more middle-brow and saccharine [sugar-sweet] nature, was the main feature of a series of Greek novels that were being launched on the world, perhaps under Egyptian influence, and were supplemented, subsequently, by spicier short stories, the *Milesian Tales*.

Chapter 4

The Coming of Rome and Downfall of the Greeks

Turning Points

IN WORLD HISTORY

Pyrrhus Fights the Romans

John Warry

Pyrrhus, king of the small Greek kingdom of Epirus, in northwestern Greece, was the first Hellenistic general to fight major battles against the Romans, whose state was rising to power in the central Mediterranean. The following concise account of Pyrrhus's Italian adventures is by former Cambridge University scholar John Warry. The ancient sources that Warry (along with other modern historians) draws on include the life of Pyrrhus by the first-century A.D. Greek biographer Plutarch, and information from two earlier Greek chroniclers, Dionysius (first century B.C.) and Hieronymous (third century B.C.).

In the middle of the fourth century BC, the Dorian Greek colonists of Tarentum in southern Italy had appealed to Sparta, their mother city, for help against the indigenous population which threatened them. At a time when northern Greece was crucially involved against Philip of Macedon, Sparta had sent a force under King Archidamus III, who had subsequently been killed fighting in Italy. Later, when Alexander the Great was in the east, his mother's brother, also named Alexander, who had made himself ruler of the tribes and cities of Epirus, gladly accepted another Tarentine invitation to intervene in southern Italy. He too was killed fighting there. A third episode of this kind occurred in 303 BC, when Cleonymus, a Spartan mercenary general, with 5,000 men, championed the Tarentines against Italian neighbours. Cleonymus used Italy as a base against Corcyra (Corfu) and eventually quarreled with the city which had engaged him. For Tarentum, the most natural sources of Greek aid in these recurrent situations were Sparta, their

Excerpted from *Warfare in the Classical World*, by John Warry. Copyright ©1980 by Salamander Books, Ltd. Reprinted with the permission of the University of Oklahoma Press.

mother city, and Epirus, conveniently situated opposite the heel of Italy across comparatively narrow seas. In 281 BC, at last in open conflict with Rome, the Tarentines issued an invitation to King Pyrrhus of Epirus. . . .

Pyrrhus Crosses to Italy

Pyrrhus inherited his title to the throne as a child and as a consequence his position long remained precarious. However, he at last enlisted the help of Ptolemy and, after establishing himself powerfully in Epirus, ruled at first jointly and then as sole monarch. In this capacity, he allied himself with the Thracian dynast Lysimachus to drive out Demetrius, who had claimed the throne of Macedon on the death of Cassander in 287 BC. Demetrius' claim was based on his marriage to Antipater's daughter Phila and he derived support from some of the Greek states, to whom he had at one time presented himself as a champion of constitutional liberty. Pyrrhus and Lysimachus, in combination, succeeded in defeating Demetrius, but when the victors competed for domination of the Macedonian kingdom, Pyrrhus was forced to withdraw. Thus frustrated, he was ready to direct his ambitions westwards.

The Tarentines, who gave Pyrrhus his opportunity, had an old treaty with Rome, perhaps describable as obsolete, according to which the Romans were not to send warships into the Tarentine Gulf. In 282 BC the Romans installed supporting garrisons in the Greek cities of Thurii, Locri and Rhegium. These measures were directed against the Italian people of Lucania, to the north. Thurii, however, lay at the western corner of the Tarentine Gulf and, probably as a demonstration of strength, the Romans sent warships there.

The matter could have been overlooked by the Tarentines, but they were already anxious at the expansion of Roman power and decided on war. They accordingly attacked and sank several Roman warships, drove the Roman garrison from Thurii and sacked the city. The violence of their reaction may be explained ideologically by the hatred of Tarentine democrats for Thurian oligarchs. Committed now to war against Rome, the Tarentines made their invitation to Pyrrhus not only in their own name but on behalf of other Greek cities in Italy. As a contribution to the common war effort, they offered both their own armed forces and substantial levies of indigenous Italian troops. . . .

Pyrrhus immediately sent Cineas, his Thessalian staff officer and diplomat on whose education and intelligence he placed great reliance, to Tarentum with an advance party of 3,000 men, while he himself assembled the main body of the invasion forces. Vessels for the convoy and an accompanying escort of war galleys were provided by Tarentum itself. In the past, Cleonymus had been similarly supplied. In a fleet which included horse-transports and a variety of flat-bottomed boats, Pyrrhus embarked 20 elephants, 3,000 cavalry, 20,000 infantry, 2,000 archers and 500 slingers. . . .

The Battle of Heraclea

As the king approached Tarentum, Cineas came out to meet him with such forces as were already stationed in the city. Whatever the precise terms of Pyrrhus' agreement with the Tarentines, he was very careful not to do anything which might offend them until his own widely dispersed fleet had at last made its way into harbour at Tarentum. He then took charge of the situation, placed the whole city on a war footing, closed all places of entertainment and sport, suspended all festivities and social events and conscripted the population for military service. Some of the citizens, who objected very strongly to this treatment, left the town.

Pyrrhus soon learned that a formidable Roman army was approaching, plundering the Lucanian hinterland on its way. The large force of allies which had been promised him by the Tarentines had not yet arrived, and Pyrrhus would gladly have waited until he had the support of greater numbers. To delay longer, however, leaving all initiative to the enemy, would clearly have been strategically inadvisable and bad for morale. He therefore led out his men to confront the Romans. Perhaps for the sake of further procrastination, he sent forward a herald to enquire whether the enemy would accept him as an arbitrator of their differences with Tarentum. The reply was, as at this stage he might have expected, that the Romans neither wanted him as an arbitrator nor feared him as an enemy.

Pyrrhus watched from his camp near Heraclea as the Romans crossed the river Siris and was impressed by their good order and military discipline, which, as he remarked to one of his officers, seemed surprising in "barbarians". More than ever, he was disposed to wait for his reinforcements, but this was precisely what the Romans were determined to prevent him from doing. Pyrrhus deployed his men along the river bank in defensive positions, but the Romans were beforehand. Their infantry crossed the river at fordable points in some strength, and Pyrrhus' men, threatened with encirclement, had to withdraw.

In the circumstances which we have just outlined, the battle of Heraclea began. Pyrrhus realized that he must seize the initiative without further delay and, adopting the time-honoured tactics of the great Alexander, left his phalanx to hold the enemy in front, while he himself led a cavalry charge at the head of 3,000 horses. But unlike Alexander, he had timed the move badly. His attack came too late. The Romans themselves were usually weak in cavalry, but on this occasion they seem to have been well supported by the horsemen of their Italian allies, and Pyrrhus' Thessalian cavalry were driven back. The king then ordered his phalangists [phalanx men] to attack, though an offensive role was not normal or suitable for them and they might well have found themselves encircled by the opposing cavalry if the enemy's horses had not taken fright at the elephants and become uncontrollable. In these circumstances, the Thessalian cavalry was able to resume the offensive and soon carried all before it.

The victory, though not decisive, was something better than what we usually describe as "Pyrrhic". Roman casualties were, according to Dionysius, 15,000; according to Hieronymus, 7,000. Pyrrhus' casualties were, by Dionysius' account, 13,000; by Hieronymus', 4,000. Perhaps we should not sneer at such widely divergent statistics. Casualty reports from modern theatres of war often show similar discrepancies. In any case, Pyrrhus possessed himself of the abandoned Roman camp, and his prestige was very much enhanced, so that many of the hesitant Lucanians, Samnites and other allies, whom he had awaited in vain before the battle, now joined him.

Another Costly Lesson

Pyrrhus did not expect to take Rome itself, but he advanced northwards, to within 37 miles (60 km) of the city walls, hoping to negotiate out of strength. However, his presence by no means intimidated the Romans. No fear that he would detach their allies from them, ravage their lands or lay siege to the city itself induced them to make peace on terms that would safeguard the Tarentines. Their friendship remained conditional on the unconditional departure of Pyrrhus and his army from Italy.

Meanwhile, two Roman consular armies had been brought up to strength and remained at large in Italy. Pyrrhus could not afford to ignore them. They might threaten his rear; they might threaten his communications; they might threaten his allies. Above all, prestige and morale were at stake. He must not appear reluctant to engage the enemy. He broke off negotiations with the Roman government and went campaigning again. Confronting the Romans at Asculum in Apulia, he fought them on rough and wooded ground which gave little opportunity to his elephants or cavalry and turned the fight into an infantry engagement. The ground seems also to have hampered the phalanx: the Romans prolonged the battle all day, and night fell without a decision having been reached.

On the following day, Pyrrhus contrived to fight on open ground which was less to the enemy's advantage, giving them no occasion for the tactics of flexible response, such as they had adopted in the wilder country. Even so, the Romans, with their short swords, striving desperately to reach a decision before the elephants could be brought into action, seem to have been a match for the long pikes of the Greek phalanx. In the end, the elephants once more gave Pyrrhus his victory—which this time was more "Pyrrhic" in character. The Romans merely retreated into their camp. Pyrrhus himself was wounded in the arm. Hieronymus' figures are of 6,000 Roman casualties, as compared with 3,550 on Pyrrhus' side. But many of Pyrrhus' ablest officers were among the dead and he was not in a position to recruit new troops, as the Romans were.

Pyrrhus was a brave and inspiring if rather flamboyant commander, who was well capable of keeping his head even in the middle of a most desperate fight. Yet he does not seem to have excelled either as a strategist or a tactician. At Heraclea, by waiting for reinforcements, he conceded a valuable initiative to the Romans, without receiving the reinforcements for which he had waited. The timing of the cavalry charge with which he had opened the battle was also tardy. At Asculum, he could not make the right choice of ground until a day of indecisive fighting had taught him costly lessons. [In another strategically questionable move, Pyrrhus suddenly moved his army to Sicily, where the local Greek cities were menaced by Carthage.] . . .

Pyrrhus Abandons the Italian Greeks

At the time of Pyrrhus' operations in Italy and Sicily (281–275 BC), Rome and Carthage were in fact associated by a series of treaties which dated from very early times. The precise number of these treaties is a subject on which neither ancient historians nor modern scholars agree. . . .

However, the first two . . . treaties seem to have been mainly commercial in scope; the third, military and naval. The underlying principle seems to have been that Carthage should offer naval aid in return for Roman military support.

It is indeed on record that, hoping to hinder Pyrrhus' intervention in Sicily, a Carthaginian admiral arrived with ships to dissuade Rome from making peace with the king. The Romans were not at first willing to commit themselves. The Carthaginians then sailed off to negotiate with Pyrrhus. These negotiations also led to nothing, but when the Carthaginian mission returned again to Rome, the Romans were more amenable. The Carthaginian negotiators had made their point. The 120 ships could be thrown into either scale: Rome continued its war against Pyrrhus' allies in Italy. In fact, the Carthaginian commander, on his way back to Sicily, even transported 500 Roman soldiers to Rhegium, on the straits of Messina, in order to reinforce the garrison.

The Carthaginian diplomatic initiative against Pyrrhus certainly seems to have borne fruit. Moreover, the Cartha-

A Pyrrhic Victory

This is Plutarch's account of the second day of fighting at Ausculum, including Pyrrhus's famous remark that later inspired the term "Pyrrhic victory," meaning something won at great cost.

The next day Pyrrhus regrouped his forces so as to fight on even terrain, where his elephants could be used against the enemy's line. At first light he detached troops to occupy the difficult ground, posted strong contingents of archers and slingers in the spaces between the elephants, and then launched his main body into the attack in close order and with an irresistible impetus. The Romans could not employ the feinting and skirmishing tactics they had used on the previous day and were compelled to receive Pyrrhus' charge on level ground and head on. They were anxious to repulse Pyrrhus' heavy infantry before the elephants came up, and so they hacked desperately with their swords against the Greek pikes, exposing themselves recklessly, thinking only of killing and wounding the enemy and caring nothing for their own losses. After a long struggle, so it is said, the Roman line began to give way at the point where Pyrrhus himself was pressing his opponents hardest, but the factor which did most to enable the Greeks to prevail was the weight and fury of the elephants' charge. Against this even the Romans' courage was of little avail: they felt as if they might have done before the rush of a tidal wave or the shock of an earthquake, that it was better to give way than to stand their ground to no purpose, and suffer a terrible fate without gaining the least advantage. . . .

The two armies disengaged and the story goes that when one of Pyrrhus' friends congratulated him on his victory, he replied, 'One more victory like that over the Romans will destroy us completely!'

Plutarch, *Life of Pyrrhus*, in *The Age of Alexander: Nine Greek Lives by Plutarch*. Trans. Ian Scott-Kilvert. New York: Penguin, 1973, pp. 408–409.

ginian navy attacked the king's forces as they returned from Sicily and destroyed a substantial number of his ships. . . .

In Italy, the Samnites, disgusted by Pyrrhus' neglect of their cause, were no longer willing to rally round him in great strength. Two Roman armies, respectively under the two consuls of the year, were now campaigning separately. Pyrrhus detached half his force to deal with the enemy in Lucania, while he himself marched northward to confront the Romans near Malventum (later renamed, more propitiously, Beneventum). Here, he attempted a night attack. Night attacks, in ancient warfare, were notoriously prone to miscarry. . . . Pyrrhus' attempt was no exception to the general rule. His advancing forces lost their way in wooded country during the hours of darkness and at dawn found themselves deployed in positions for which they had never bargained. The Romans, at first alarmed by the unexpected presence of the enemy, soon realized that it was possible to attack the isolated vanguard and rout it. Thus encouraged, the cautious consul gave battle to Pyrrhus' main body in the open plain. On this occasion, the Romans seem to have discovered a method of dealing with elephants: though the animals at first moved onward with their usual irresistible momentum, they were eventually frightened and induced to turn against their own troops. As a consequence, Pyrrhus was obliged to retreat.

He was now left in command of 8,000 infantry and 500 cavalry and, as Plutarch convincingly assures us, for lack of money to pay them, he was obliged to look for a new war. This he found in Macedonia, which Antigonus Gonatas, Demetrius' son and successor, proceeding from his rather precarious foothold in Greece, now occupied. . . . Pyrrhus was successful against Antigonus' elephants and won over the opposing Macedonian infantry by an appeal made to them on the battlefield. Antigonus fled, but the Macedonian population was soon alienated from Pyrrhus. . . .

As ever, turning from a task which, left uncompleted, would have been better unattempted, Pyrrhus answered an invitation to meddle in Spartan politics, hoping thereby to make himself master of the Peloponnese. He was killed in

Argos during a street fight, having been felled by an accurately aimed tile from a woman's hand.

Meanwhile, in Italy, the garrison which Pyrrhus had left at Tarentum defied the Romans until 272 BC. It then surrendered, but was allowed to withdraw on honourable terms, while the Tarentines gave hostages to Rome and accepted a Roman garrison. The Romans dealt sternly but not vindictively with the Italian populations which had supported Pyrrhus. Important sectors of their territory were confiscated in order to provide for Latin colonial settlements. . . .

Rome now dominated southern and central Italy, including . . . the Greek cities.

Rome Expands into the Mediterranean

Chester G. Starr

After clashing with the Greek general Pyrrhus in the 270s B.C., the Romans saw firsthand just how formidable the Greek armies of the day were, and also how uncomfortably close the Hellenistic realms were to the Roman sphere of influence. This realization was reinforced a few decades later when Macedonia's king, Philip V, allied himself with Rome's enemy—Carthage. The wars between Rome and Carthage constituted the beginning of Roman expansion into the Mediterranean, a process that would soon spread to the Greek East. This early phase of Roman expansion is chronicled here by Chester G. Starr, former Bentley Professor of History at the University of Michigan.

During the period 264–133 B.C., Rome strode out of Italy into the broad Mediterranean world. This expansion was not deliberately planned; many Roman leaders, indeed, spoke against foreign entanglements and commitments in terms we might well call "isolationist." Yet internal expansive forces were strong and were further intensified by the unstable political conditions which existed elsewhere in the Mediterranean.

First the Romans fought two great wars with Carthage, which gave them control of the western Mediterranean by 201. Thenceforth Rome had the enduring problems of pacifying and civilizing districts which were less civilized than itself.

After 200 the Romans also looked eastward, where the Hellenistic political structure was falling to pieces. The wars of the great monarchies after Alexander had by this time

Excerpted from *A History of the Ancient World*, by Chester G. Starr. Copyright ©1997 by Oxford University Press, Inc. Reprinted with the permission of the Oxford University Press, Inc.

worn down their strength, and the lower classes grew ever more restive at the exploitation by the Greek bureaucrats and by the city-dwellers. From the Iranian plateau a new dynasty, that of Parthia, expanded by land into Mesopotamia; from the west Rome advanced swiftly to take control of the coastal districts of the Hellenistic world. By 133 the state on the Tiber held virtual mastery over all the Mediterranean world, though it was not yet ready to assume direct responsibility for the governance of this empire.

The expansion of Rome had other than military aspects. The continuing economic, social, and internal political developments of Rome must be considered . . . in connection with their enduring effects after 133. Culturally . . . the Roman upper classes became ever more receptive to the attractive, if somewhat superficial, qualities of Hellenistic civilization. Some dogged Romans were deeply suspicious of these foreign ways, but Roman society as a whole accepted sophistication with enthusiasm. In every respect the period witnessed a growing unification of the Mediterranean world, which was to produce the last great phase of ancient history.

The Western Mediterranean Scene

By 264 Rome had developed a system of government which was technically a democracy but in which the actual exercise of power was primarily in the hands of a landed aristocracy, accustomed to military activity. It had also gained mastery over the Italian peninsula and had bound its allies, or subjects, to it by a pattern of varied privileges and responsibilities.

Across the Mediterranean in north Africa, Carthage had also been expanding. . . . The aristocratic families of Carthage held extensive lands in the neighborhood but also had commercial interests to a greater degree than did their peers in Rome, for Carthage dominated a great trading empire in north Africa, south Spain, western Sicily, and Sardinia and Corsica. Some of the products which it sold for metals and other raw materials were made in Carthage; others came from the east or from Campania [a region of southwestern Italy]. Like the Romans, the Carthaginians were more and more influenced by Greek culture from the fourth century onward.

To maintain its position Carthage relied largely upon a mercenary army, some naval power—though its navy had fought no battles for a long time—and diplomatic guarantees of its closed commercial sphere. Whereas the Romans exacted troops rather than money from their subjects in Italy, the Carthaginians required from their dependents a heavy tribute in grain and precious metals in order to defray the expenses of their empire. The population of the Carthaginian domains is estimated at about 3,000,000, approximately the same as that of Roman Italy.

At the very beginning of the Roman Republic, Carthage and Rome had contracted a treaty which banned Roman traders from most of the Carthaginian shoreline, while Carthage agreed not to interfere in the Roman sphere of interest in Latium. Other treaties of similar nature had been made later, in 348 and 306. In the war with Pyrrhus Carthage had offered financial and naval assistance to Rome. Between Roman and Carthaginian interests lay a buffer of Greek states, that is, Massilia and its dependencies in Gaul [what is now France] and north Spain and the Greek cities of Sicily. From these states, however, were to spring the conditions which led Rome and Carthage into decisive struggles, called Punic wars because the Greek name for Carthaginians was "Poeni."

The spark which kindled the first struggle came from an attack by Hiero, king of [the Greek Sicilian city of] Syracuse, on some Campanian mercenaries who had seized Messana at the northeast tip of Sicily. In their plight these "Mamertines" appealed to both Carthage and Rome. The former sent naval aid at once; the Roman Senate debated the issue in a quandary. If Rome allowed Carthage to have a foothold so close to Italy, it could hamper the trade of the south Italian subjects of Rome; but Roman naval interest had always been so slight that the Senate hesitated to move into Sicily. An answer to the appeal, which was one of the most critical decisions in all Roman history, was referred to the assembly. The people, spurred by the consuls, voted to protect the Mamertines.

An advance Roman detachment threw out the Carthaginian garrison already in Messana; but when the Roman consul Appius Claudius appeared, he found himself in open fighting with Carthaginian reinforcements. The war which thus resulted was to lead to the beginning of Roman overseas empire.

The First Punic War (264–241 B.C.)

Initially the Roman army scored great successes in Sicily, for the Carthaginians had no nearby naval bases to check Roman troop movements across the Sicilian straits. . . . But the other coastal towns in Carthaginian hands could not be easily taken so long as the Punic fleet supplied them by sea, and coastal raids on Italy itself pointed to the dangers of a Roman naval weakness.

The clear-headed Roman strategists saw the need and in 261 set about building a fleet of 20 *triremes* [warships with three banks of oars] and of 100 heavier *quinqueremes*, in which each oar was pulled by five men. Crews were trained in mock-up ships on land, and the Romans devised a secret weapon, the "crow" *(corvus)*. This was a gangway held upright until a Roman ship was next to its enemy, whereupon it was suddenly lowered so that Roman soldiers could pour onto the foe's vessel. So equipped, the Roman fleet under the consul C. Duilius rowed to Sicily in 260 and won a smashing victory at Mylae over the Carthaginians under Hannibal, whose ships were caught one by one. Soon Carthage held only the base of Lilybaeum in western Sicily.

The triumphant Romans, rather than wasting time here on a difficult siege, decided in 256 to strike directly at Carthage. Their fleet, under the consuls M. Atilius Regulus and L. Manlius Vulso, defeated the Carthaginians under Hamilcar in the great battle of Ecnomus, then landed a Roman army near Carthage. In their desperation the Carthaginians turned to a Spartan mercenary general, Xanthippus, who was versed in Hellenistic tactics. Xanthippus skillfully combined the Carthaginian infantry with Numidian cavalry and elephants to defeat the Romans. Regulus was taken prisoner, and the remnants of his forces were evacuated by the Roman navy.

Thereafter the Romans suffered naval disaster after disaster in storms, which sank all-told about 600 warships and 1000 transports; probably no naval war in all history has seen such casualties by drowning. The Roman state and treasury were close to exhaustion, but finally in 244 the Senate assessed itself for a public loan to build a last fleet of 200 warships, which omitted the top-heavy *corvus*. This squadron C. Lutatius Catulus led down to Sicily to blockade Lilybaeum. In 241 he took his ships out to sea, despite stormy weather to meet and crush the relief fleet sent from Carthage in the battle of the Aegates islands.

Carthage was equally exhausted by the long war and now made peace. It surrendered Sicily to the Romans and paid an indemnity of 3200 talents over the next 10 years. . . .

New Suspicions and Tensions

Both Sicily and Sardinia-Corsica were formed into [Roman] provinces. . . . In creating provinces . . . the Romans broke with their Italian policy and began to lay the patterns which governed their further imperial expansion.

The expansive forces inherent in the Roman system of government and alliances soon led the Romans into other areas. To the north lay Cisalpine Gaul or the fertile Po valley, occupied by the barbaric Gauls but coveted by the Roman farmers. The popular hero C. Flaminius, tribune in 232, secured a law against the opposition of the more far-seeing Senate, which divided some of the southeastern part of the valley into new farms. After a Gallic rebellion in 225, Cisalpine Gaul was conquered by 220.

To the east, across the Adriatic, a number of minor principalities were engaged in piratical activity which disturbed the south Italian cities. In 229–28 and again in 219 the Roman fleet operated in the Adriatic and established a Roman sphere of influence along the Dalmatian coast. This pacifying activity was generally approved by the Greeks proper, but the kings of Macedonia, just to the east, began to grow suspicious of the Romans. . . .

Carthage, meanwhile, licked its wounds and began to build up a strong position in Spain, which it had virtually lost during the strains of the First Punic war. This purpose-ful expansion, carried on by the general Hamilcar, then his son-in-law Hasdrubal, and finally his son Hannibal (245–183) from 221, seriously alarmed Massilia, which made representations to Rome. In 226 the Romans dictated an agreement with Carthage which set the limit of its northward expansion at the Ebro river, but the suspicious Romans continued to watch developments in Spain with concern. They contracted an alliance with the native state of Saguntum, though it lay south of the Ebro, and encouraged the Saguntines in anti-Carthaginian activities. The fiery young Hannibal refused to tolerate this interference and took Saguntum after siege in 219. The Romans had done nothing to aid their ally but now sent ambassadors to Carthage with the ultimatum to surrender Hannibal. On its refusal the ambassadors declared war in March 218.

The Second Punic War (218–201 B.C.)

The Romans went into the Second Punic war confident of victory. They had retained the naval mastery which they had gained in the previous war and launched two squadrons at once. The first was to take a Roman army under the consul P. Cornelius Scipio to Spain to pin down Hannibal; the second was to ferry an army under the other consul Ti. Sempronius Longus to Africa in order to conquer Carthage itself.

Unfortunately for the Romans, they moved too slowly—their enemy had plans of his own. Hannibal calculated that if he could invade Italy and defeat the Romans their subjects would revolt and so end Roman power. He was confident in his own powers of generalship and in the quality of his veteran army; he could secure a base among the disaffected Gauls of the Po valley; all that remained was to get from Spain to Italy. As early in the spring of 218 as the Pyrenees were open he marched into southern Gaul, dextrously made his way across the Rhône despite native opposition, and crossed the Alps into Italy in September, just after the first snows had fallen. Hannibal had had to march by land both because the Romans held the sea and because he brought with him a large force of cavalry and elephants; but by the late fall he stood among friendly Gauls in the Po valley with an army of 20,000 foot and 6,000 horse.

While Scipio was at Massilia, he learned of the Carthaginian march, too late to stop Hannibal. The consul sent his army on to Spain, an important step later in preventing easy reinforcement to Hannibal, and returned to Italy. Sempronius abandoned his attack on Carthage and marched north to meet his colleague in the Po valley. In December 218, in battle in the mists on the Trebia river, the Romans lost two-thirds of their force in a Carthaginian ambush. The Po valley now had to be yielded to Hannibal.

The Roman people, much disturbed by the situation . . . rallied behind the popular hero Flaminius and elected him as one of the consuls for 217. . . . Hannibal drove his men southward behind Flaminius, who hurried to catch up with his two legions. The result was another Carthaginian trap on the north shore of Lake Trasimene, from which none of the Romans (including their general) escaped. Hannibal released those prisoners who were from the Italian allies and moved south to Campania, awaiting in vain the expected revolt of the Roman subjects. . . .

For the year 216 the Romans elected L. Aemilius Paullus and C. Terentius Varro as consuls. Rather than dividing their forces, they sent out an army of at least 60,000 under both consuls, with orders to meet and defeat Hannibal once and for all. The consuls had first to train their troops, but by late summer moved down near Hannibal at Cannae, in northern Apulia. On August 2 the Romans arranged their army in compact mass on the south bank of the Aufidus river, in open terrain where no mists would occur. Hannibal, likewise eager for battle, ordered his army, of no more than 45,000 men, in a long line, with his superior cavalry on the flanks. When the battle began, his infantry center of half-civilized Spaniards and Gauls deliberately retreated under Hannibal's personal supervision so as to lure the Romans forward. His cavalry meanwhile won first on the left, then on the right flank. Thereupon his African infantry, farther out in the line, wheeled in, and his cavalry closed behind the close-packed Roman infantry, blinded by the dust of the battle; only about

10,000 Romans managed to break their way out of the trap. This double envelopment of a superior enemy was one of the greatest tactical masterpieces in all military history. . . .

After the battle of Cannae Hannibal's basic strategy at last gained part of its objective, for a great deal of southern Italy revolted from Roman rule. Capua, the greatest city in Campania, joined the revolt, as did eventually Syracuse, the principal city of Sicily. The Gauls of the Po valley had already rebelled, and shortly after Cannae came the news that the Roman army of reconquest in the Po valley had been wiped out. The young king of Macedonia, Philip V, contracted an alliance with the victorious Hannibal and began the First Macedonian war (215–05) against Rome with the object of taking the Roman protectorate on the Dalmatian coast.

Yet most of the Roman subjects in central Italy remained loyal, and the Romans themselves fought on stubbornly. Never again did their commanders allow themselves to be drawn into open battle in Italy with Hannibal. After 216 one Roman army continually watched the great Carthaginian, while others set about the grim task of conquering the Italian rebels. . . .

In Spain, meanwhile, the Roman army which had been sent out in 218 continued to put pressure on the Carthaginian domains and pinned down troops that would have been valuable to Hannibal. In 211 the two Roman commanders, both Scipios, were caught and killed; but the next year the son of one, P. Scipio (eventually called Africanus), was assigned as commander in Spain, though he was only 24 or 25. A sudden, brilliant dash in 209 far behind the Carthaginian lines gave him the hub of Carthaginian power, New Carthage (Cartagena), whereafter he began to gain the upper hand. . . .

Now, once again, the way was open for the Romans to return to their initial strategy of crushing Carthage by direct attack. Both the Roman treasury and the people, however, were themselves close to exhaustion. Their most experienced general, M. Claudius Marcellus, who had taken Syracuse, had been surprised and killed in 208. At this critical juncture the young Scipio Africanus, who had returned to Rome from his Spanish victories, stepped forward and secured the command. His army consisted mainly of volunteers and was equipped by loans.

In 204 Scipio landed in Africa and after some success granted a tentative peace treaty to Carthage, one condition of which was that it evacuate Hannibal from Italy. So Hannibal left in 203 a land where he had never been defeated in battle, yet could not win in war. After his return the armistice was broken, and the decisive battle took place at Zama in 202. This time Scipio had the advantage in cavalry, for the Numidians had joined him; and, using Hannibalic tactics against Hannibal, won.

The peace was harsh. Carthage yielded its elephants and all but 10 of its warships, formally surrendered Spain to Rome, and promised to pay 10,000 talents over the next 50 years. In the further agreement not to wage war in Africa itself without Roman approval lay seeds for later troubles which eventually were to bring the utter destruction of Carthage.

Comparison of the Greek and Roman Military Systems

Archer Jones

This examination of the two most powerful military systems of the Hellenistic period is by Archer Jones, a noted military historian who has taught at several universities. He begins with a brief overview of the combined, or integrated, military system developed by Philip and Alexander of Macedonia; with some minor modifications, this was the system used by the Hellenistic generals. Jones then describes the Roman system, perfected little by little in costly encounters with various enemies, notably the Greek general Pyrrhus and Carthaginian general Hannibal (who after a long string of stunning victories met defeat at the hands of Rome's P. Cornelius Scipio, later called "Africanus"). Finally, Jones cites some of Rome's first battles fought on Greek soil to show how the Roman system proved more flexible and effective. (The terms "heavy" and "light" in reference to infantry and cavalry generally differentiate heavily armored fighters from those wearing little or no armor. The quotes that appear throughout the essay are by the second-century B.C. Greek historian Polybius.)

Philip bequeathed to Alexander a force of heavy cavalry. Whereas Greek and Persian cavalry used the javelin or the bow and were prepared to thrust with a javelin or light spear, some Macedonian cavalry relied primarily on shock action [frontal assaults on enemy infantry and cavalry]. Like the heavy infantry, these men wore armor and carried shields and a short lance, a cavalry spear. About nine feet long and

Excerpted from *The Art of War in the Western World*, by Archer Jones. Copyright ©1987 by the Board of Trustees of the University of Illinois. Reprinted with the permission of the University of Illinois Press.

weighing four pounds, the lance had an iron point on each end. Though the horseman lacked a stirrup, training and practice enabled him to keep his seat reasonably well in combat at close quarters. When he thrust with his lance, he released it at or just before the moment of impact to avoid transmitting to himself the shock of the blow. He thus escaped the danger of losing his seat on his mount.

The Macedonian Combined Weapons System

Macedonian horsemen also differed from Greek cavalry in that they were thoroughly disciplined and trained to work together in groups and to respond to commands. They thus had better articulation, training, and skill in addition to their primary reliance on shock action. Over cavalry relying on javelins and rarely closing with the enemy, this doctrine enabled them to enjoy the same advantage as Greek heavy infantry held over light infantry in shock combat. Cavalry unprepared for determined shock action could not resist their charge. Heavy cavalry had the same dominance over light infantry as did heavy infantry, with an important difference—light infantry could not escape by running away. Only the heavy infantry, a formation of armored hoplites with their spears, could resist the charge and best them in hand-to-hand combat.

This Macedonian heavy cavalry, a small elite group, was called Companions of the King. The Macedonian army also had far more of the traditional, hybrid, or general-purpose cavalry, which largely relied on missile action, principally the javelin. And the bulk of the Macedonian army remained infantry. Light infantry had an important role: in battle it deployed in front of the heavy infantry where it could use its traditional tactics of slinging missiles, shooting arrows, or hurling javelins while keeping away from its heavy infantry opponents. Before the lines of hoplites clashed, the light infantry withdrew out of harm's way, its usefulness ended. Thus the tactics involved an initial reliance on the intrinsic ascendancy of the light over the heavy infantry.

The Macedonians changed the heavy infantry by doubling the length of the spear, at least for the ranks behind the first two. The longer spear enabled those of several ranks to project beyond the front, utilizing more rear-rank men and making an advance by this phalanx formidable indeed. Even if the front ranks did not use shorter spears and the rear ranks progressively longer spears, a united push by several ranks almost always drove back the opponents. The longer spears also made body armor less important, the rear ranks requiring none at all, a substantial saving in equipment costs. Relying more on the action of the group, individual soldiers needed less skill. Still the Macedonians made a virtue of the tactical innovation of the long spear and drilled their phalanx of professional soldiers so that it could function as a unit. In addition, they subdivided their troops, giving some articulation and maneuverability to an inherently unwieldy formation. But the longer spear reflected a subtle change, placing greater reliance on the advance of a wall of spears and less on the individual effort by the men in the front rank.

The creators of this army, the astute Philip and his son, Alexander, integrated these four weapon systems into a mutually supporting combat team. Heavy and light infantry each had its role as did the light and heavy cavalry, with the shock action of the elite Companions of the King held for a decisive blow. No weapon system had primacy, and none a merely auxiliary role; all had a significant part to play. . . .

Roman Weapons and Battlefield Units

While the Macedonians were perfecting the art of war in their fashion, the army of Rome, a small Italian city-state, evolved in a different direction. Like the Greeks, the Romans fought with a phalanx of hoplites assisted by light infantry and a general-purpose cavalry. But the Romans abandoned the spear as their principal weapon fairly early and adopted versatile offensive arms. For defense, they placed heavy reliance on a large convex shield, two and a half feet wide and four feet high. This wooden shield, covered with cloth and then with calf skin and reinforced in the center with iron, could turn "aside the more formidable blows of stones, pikes, and heavy missiles in general." A contemporary explained that "its upper and lower rims are strengthened by an iron edging which protects it from descending blows and from injury when resting on the ground." Since the Romans engaged in many sieges, faced the long pikes or spears of the Greeks, and fought the Celts who wielded a two-handed cutting sword, they eventually devised a shield effective against all opponents. They completed their protection with a helmet and a brass breastplate or, for the wealthier, a coat of chain-mail.

For attack the Romans depended for shock combat on a short sword, "excellent for thrusting, and both of its edges cut effectually, as the blade is very strong and firm." Such a sword would prove its worth at close quarters with an opponent whose two-handed sword or long pike could be turned aside by the shield. The bulk of the infantry also carried two of a javelin called a pilum. This had a point that bent or broke if it struck a hard object so that "the enemy is unable to return it. If this were not so, the missile would be available to both sides." This suited Roman tactics, which consisted of throwing the javelin and then closing quickly to fight with sword and shield.

The distinctive organization matured by the Romans proved more fundamental than their use of the sword. Arraying their army in three successive lines, each six ranks deep, they subdivided these lines into maniples, each maniple having two centuries of sixty men each. This subdivision provided rudimentary articulation and promised some maneuverability. The Romans exploited this organization by leaving gaps between each maniple in each line; the maniples of the second line were staggered so that they covered the gaps in the first. The third line differed from the first two as its maniples had only half the front, with sixty rather than 120 men. The men of the third line were the older citizens and still used the spear as their principal weapon. The maniples of the third line positioned themselves behind the holes in the second line, making the whole formation somewhat like a checkerboard. This was the basic formation in which the Romans advanced to the fight. Since gaps would almost certainly form in any line of battle as it advanced, the Romans anticipated this by providing the intervals systematically. Before the Roman line closed with the enemy in combat, the second line filled the breaks in the first with either a century or a full maniple pushing into the spaces in the front line. The third line moved up into the vacant positions in the second line and, with the remainder of the second line, constituted a reserve if not needed to help fill a large gap in the first line. This organization gave the Roman line of battle a flexibility and responsiveness that the phalanx lacked.

The administrative organization provided another element of strength in the Roman system. Ten of the first- and second-line maniples of 120 men each and ten of the sixty-man third-line maniples comprised an administrative organization called a legion. With a proportion of orderlies, clerks, porters, etc., some of whom doubled as light infantry, and a small amount of cavalry, the legion numbered over 4,000 men. When the Romans expanded their army, they added legions, thus providing good administration and organization for any large field army. . . .

The Romans practiced a slow but sure strategy, and gradually Rome dominated much of Italy. Since political astuteness complemented military skill, they bound to themselves as firm and willing allies the areas they controlled and extended to these allies the Roman organization and style of warfare. By the time of Alexander the Great, Rome had become a formidable power, ready to come into military contact with others in the Mediterranean.

Rome's First Encounters with the Macedonian System

The Macedonian system as used by Alexander became the standard for the eastern Mediterranean and much of the old Persian Empire. The difference between the Macedonian and Roman systems lay not primarily in the Roman use of swords and the Macedonian reliance on the spear; the difference was more subtle. The Roman army depended on their sword-wielding, partially articulated heavy infantry with their light infantry and cavalry filling the roles of auxiliaries. In their evolution from the phalanx to the manipular array, they had improved the infantry but had not developed in the direction of the Macedonian system of Alexander, which relied on the combined effect of all arms, including a cavalry force trained for real shock combat.

In the first major Roman combat with the Macedonian or Alexandrian system the combined-arms force won. The particulars of these battles with King Pyrrhus of the Greek Kingdom of Epirus are obscure, but, in Pyrrhus, the Romans faced not only a relative and disciple of Alexander the Great but also a general whose many campaigns had earned for him a most exalted reputation. The Romans attributed much of Pyrrhus's success to his use of elephants, which Alexander's successors had incorporated into the Macedonian system after Alexander faced them in India. Often unreliable, occasionally stampeding through their own infantry when attacked by javelins and other missiles, elephants proved most effective against cavalry because they frightened the enemy's horses. Pyrrhus based his successful battles with the Romans not on his elephants but on the success of his cavalry, presumably aided by elephants, in defeating the Roman cavalry and attacking the Roman infantry in flank and rear. But in defeat the Romans inflicted such severe casualties on Pyrrhus that he remarked that more such victories would force him to return to Greece alone.

In its first contest with the Romans, the African power Carthage copied the Macedonian system of war, even retaining a Greek general to command the army in the campaign to drive back the Roman invasion of Africa. Stationed as usual, on the flanks, the more powerful heavy cavalry of the Carthaginians defeated the Roman cavalry on the flanks and attacked the Roman infantry in the rear. The articulation inherent in the Roman three-line system meant that the rear maniples could turn about to fend off this assault, but this effective defensive tactic did not save the Romans: the Carthaginians won the Battle of Tunis and captured the Roman commander. . . .

The Roman System Proves Itself at Zama

[After more defeats, including the loss of some 50,000 men at Cannae, in 216 B.C.] the Romans avoided battle with Hannibal for fourteen years. When they again met him, they had in their commander, Scipio, a brilliant general who, though in his early thirties, had ample experience. . . . In spite of his taste for luxury and his Greek culture, Scipio easily instilled confidence in his troops. He then led his army into Africa while the steadfast Hannibal still remained in southern Italy. By this time the Romans no longer fielded militia, and Scipio commanded and inspired the devotion of an army largely composed of well-trained and disciplined veterans of many campaigns. Scipio and Hannibal met in Africa in 202 B.C. at the Battle of Zama, where each exhibited his genius. The contest between these two masters advanced the art of war. . . .

The Roman army had decisive superiority in cavalry, an advantage that usually belonged to Hannibal. But Scipio did not rely exclusively on his cavalry for success. He deployed his infantry in a manner that he had developed in Spain. Instead of having the maniples of the second and third lines close to and covering the intervals in the first line, he kept them back a distance of probably several hundred feet. He correctly believed that when the six-deep first line engaged the enemy infantry, the veterans would manage well without additional ranks behind them. The rear ranks constituted Scipio's reserve. . . .

But Scipio also had to cope with the Carthaginian army's eighty elephants. For this reason he abandoned the usual Roman initial array in a checkerboard formation and stationed the second and third lines of maniples directly behind those of the first. The intervals of the first he filled with the light infantry, "ordering them to open the action, and if they were forced back by the charge of the elephants to retire, those who had time to do so by the straight passages as far to the rear of the whole army, and those who were overtaken to right or left along the intervals between the lines."

Hannibal, realizing that he could not rely on his cavalry for victory, also had in a rear line of infantry a reserve that he could deploy. As at Cannae his best troops made up this reserve, but he altered his disposition of them. At Cannae he had placed the reserve in a column on each flank of his infantry line, ready to advance, face, and attack the Romans in their flank. But, since such a disposition was too obvious against Scipio, he kept this reserve in line, behind and parallel to his main infantry line. Superior in infantry, Hannibal counted on winning by using his reserve to envelop the Roman infantry line.

When the battle opened and as the light cavalry skirmished between the lines, "Hannibal ordered the drivers of the elephants to charge the enemy. When the trumpets and bugles sounded shrilly from all sides, some of the animals took fright and at once turned tail and rushed back" upon the Carthaginians. But some of the unpredictable and dangerous beasts did go forward against the Roman line, faced the javelins of the courageous Roman light infantry, "and finally in their terror escaped through the gaps in the Roman line which Scipio's foresight had provided." Others fled to the flanks, clearing the field for the serious engagement of the infantry and cavalry.

Then the imposing lines of the Roman and Carthaginian heavy infantry joined battle. Meanwhile, the Roman . . . cavalry had driven Hannibal's cavalry from the field and, as Hannibal doubtless had anticipated, instead of attacking the Carthaginian infantry, had pursued the fleeing enemy cavalry far from the field of battle. This often happened in battle, commanders being unable to control their cavalrymen who naturally sought to follow their beaten foes. At Cannae Hannibal's well-disciplined and well-led professional cavalry had immediately turned against the rear of the Roman infantry, but at Zama the Roman and allied cavalry lacked the discipline, restraint, and leadership to enable them to make this critical maneuver.

With all cavalry off the field of battle, Hannibal had an infantry battle alone and moved promptly to exploit his numerical superiority and the articulation provided by his reserve of veterans. He moved out his rear infantry formation, extending its line preparatory to enveloping the flanks of the Roman infantry. But Scipio saw the maneuver in time to commit his rear-line reserve, extending his line equally, and the infantry of the two armies remained locked in a frontal battle of doubtful outcome. Then, before the infantry battle reached a decision, the Roman . . . cavalry returned to the battlefield and carried out their mission of attacking the rear of the relatively thin, fully committed line of Carthaginian infantry. This decided the battle, the Romans . . . virtually annihilating the Carthaginian army, leaving a field covered with "slippery corpses which were still soaked in blood and had fallen in heaps."

The role of the cavalry in the Roman victory at Zama revealed that the Romans had adopted the Macedonian system. But the use of a reserve by both combatants and the superior articulation that made this possible shows that the art of war had surpassed that of Alexander's era. Neither Hannibal nor Scipio had participated in the battle, both remaining where they could manage the contest and commit their reserves at the critical time and place. This represented a major advance over Alexander's preplanned battles, as did the concept of the subtracted or uncommitted reserve and the improved articulation of the infantry that enabled the reserves to maneuver on the battlefield. The excellent articulation of the Roman army had done much to permit Scipio to command all of the army in battle rather than, as had Alexander, only a part. . . .

Roman Legions Against the Hellenistic Phalanx

When the Romans fought in Greece and Asia, they again confronted the Macedonian system of war. Although the Romans also used this combined-arms method, they still stressed their heavy infantry and never raised their cavalry to the quality or the importance that it had with Alexander. But they also never had to make war with the united forces of Alexander's by-then divided empire, and they almost always fought with the aid of local allies. The Romans had critical help from an ally in their major battle against their most-imposing opponent, Antiochus the Great, ruler of Syria and much of Asia to the east. In the conflict in 190 B.C. at Magnesia in Asia Minor, they faced a formidable army under Antiochus himself with the exiled Hannibal as his advisor. The details of the battle are vague, but clearly the powerful cavalry of the Roman ally, the king of Pergamum, played an important role in the Roman victory. Increasingly the Romans relied on their allies to provide cavalry.

The apparent challenge to the dominance of the Romans' tactical system came not from the possibility that their opponents might have superior cavalry but from a further development of the Macedonian phalanx. When in 197 B.C. the Romans faced an army of the Macedonian kingdom, they found that the phalanx had lengthened at least some of its spears to twenty-one feet. Apparently the front ranks had shorter spears, probably nine feet, which they held in one hand; the fifth rank used both hands to carry twenty-one-foot spears that projected beyond the front rank; the intermediate ranks seem to have had spears of varying lengths so that all the spear points projected about the same distance beyond the front rank. The front ranks carried shields; the rear rank, using both hands to hold their long spear, had either no shields or very small ones slung on a strap across their chests. Behind the first five ranks the phalanx had an additional eleven ranks, the men holding their spears elevated until needed.

This formation marched shoulder-to-shoulder and for its effectiveness relied on the combined effect of the spears; the individual had no role except to hold his spear and keep his formation. Since the Romans fought with swords and so needed more space between them than the men in the phalanx, the phalanx had two men in front for every Roman. Each Roman thus faced ten spears. According to the historian Polybius, "It is both impossible for a single man to cut through them all in time once they are at close quarters and by no means easy to force their points away." It seemed, therefore, that this new phalanx could bear down all opposition, giving the Macedonians victory because of their better infantry.

But the articulated Roman infantry easily defeated this apparently invincible tactical innovation. In connection with their success at the Battle of Zama, Polybius had pointed out that the subdivided Roman tactical organization enabled "every man individually and in common with his fellows to present a front in any direction, the maniples which are nearest to the danger turning themselves by a single movement to face it. Their arms also give the men both protection and confidence owing to the size of the shield and owing to the sword being strong enough to endure repeated blows." Thus the Roman could maneuver, and if he could get past the hoplite's spear, he had overwhelming superiority at close quarters, especially against the shieldless men with the two-handed spears.

In the first conflict the Romans won the infantry combat because they caught the phalanx before it had formed and while some of its members were still marching to the place of battle. But even under favorable conditions the phalanx depended so much upon keeping its formation that it could never have succeeded against the Roman infantry. Polybius pointed out, "The phalanx requires level and clear ground with no obstacles such as ditches, clefts, clumps of trees, ridges and water courses, all of which are sufficient to impede and break up such a formation." Of course, gaps in a phalanx would enable the Roman swordsmen to come to close quarters with disastrous consequence for the hoplites in the phalanx.

Even on level ground the phalanx proved vulnerable, for, Polybius wrote, "the Romans do not make their line equal in force to the enemy and expose all of the legions to a frontal attack by the phalanx, but part of their forces remain in reserve and the rest engaged the enemy. Afterwards whether the phalanx drives back by its charge the force opposed to it or is repulsed by this force," the phalanx exposes itself either "in following up a retreating foe or in flying before an attacking foe." When this happens, the phalanx then leaves "behind the other parts of their own army, upon which" the Roman "reserve have room enough in the space formerly held by the phalanx to attack no longer in front" but appear "by a lateral movement on the flank and rear of the phalanx" and so with sword and shield at close quarters on the flank slaughter the hoplites whose formation and weapons made them almost defenseless.

Thus the improved infantry of the Romans helped Rome establish its mastery over the Mediterranean basin. The Romans had incorporated all of the features of the Macedonian system and had learned from Hannibal the value of an infantry reserve and the concept of a general who kept out of combat so that he could control the reserve and direct the battle.

Roman Armies Enter Greece

Arthur E.R. Boak and William G. Sinnigen

Eager to punish Macedonia's king, Philip V, for helping Carthage during the Second Punic War, late in 200 B.C. the Romans crossed the Adriatic Sea into Illyria (Illyricum), the Balkan region bordering Macedonia in the west. Soon afterward they entered Greece, and within only a few years managed to defeat not only Philip, but the able and energetic Seleucid ruler Antiochus III and the feisty Aetolian Confederacy (or League) as well. This synopsis of these initial Roman interventions in Greek affairs is by former University of Michigan professor Arthur E.R. Boak and former Hunter College professor William G. Sinnegin.

During the thirty-five years which followed the battle of Zama, Rome attained the same dominant position in the eastern Mediterranean that she had won in the West as a result of the First and Second Punic Wars. The explanation of Roman interference in the East and the rapid extension of her authority there lies in the political situation of the Hellenistic world at the close of the third century, one which Rome exploited by virtue of her increasingly important role as patron to states east of the Adriatic. . . .

Down to the year 201 Rome can hardly be said to have had any definite eastern policy. Diplomatic intercourse with Egypt had followed the visit of an Egyptian embassy to Rome as early as 273, but this had had no political consequences. Since that date she had come into conflict with the Illyrians and with Macedonia and had established a small protectorate across the Adriatic, but in so doing her actions had been spasmodic and had been brought about by the attacks of the Illyrians and Macedonians upon her allies or herself and were not the result of any aggressive policy of her own. The interest and outlook of Rome's agrarian oligarchy did not include Hellas [Greece] as a whole or the Greek East. This may be seen in the favorable peace terms granted Philip V of Macedonia in 205, by which Rome abandoned her formal alliances with Philip's enemies, especially the Aetolians. This is the first known instance in which Rome failed to fulfill to the letter her written agreements with her friends, and marks an important stage in the growing sophistication of her foreign policy. These actions made her very unpopular in most of Greece. Her erstwhile allies, especially the Aetolians, protested that they had been left in the lurch, while other Greek states felt antagonistic because Rome had permitted the Aetolians to treat them brutally during the recent war. Rome still found it possible to maintain friendly relations, albeit without formal and possibly entangling treaties, with Pergamon, the Illyrians, some city-states of the Peloponnesus, and possibly Athens. Rome's general attitude toward the Greek world in the period 205–201 was watchful rather than disinterested; she had no vital or definite commitments in the area except the defense of her Illyrian clients.

The Romans Turn Eastward

A combination of circumstances involving Illyria brought about the Second Macedonian War. After the peace of 205 Philip apparently misread the Roman attitude toward Greece as one of total disinterest and attempted by diplomacy to seduce the Illyrians from their connection with Rome. Just as Rome was observing the Illyrian situation with increasing disquiet in 202, the envoys of Rhodes and of Attalus I, King of Pergamon, arrived to inform the Senate of Philip's aggressions in the East and of his alleged pact with Antiochus to partition the Egyptian Empire. They requested Roman help. The Senate, basically unconcerned with what was going on in the Aegean and undisturbed by the unlikely prospect of the "alliance" between Philip and Antiochus being directed against Italy at some future date, was interested, however, in humbling the king who had stabbed her in the back during the recent war with Hannibal and who was now tampering with her Illyrian clients. It seized upon Philip's aggressions against Attalus as possible *casus belli* [justification for war]. Roman ambassadors were sent to Greece in 201/200 to proclaim a basic change in Roman policy—protection of all Greeks against future Macedonian aggression—and to mobilize Greece under the Roman aegis against Philip. They also carried an ultimatum for Philip which they delivered to one of his generals, a demand that he refrain from war with any Greek state and that he submit his differences with Attalus to arbitration. The ultimatum revealed Rome's new aims: the reduction of Philip to the status of a client prince and the consequent conversion of Greece into a Roman protectorate. Although the Senate was apparently committed to war when these demands were not met, the Roman people as a whole shrank from embarking upon another war so soon after the close of the desperate conflict with Carthage. At first the Centuriate Assembly voted against the proposal, and at a second meeting was induced to sanction it only when the people were told they would have to face another invasion of Italy if they did not anticipate Philip's action. When the Assembly finally gave its approval, one of the Roman ambassadors whom the Senate had already sent to Greece to threaten Philip and encourage his opponents presented the formal declaration of war to the king, who was at that time engaged in the siege of Abydos on the Hellespont, whereupon the conflict began. In accordance with their instructions the ambassadors then visited Antiochus in Syria, perhaps to intercede on behalf of Egypt or to assure him of the good will of Rome so that he might not abandon his Syrian campaign and unite his forces with those of Philip in Macedonia. Roman diplomacy leading up to the war shows that at this stage of her history Rome took states unilaterally under her protection without the formality of a treaty and tended to regard her friends not as equals but as clients.

The Second Macedonian War

Late in 200 a Roman army under the consul Sulpicius Galba crossed into Illyricum and tried to penetrate into Macedonia. Both in this and in the succeeding year, however, the Romans, although aided by the Aetolian Confederacy, Pergamon, Rhodes, and Athens, were unable to inflict any decisive defeat upon Philip or to invade his kingdom.

With the arrival of one of the consuls of 198, Titus Flamininus, the situation speedily changed. The Achaean Confederacy was won over to the side of Rome, and Flamininus succeeded in forcing Philip to evacuate Epirus and to withdraw into Thessaly. In the following winter negotiations for peace were opened. At the insistence of her Greek allies, Rome now demanded not merely a guarantee that Philip would refrain from attacking the Hellenes but also the evacuation of Corinth, Chalcis, and Demetrias, three fortresses known as "the fetters of Greece." Philip refused to make this concession.

The next year military operations were resumed with both armies in Thessaly. Early in the summer a battle was fought on a ridge of hills called Cynoscephalae (the Dogs' Heads), where the Romans won a complete victory. Although the Aetolians rendered valuable assistance in this engagement, the Macedonian defeat was due primarily to the superior flexibility of the Roman legionary formation over the phalanx. Philip fled to Macedonia and sued for peace. The Aetolians and his enemies in Greece sought his destruction, but Flamininus realized the importance of Macedonia to the Greek world as a bulwark against the Celtic peoples of the lower Danube and would not support their demands. The terms fixed by the Roman Senate were: autonomy of the Hellenes, in Greece and Asia; evacuation of the Macedonian possessions in Greece, in the Aegean, and in Illyricum; an indemnity of 1,000 talents; and the surrender of nearly all his warships. These conditions Philip was obliged to accept (196). Soon afterwards he became a Roman ally.

At the Isthmian games of the same year Flamininus proclaimed the complete autonomy of the peoples who had been subject to Macedonia. The announcement provoked a tremendous outburst of enthusiasm among most of the Greek states. After spending some time in effecting this policy and in settling the claims of various states, Flamininus returned to Italy in 194, leaving the Greeks to make what use they would of their freedom. The dramatic proclamation of Flamininus is often attributed to the cultural philhellenism [admiration for Greek culture] increasingly noticeable at this time among the Roman ruling class. Rome's interest in Greek freedom was not sentimental, but was rather the natural result of political and strategic considerations growing out of the recent war. Rome was now merely applying throughout Greece a policy that she had previously used in Messana, Saguntum and Illyria. If the Greeks were free, from the Roman point of view they enjoyed the freedom of client states, which, as a matter of course, would pursue a foreign policy compatible with Roman interests and which would form a bulwark against any hostile action on the part of Philip or Antiochus.

Antiochus and the Aetolians Stir Up Trouble

Even before Flamininus and his army had withdrawn from Greece, the activities of Antiochus had awakened the mistrust of the Roman Senate and threatened hostilities. The Syrian king had completed the conquest of Lower Syria in 198. Profiting by the difficulties in which Philip of Macedon was involved, he had then turned his attention toward Asia Minor and Thrace with the hope of recovering the possessions once held by his ancestor, Seleucus I. The Romans were at the time too much occupied to oppose him. Outwardly he professed to be a friend of Rome and to be limiting his activities to the reestablishment of his empire's former extent. Eventually, in 196 he crossed over into Europe and took Thrace. The Romans tried to induce him to withdraw but were unsuccessful. Two years later Antiochus himself opened negotiations with the Senate to secure Roman recognition of his claims to Thrace and to certain cities in Asia Minor which, relying upon Roman support, refused to acknowledge his overlordship. The Roman government, cynically enough, was willing to abandon its self-proclaimed status as protector of the Greeks in Asia if Antiochus would evacuate Thrace. Since Antiochus, although harboring no designs against Rome, refused to be forced out of his European possessions, he decided to support the anti-Roman elements in Greece to force Rome to yield the points at issue. Accordingly, he willingly received deputations from the Aetolians, who were the leading opponents of Rome among the Greeks.

The Aetolians, Rome's allies in the war just concluded and greatly exaggerating the importance of their services, were disgruntled because Macedonia had not been entirely dismembered and they had been restrained from enlarging the territory of the Confederacy at the expense of their neighbors. In short, they wished to replace Macedonia as the leading Greek state. Accustomed to regard war as a legitimate source of revenue, they did not easily reconcile themselves to Rome's imposition of peace in Hellas. Ever since the battle of Cynoscephalae they had striven to undermine Roman influence among the Greeks, and now they sought to draw Antiochus into conflict with Rome.

In 192 they brought matters to a head by unexpectedly attacking some of Rome's supporters in Greece and seizing the fortress of Demetrias, which they offered to the king [Antiochus], to whom they also made an unauthorized promise of aid from Macedonia. Trusting in the support promised by the Aetolians, Antiochus sailed to Greece with an advance force of 10,000 men. Upon his arrival the Aetolians elected him their commander in chief. . . .

The Defeat of Antiochus

In 191 a Roman army under the consul Acilius Glabrio appeared in Greece and defeated the forces of Antiochus at Thermopylae. The king fled to Asia. Contrary to his hopes he had found little support in Greece. Philip of Macedon and the Achaean Confederacy adhered to the Romans, and the Aetolians were made helpless by an invasion of their own country. The Rhodians and Eumenes, the new king of Pergamon, joined their navies to the Roman fleet.

As Antiochus would not listen to the peace terms laid down by the Romans, the latter resolved to invade Asia Minor. Two naval victories, won with the aid of Rhodes and Pergamon, secured control of the Aegean, and in 190 a Roman force crossed the Hellespont. For commander the

Senate had wished to designate Scipio Africanus, the greatest Roman general. As he had recently been consul he was now ineligible for that office. The law was circumvented by election of his brother Lucius to the consulate and his assignment to the command, and by the appointment of Publius to accompany him, apparently as a legate. This arrangement permitted Publius to assume practical direction of the campaign.

One decisive victory over Antiochus at Magnesia [in western Asia Minor] in the autumn of 190 brought him to terms. He agreed to surrender all territory north of the Taurus mountains and west of Pamphylia, to give up his war elephants, to surrender all but ten of his ships of war, to pay an indemnity of 15,000 talents in twelve annual instalments, and to abstain from attacking the allies of Rome. . . . He was still at liberty to defend himself if attacked. Peace upon these conditions was formally ratified in 188. This time Rome did not "free" all the Greeks as she had done in 196, since such an action would have produced too many petty states and future imbroglios [entanglements]. Some of the Greek city-states did receive their freedom, but Rhodes and Pergamon were the principal beneficiaries of the peace, which brought them an accession of territory at the expense of neighboring Greeks and non-Greeks alike. . . .

Rome Subdues the Aetolian Confederacy

The Roman campaign of 191 against the Aetolians had caused the latter, who were also attacked by Philip of Macedon, to seek terms. The Romans demanded unconditional surrender, and the Aetolians decided to continue the struggle. No energetic measures were taken against them at once, but in 189 the consul Fulvius Nobilior pressed the war vigorously and besieged their chief stronghold, Ambracia. Since the obstinate resistance of its defenders defied all his efforts and since the Athenians were trying to act as mediators in ending the war, the Romans abandoned their demand for unconditional surrender. The Aetolians proved that they had not understood the meaning of clientship, and the Romans were determined that any peace treaty with them should express their dependent status. Peace was finally made on the following conditions: the Aetolian Confederacy was granted a permanent alliance with Rome on an unequal footing, with the obligation to support Rome against all her enemies; the Confederacy gave up all territory captured by its enemies during the war; Ambracia was surrendered and sacked. . . .

Although by her alliance with the Aetolians Rome had planted herself permanently on Greek soil and in the war with Antiochus had claimed to exercise a protectorate over the Greek world, the Senate as yet gave no indication of reversing the policy of Flamininus, and the Greek states remained friends of Rome in the enjoyment of political "independence." It was not long, however, before these friendly relations became seriously strained and Rome was induced to embark upon a policy of political and then military interference in Greek affairs, which ultimately put an end to the apparent freedom of Hellas.

Rome Takes Control of Mainland Greece

Max Cary

This account of the last few years of liberty for the inhabitants of mainland Greece (including Macedonia) is by the
late, distinguished University of Michigan scholar Max
Cary. He begins with the resistance offered to Rome by
Macedonia's new king, Perseus, son of Philip V (who had
signed a treaty with the Romans after they had defeated
him in 197 B.C.). Cary then gives an overview of the main
events of the Third Macedonian War (171–168 B.C.), including a very clear description of the pivotal battle of
Pydna, and goes on to chronicle the demise of the
Achaean League.

Philip's successor Perseus inherited the cautious tempera-
ment of the true Antigonid breed, but was trained in the self-
assertive traditions of his father. His early policy was an un-
steady compromise between these conflicting tendencies. At
the outset of his reign he conciliated the [Roman] Senate by
applying for a renewal of his father's treaty, and to the Greek
cities in his dominions he was more considerate than Philip.
But he placed himself in a false position by his ostentatious
promises to bankrupts and political outlaws from the towns
of the Greek Homeland. These appeals to the political and
economic underworld brought him no solid support, while
to the Romans they appeared as an attempt to overthrow
their settlement of Greek affairs. Renewed visits by senatorial commissions, before whom Perseus failed to clear himself, gave rise in turn to fresh accusations from the king's
malevolent neighbours. In 172 [B.C.] king Eumenes of Per-

Excerpted from *A History of the Greek World from 323 to 146 B.C.* (London:
Methuen, 1968), by M. Cary. Reprinted with the permission of Taylor & Francis
Books, Ltd.

gamum made a journey to Rome to present a crime-sheet against Perseus. Returning home by way of Delphi, he was all but killed by a falling rock from [Mount] Parnassus [near Delphi, in central Greece], and he used this incident—which may quite well have been due to natural causes—to pillory the Macedonian king as an assassin. Hereupon the Senate resolved its doubts by sending an order to disarm as an ultimatum to Perseus, and thus virtually forced on the Third Macedonian War. Like the Third Punic War, this conflict was the outcome of ill-defined suspicions rather than of clearly proved guilt.

The Fall of Macedonia

The Third Macedonian War was a plain trial of strength between Macedon and Rome. Perseus received no Greek support save from a few minor towns of Boeotia. The Epirotes [inhabitants of the kingdom of Epirus] declared themselves sufficiently to draw Roman vengeance upon their country, but gave Perseus no effectual aid. The abstention of the Greeks was partly due to Perseus' parsimony [stinginess], which deterred him from spending the accumulated funds of the Macedonian treasury in a timely diplomatic offensive. But it is highly unlikely that he could have bought many Greek states for a war against Rome. Apart from the Greek exiles and debtors, he had on his side some political leaders who chafed at the inevitable restrictions entailed with Rome's gift of freedom to the Greeks. But the governing classes in general acquiesced in [gave in to] a Roman suzerainty [domination] which greatly added to their security, and they had not forgotten Cynoscephalæ [the battle in which the Romans had decisively defeated Philip V]. Under these conditions a general Greek rally to Macedon was out of the question. On the other hand Perseus had scrupulously avoided those blunders of policy which had brought the Greeks into the field against Philip. The Romans therefore received no Greek assistance except from the Achæan League, which supplied a small contingent, and from Pergamum and Rhodes, which furnished a few warships and transports. Their total field force, numbering some 35,000, hardly exceeded that of Perseus.

The Romans and Perseus, having fumbled into war, spent three years in trying to fumble out of it. Though the Roman generals had a fleet at their disposal, they derived scarcely any benefit from it. For two years they made vain endeavours to force the Olympus range between Thessaly and Macedonia. In 169 the consul Marcius Philippus carried the barrier, but more by luck than by management. On the other hand Perseus' congenital cautiousness recovered possession of him on the field of battle. A victory gained by him in a cavalry action near Larissa in 171 frightened him into making two successive attempts at negotiation, and in 169 he abandoned the Olympus position before the Romans had extricated [removed] their columns from the mountain defiles. It was not until 168 that the Roman army and fleet, brought into effective co-operation by the consul Æmilius Paullus, were able to acquire a definite foothold in Macedonia.

In 168, however, the war was decided in the course of a few minutes. The battle of Pydna, in which Perseus' army was virtually annihilated, was in essentials a replica of Cynoscephalæ. Developing by chance from an affair of outposts, it began with a mass attack by the Macedonian phalanx, which Paullus, a seasoned veteran, declared to have been the most terrifying sight in his ample experience. The Roman legions, which never proved their elasticity and manoeuvring power more brilliantly than on this field, fell back in good order upon higher ground, and as the momentum of the charging phalanx dislocated its ranks, they thrust themselves, company by company, into its gaps or round its flanks. The Macedonian infantry, unable to reform its line, and left unprotected by its mounted flank guards, was quickly killed off in a veritable battue.

Macedonia Dismembered, Epirus Desolated

During the Third Macedonian War anti-Roman feeling among the Greeks had been strengthened by the failure of the earlier Roman commanders to protect the civilian population against marauding troops and by their own excessive requisitions. But Greek resentment was allayed by the exemplary discipline enforced by Paullus upon his soldiery.

Besides, the massacre of Pydna relieved the Romans of all further reason for fearing the Greeks. Nevertheless the generosity . . . with which the Senate had hitherto treated Greek affairs now gave way to anxious suspicion. Though for the

The Destruction of Corinth

In his Guide to Greece, *the second-century* A.D. *Greek writer Pausanias provided this brief description of Rome's sack of Corinth after its defeat of the Achaeans (or Achaians) and Greece's overall loss of freedom.*

The Achaians who escaped to Corinth after the battle ran away during that night, and many of the Corinthians fled at the same time. Mummius held back from entering Corinth even though the gates were open, suspecting there might be an ambush inside the walls, but two days after the battle he took possession in force and burnt Corinth. Most of the people who were left there were murdered by the Romans, and Mummius auctioned the women and children. He auctioned the slaves as well, those of them I mean who were set free and fought beside the Achaians, and were not killed at once in the fighting. He collected the most marvellous of sacred dedications and works of art, and gave the less important things to Attalos's general Philopoimen: and in my time at Pergamon they still had the spoils of Corinth. Mummius broke down the walls and confiscated the armaments of every city that had fought against the Romans even before Rome sent out its advisory commission, and when his commissioners arrived he put an end to the democracies and established government by property qualification. Greece was taxed and the monied classes were barred from the acquisition of property abroad. All national leagues alike were put an end to, Achaian and Phokian or Boiotian or anywhere. . . .

At this time more than any other, Greece sank into the last stages of weakness: crippled and utterly devastated from the beginning in this part or that by a daemonic spirit.

Pausanias, *Guide to Greece.* 2 vols. Trans. Peter Levi. New York: Penguin Books, 1971, vol. 1, pp. 266–268.

third time they left the Greeks free and withdrew their troops, they took precautions, wise and unwise, against future misuse of their liberty. In Macedonia they dethroned the Antigonid dynasty and set up four federal republics extending in a line from the Illyrian frontier to the river Nestus. The new federations were in themselves a justifiable experiment, for the growth of town life in Macedon had made the people ripe for a measure of self-government. Moreover, in fixing the yearly rate of war-indemnity at a mere half of the former royal land-tax, they left Macedon in a better financial position than under the Antigonids. But in prohibiting all intercourse, political or economic, between the four succession-states, they violated the legitimate sense of nationhood among the Macedonians; and in deporting to Italy not only Perseus but all the royal officials they left the republics without political leadership.

In Greece the Romans made no alterations in the governments and but few changes in the frontiers. But they took strong measures to purge the cities of declared or suspected sympathizers with Macedon. In Ætolia they furnished troops to their principal supporters, who executed five hundred antagonists after a farcical trial. In Achæa, where a party led by Lycortas and his son Polybius (the future historian) had unsuccessfully advocated neutrality, they first demanded a judicial massacre on the Ætolian pattern; on discovering that they could not carry this point they deported one thousand suspects . . . under pretence of arranging for their trial in Italy. In Epirus the ex-consul Paullus was bidden to punish the ineffective sympathies of the people for Perseus with a systematic dragonade [persecution] in which he carried off 150,000 souls to the Roman slave-market. This utterly inexcusable brutality, which left Epirus half-desolate, was never requited [avenged] upon the Romans. Their more venial mistakes in Macedon and Achæa brought their revenge with them.

The Fourth Macedonian War

In Macedon the new federations so far proved their capacity to govern, that in 158 B.C. the Senate removed some of the previous commercial embargoes. But the restriction of intercourse between the four republics prevented their taking adequate measures for common defence. By a fortunate chance the Dardanians [neighboring Balkan tribesmen], having recently been engaged in a murderous war in the Balkan hinterland, were slow to seize their opportunity. But in 150 an adventurer named Andriscus, who claimed to be a son of Perseus, won enough adherents to gain successive battles against the . . . levies [troops] on either side of the river Strymon [running through central Macedonia]. From a reunited Macedon the pretender mustered sufficient troops to defeat a small Roman force which the Senate hastily sent against him. But his improvised levies were easily disposed of by an augmented Roman army under Cæcilius Metellus (148), and Macedon made its final surrender to Rome. After the Fourth Macedonian War the Senate did not repeat the mistake of partitioning Macedon, yet it dared not entrust the entire country to a native administration. It therefore broke with its long-standing policy of leaving Greek lands ungarrisoned and converted Macedon into a Roman province. By this act it virtually closed the book of Macedonian history.

The Achæan League Rebels

In Peloponnesus the deportations of the Achæan suspects, far from cowing the League, drove it to open hostility against Rome. For sixteen years the Senate turned a deaf ear to the League's protests against the detention of its citizens; in 151 it released without trial the surviving remnant of the prisoners. But this act of grace came too late to appease Achæan resentment. Since the Third Macedonian War the revolutionary element, whose chief strength lay in the proletariate of Corinth, had gained steadily upon the friends of Rome and of domestic peace. . . . The stalwarts of the League fixed a fresh quarrel upon Sparta over the thorny question of its special privileges, and thus provoked a direct conflict with the Senate, to which the Spartans as usual carried their complaints. The extremist leader Diæus prepared a military execution upon Sparta without awaiting the Senate's decision, which was delayed through its preoccupation with the Macedonian and the Punic Wars. The Senate eventually answered his contumacy [stubbornness] with an order to the Achæans to restore full independence to Sparta, which desired it, and to Corinth and Argos, who had no wish to secede. With this sentence of mutilation it finally threw the League into the hands of the extremists, and the Senate's envoys barely escaped death at the hands of the Corinthian mob. In 147 the Senate endeavoured to re-open negotiations by tacitly rescinding its previous instructions, while Metellus sent a conciliatory message from Macedon. But the new Achæan general Critolaus, mistaking the Senate's overture for a confession of weakness, played off its commissioner with impudent chicanery [trickery], and the mob of Corinth hooted Metellus' envoys off the platform. To cut off the League's retreat, Critolaus had himself proclaimed dictator by tumultuary procedure. With his usurped powers he compelled the wealthier citizens to contribute heavy taxes and to set free a quota of slaves for military service; and in 146 he directed an expedition against Heracleia-ad-Œtam [a town near the pass of Thermopylæ, in central Greece], which had under unknown circumstances been annexed to the League, but had profited by the Senate's recent pronouncement to re-assert its independence. He was joined on the way by contingents from Thebes and other Central Greek towns, where the party of social revolution was in the ascendant. But while he lay before Heracleia he was taken unawares by Metellus, who put the Achæan forces to headlong rout and flung them right back upon Corinth. Meanwhile Diæus had collected a second forced levy of freemen and slaves, amounting to some 15,000 men. With this scratch force he offered a desperate resistance to Metellus' successor Mummius, who had brought up large Roman reinforcements. In a battle on the Isthmus [of Corinth, the narrow land bridge connecting the Peloponnesus to the Greek mainland] the raw Achæan levies proved once more—if proof were needed—that Greeks under firm leadership could fight without flinching; but in the face of hopeless odds they met with irretrievable defeat.

The End of Greek Liberty

In Greece, as in Macedon, the Senate decided to take no further chances. By way of upholding the sanctity of ambassadors, it ordered the inhabitants of Corinth to be sold into
slavery, and the town to be levelled to the ground. It dissolved the Achæan League and annexed its component states
to the province of Macedonia. These states henceforth paid
tribute to Rome and in some cases had their constitutions
remodelled. Athens retained its full freedom; the small local
leagues in which the states of Central Greece and Thessaly
had been grouped by previous Roman action retained their
autonomy under the supervision of the governor of Macedonia. Under this settlement the Greek ideal of local autonomy was in large measure realized, and for the first time in
its history the country enjoyed an enduring peace. But the
ideal of a United States of Greece was finally shattered, and
the era of liberty and of fertile political experiment in Greek
lands gave way to two thousand years of forced inertia.

Cleopatra: Last of the Greek Hellenistic Rulers

Peter Green

The last Hellenistic realm to maintain a semblance of independence, the Ptolemaic Kingdom, had, by the mid-first century B.C., degenerated into a third-rate power cowering in Rome's mighty shadow. This was the age of devastating civil wars and power struggles among powerful individuals, including the renowned Roman generals Julius Caesar and Gnaeus Pompey; Caesar's lieutenant, Marcus Antonius (Mark Antony); and Caesar's adopted son, Octavian (the future emperor Augustus). To their number must be added one Greek, who was every bit as talented and ambitious as they—Cleopatra VII, daughter of Ptolemy XII. After she and her lover/ally Antony went down to defeat at Actium in western Greece, in 31 B.C., she became the last of the Ptolemies and the last independent Greek ruler of antiquity. As Peter Green, of the University of Texas at Austin, points out in this excerpt from his definitive study of the Hellenistic Age, it was perhaps poetically fitting that the era's first and last great Greek figures—Alexander and Cleopatra—both became, and remain, legendary.

One of the more tempting excuses for Rome's progressively more radical, steadily less reluctant policy of intervention and eventual takeover in the eastern Mediterranean was, beyond any doubt, the patent inability of the rulers *in situ* [then in place] to manage their own affairs. This not only encouraged what Rome, and conservatives generally, saw as dangerous sociopolitical trends—mass movements by the dis-

Excerpted from *Alexander to Actium: The Historical Evolution of the Hellenistic Age*, by Peter Green. Copyright ©1990 by Peter Green. Reprinted with the permission of the University of California Press.

possessed, encroachment by non-Mediterranean tribal elements—but, worse, proved disastrous for trade, a fault that Roman administrative paternalism could seldom resist the temptation to correct. In addition to the rampant scourge of piracy . . . a general condition of acute economic and, intermittently, political anarchy now afflicted both Syria and Egypt. Cities, local chieftains, and individuals all broke away when they could from a now highly inefficient (though no less captious and oppressive) system of central bureaucracy. Endless . . . dynastic conflicts, combined with relentless extortion (to pay for these and other excesses), had all but destroyed the countryside.

Since both Syria and Egypt were potentially the most fertile and productive areas imaginable, this represented a more than usually monumental feat of shortsighted stupidity—and indeed one is constantly amazed at just how much, even *in extremis* [in desperate straits] could still be extracted from the inhabitants to meet yet another crisis. Alexandria, of course, had the advantage, in addition, of still-substantial royal treasures. In 59 Ptolemy XII Auletes raised almost six thousand talents, perhaps a year's revenue, perhaps less, to bribe Caesar, now consul, into successfully upholding his claim to recognition by the Senate. . . . Though some of this money was raised through a loan, or loans, from the Roman banker Gaius Rabirius Postumus, the rest came from Ptolemy's own resources, while the loans were recouped by extorting extra funds from his long-suffering subjects. His annual revenues, indeed, were variously estimated at between six and twelve and a half thousand talents. . . .

This was a situation that positively invited Rome's attention. Unfortunately . . . the profit principle proved no less irresistible to Roman administrators, businessmen, and, all too soon, senators than it had done to the Macedonians. The tradition, after all, was well established. It had been what panhellenism was all about, as early as the fourth century: a united ethnic crusade against the East, with wealth and power as its objectives, cultural superiority (and Xerxes' long-past invasion) as its justification. That had been the whole moral basis of Alexander's expedition, of the sharing of the spoils by his successors. Material greed and racial contempt had been the fuel that maintained Macedonians in power, from the Nile to the Euphrates, for three centuries—while their own *mores* steadily degenerated, and, more subtly, were infiltrated by the culture of those whose capital they stole, whose languages they ignored. Now, with the Romans—whom Alexander's descendants, prematurely, also dismissed as mere barbarians—the situation was abruptly reversed: it was Rome that very soon began to display contempt for these effete and fractious dynasts. . . .

The Ptolemies in Egypt

Behind the last convulsive struggles of Seleucids and Ptolemies Roman policy—or, worse, free enterprise minus a policy—can always be sensed in the background. Worse still, from the viewpoint of the Greeks in particular, was the imposition of rival foreign warlords—Caesar and Pompey, Octavian and Antony—who not only fought out their own dynastic struggles on Greek soil and in Greek waters, but bled the inhabitants white for supplies, from grain to warships, and had an unnerving habit of executing those who chose the wrong (i.e., the unsuccessful) side. Roman egotism was matched, as so often, by Greek cynicism: survival became the prime objective. . . .

If Ptolemy Auletes . . . enjoyed a relatively undisturbed reign of almost thirty years (80–59/8, 55–51) in which to indulge his passion for flute playing (*Aulētēs* means "Piper") and other, less mentionable, habits, that was no tribute to his strength of character. . . . There were, in fact, two good reasons why Ptolemy Auletes, and his kingdom, survived as long as they did. To begin with, he had no serious rivals for the throne. This did not mean he was popular—far from it—but it did set his enemies a problem when it came to replacing him. At the time of his enforced exile in 59/8 . . . the Alexandrians—who had thrown him out . . . scraped the very bottom of the dynastic barrel trying to find any acceptable substitute for him.

After a little-known son of Cleopatra Selene [a former royal princess, daughter of Ptolemy X] had died on them during negotiations . . . in desperation they picked on an alleged royal claimant whose chief title to consideration was the name of Seleucus. His appearance, and oafish manners, got him the nickname in Alexandria of *Kybiosaktēs*, "the Salt-Fish Hawker." The ulterior purpose of this frantic search was to find a male consort for Auletes' daughter Berenice, who had been proclaimed queen in her father's absence, perhaps at first as a temporary measure. The evidence is patchy. . . . Auletes left behind, as co-regents in his absence, his wife (and sister) Cleopatra V Tryphaena, together with their eldest daughter, Berenice IV. Two other daughters, Arsinoë and Cleopatra VII, the future queen, were barely adolescent, while the boys, Ptolemy XIII and Ptolemy XIV, were still infants. . . .

Enter Cleopatra

[These last members of the long-lived Ptolemaic dynasty] went out in a blaze of glory that has inspired great poetry down the ages. In the spring of 51 Ptolemy Auletes died, leaving the kingdom in his will, jointly, to his eighteen-year-old daughter Cleopatra, and her younger brother Ptolemy XIII, then about twelve. In Cleopatra the tradition of brilliant, strong-willed Macedonian queens reached its apotheosis [height]. With Cyprus, Coele-Syria, and Cyrenaica gone, with the world her ancestors had known crumbling about her, with famine at home and anarchy abroad, this astonishing woman not only dreamed of a greater world empire than Alexander had known, but came within an iota of winning it. . . . No one could fail to take her seriously. How far her sexual allure was exercised for its own sake, and how far in pursuit of power, we shall never know for certain. But there are one or two pointers. Like many Hellenistic queens, she was passionate, but never promiscuous. Caesar and Antony apart, we hear of no other lovers. . . . The wretched surviving iconography [surviving images of her on coins and so on] . . . suggests neither a raving beauty nor a voluptuary. . . . There is also her choice of lovers to consider. Anyone who so consistently aimed for the top is unlikely to have been motivated by nothing apart from sheer unbridled passion. . . .

She was, in short, a charismatic personality of the first

order, a born leader and vaultingly ambitious monarch, who deserved a better fate than suicide. . . .

The times, however, were hard, and she was forced to make of them what she could—which was a great deal. The civil wars in Italy [between Caesar and Pompey] broke out in 49, two years after she came to the throne. She made her independent spirit clear from the start. By August 51 she had already dropped her young brother's name from official documents, despite traditional Ptolemaic insistence on titular male precedence among co-rulers. (Throughout her reign, independent or not, Cleopatra was always forced to accept either a brother or a son, however underage or otherwise ineffectual, as obligatory consort: there were some traditions not even she could ignore.) She also, exceptionally, put her own portrait and name on her coinage, again ignoring those of her brother. This, not surprisingly, alarmed the more powerful court officials in Alexandria. . . . Such behavior very soon brought opposition to a head. Certainly by 48, and in all likelihood two years earlier, a palace cabal [plot], led by Theodotus, the eunuch Pothinus, and a half-Greek general, Achillas, ousted Cleopatra in favor of her more pliable younger brother, with themselves as a council of regency. . . .

Enter Caesar

Meanwhile Pompey, defeated at Pharsalus (Aug. 48), took ship for Alexandria. He was relying, unwisely, on his position as backer, indeed as Senate-appointed guardian, of young Ptolemy XIII. . . . He seems not to have realized, till it was too late, just how far Pharsalus had destroyed his international reputation and credit. Achillas and his fellow regents were already working out their best approach to Caesar; in their eyes Pompey was nothing but a dangerous embarrassment. They had him murdered as he stepped ashore, an object lesson for the precocious boy king, who watched this scene from the dockside, arrayed in his diadem and purple robes. Pompey's severed head was pickled, and afterwards presented, as an earnest of good will, to his conqueror, who at least had the grace to shed tears at the sight. Caesar may have been only too glad to have Pompey thus providentially put out of the way, but the circumstances of his death were appalling, and Caesar himself knew this better than anyone. At the same time the episode encouraged him in what was to prove a near-fatal Egyptian adventure. When he came ashore himself at Alexandria four days later, he was in a mood of careless and arrogant confidence, with an escort of no more than thirty-two hundred legionaries and eight hundred cavalry. His public reception was anything but ecstatic. . . . Riots followed.

Ptolemy XIII was away at Pelusium, ready to defend the frontier against his elder sister. Caesar coolly installed himself in the royal palace and began issuing orders. Pothinus the eunuch . . . brought Ptolemy back to court, but took no steps to disband his army. At this point Cleopatra, anxious not to be left out of any deal being cut, had herself smuggled through these hostile lines, like contraband, and turned up in her carpet. Both she and her brother were invited to appear before Caesar's *ad hoc* judgment seat the following morning; but by then Caesar, who was instantly captivated by Cleopatra's insistent charms, had already made her his lover, as she doubtless intended he should. Young Ptolemy instantly grasped the situation (hardly difficult, in the circumstances), and rushed out in a fury, screaming that he had been betrayed, to rouse the Alexandrian mob. . . .

The so-called Alexandrian War, which followed . . . came as near to destroying Caesar himself, let alone his reputation, as any campaign, military or political that he ever fought. Once he had to swim from the mole to save his life, leaving his purple general's cloak behind as a trophy for the enemy. The warehouses and some part of the great Alexandrian Library went up in flames. Caesar managed to capture the Pharos lighthouse, which safeguarded his control of the harbor. Arsinoë, meanwhile, contrived to escape from the palace, fled to Achillas, and was promptly proclaimed queen by the army and the Macedonian mob, an act for which her sister never forgave her. All through that winter fighting and intrigue sputtered on. . . . [Eventually, Caesar's forces prevailed and] Ptolemy XIII fled and was drowned in the Nile. Thus Cleopatra, whom Caesar had restored, officially, to joint occupancy of the throne of Egypt, now, in effect, indeed became sole ruler—although as a sop to tradition she was duly married off to her younger brother Ptolemy XIV, now aged eleven. . . .

Rather than make Egypt a province, with all the senatorial intrigue and rivalry that this was bound to entail, Caesar had every intention of shoring up the Ptolemaic regime, on his own terms. To have a son in line for the throne would by no means come amiss, whatever the status of consort and heir in Rome. Meanwhile, to placate the Alexandrians and the Egyptian priesthood, Cleopatra obligingly wed her sibling co-regent, while her younger sister, Arsinoë, languished under arrest with a charge of high treason pending against her. . . .

In July 46, after his successful African campaign, Caesar returned to Rome, to be showered with unprecedented honors, including four successive triumphs and a ten-year dictatorship. During these celebrations (Sept.–Oct.) he brought over Cleopatra and her entourage, establishing them in his own town house, a return of hospitality that caused considerable offense among conservative Republicans. . . . By then he was mulling over ideas about deification and world empire that seemed, or were thought, to include the establishment of Alexandria as a second capital, and of Cleopatra herself as some kind of bigamous queen-goddess, the New Isis, as she styled herself. Rome buzzed with gossip. . . .

Exit Caesar, Enter Antony

But the Ides of March 44 [when Caesar was stabbed to death in the Senate] put an end to all these grandiose dreams. Two weeks after Caesar's assassination, when the will was known and Caesarion [her young son by Caesar], inevitably, had no place in it, Cleopatra, with more speed than dignity, and perhaps in real danger of her life, left Rome and returned to Alexandria. . . . On her arrival Cleopatra lost no time in having her sibling consort, Ptolemy XIV, assassinated, and Caesarion established, at the tender age of four, as her new co-regent. [Soon afterward, Octavian and Antony defeated Caesar's assassins and Cleopatra, like many others at the time, saw Antony as the most likely person to control the Roman sphere.] . . .

By the time that Antony summoned her to that fateful meeting at Tarsus, in 41, she already knew more than enough about him: his limited tactical and strategic abilities, his great popularity with his troops; his blue blood, which was so embarrassingly offset by financial impoverishment; the drinking, the womanizing, . . . the Herculean vulgarity, the physical exuberance and brutal ambition, the Dionysiac pretensions to godhead. . . .

Antony was tickled by the idea of having a blue-blooded Ptolemy (his previous mistresses, not to mention his present wife, Fulvia, a powerful termagant, all seem to have been shrewishly middle-class), and by the coarse implications of all this royal finery: eight or nine years later we find him writing to Octavian, asking him why he has changed so much, turned so hostile—"Is it because I get into the queen?". . .

Both Cleopatra and Antony, then, had highly practical ulterior reasons for cultivating one another; how much personal chemistry helped the equation is hard to tell. Nor can anyone be certain how soon Antony planned to return when he left Cleopatra in the early spring of 40, or what he told her—not necessarily the same thing. Her magnetism was by no means irresistible, since in the event he did not see her for another four years. . . . Public considerations once more came first. That same autumn Antony made his peace with Octavian at Brundisium (Brindisi), cemented the alliance by marrying his fellow triumvir's sister, Octavia—a beautiful and high-minded young intellectual, recently widowed, and with three children from her first marriage. . . . Meanwhile in Alexandria, Cleopatra, never one to do things by halves, bore Antony twins, a boy and a girl. His first child by Octavia, a girl, was born in 38.

Just what Antony thought he was doing at this point is not wholly clear. He may have been playing the Roman card; he may have thought he could finesse Cleopatra against Octavia, in whose company, during the winter of 38–37, he played the dutiful intellectual in Athens, attending lectures and going the rounds of the philosophical schools. . . . Octavian's growing enmity also must have turned him back toward the idea of playing winner-take-all, with Alexandria as his base. If Octavia had borne him a son, things might have been different; but she had not, and Cleopatra had. Cleopatra also held the still-impressive accumulated treasure of the Ptolemies, something that Octavian, too, kept very much in mind. . . .

So Antony left Italy and went east, with the Senate's authority to reallocate client kingdoms—a commission that, as we shall see, he proceeded to interpret in a more than liberal fashion. . . . The first thing that Antony did, on reaching Antioch, was to send for Cleopatra. After their long separation it was now that his, or their, schemes for . . . a "Romano-Hellenistic Orient" began to take shape.

Antony proceeded to lavish on the queen not only Cyprus . . . but also the cedar-clad Cilician coast, so ideal for ship-building, not to mention Phoenicia, Coele-Syria, and the richest spice-bearing regions of Judaea and Arabia, dispositions that not unnaturally caused vast offense in Rome, and not only because of Cleopatra's personal unpopularity there: these provincial areas were in fact not in his authority to dispose of, and the obvious purpose of their allocation to Cleopatra, Egypt itself being virtually without timber, was to provide lumber and shipyards for the creation of a large Egyptian fleet. The twin children were also now acknowledged by Antony, and officially named Alexander Helios and Cleopatra Selene, titles powerfully evocative of Hellenistic dynastic ambition. . . .

So it came about that in 34 Antony committed himself still further to his independent Graeco-Roman dream. After a successful—and financially rewarding—Armenian campaign he celebrated a triumphal parade through Alexandria, playing the role of the New Dionysus, while Cleopatra, enthroned as the New Isis, presided over the ceremony. (Inevitably, when the news reached Rome, this occasion was misinterpreted as an unauthorized and improper Roman triumph.) Only a few days later a yet more explicit political ceremony took place. In the great Gymnasium of Alexandria, with Cleopatra once more robed as Isis, and Antony enthroned by her side, titles were bestowed upon the royal children. Ptolemy XV Caesar (Caesarion)—though carefully subordinated to the royal pair—was made joint ruler of

Egypt with his mother and proclaimed King of Kings (she became Queen of Kings, a higher honor still). Alexander Helios . . . was declared Great King of what had been the Seleucid empire at its zenith. . . . His sister, Cleopatra Selene, was instated as Queen of Cyrenaica and Crete. The youngest son of Antony and Cleopatra, Ptolemy Philadelphos . . . was proclaimed, at the age of two, King of Syria and Asia Minor: he was also dressed in Macedonian royal robes.

[These ceremonies] not only laid improper claim to territories that were either outside Rome's control or, worse, already under Roman administration; they also made it only too clear that Cleopatra and the formidable resources of Egypt were backing Antony's dreams. Once again the irresistible lure of world empire was in the air: the grim lessons of the past three centuries had been quickly forgotten. . . .

Enter Octavian, Exit Antony, Cleopatra, and the Hellenistic Age

In 32/1 Antony formally divorced Octavia, thus forcing the West to recognize his relationship with Cleopatra; he had already, unprecedentedly, put the Egyptian queen's head and name on his official Roman coinage, the silver denarii that enjoyed an enormously wide circulation throughout the eastern Mediterranean. These acts also terminated even the pretense of his Roman allegiance, and Octavian . . . formally declared war on Cleopatra, and on her alone; no mention was made of Antony. The whipped-up hysterical xenophobia [anti-foreign] current in Rome at the time can be sensed from the (largely factitious) propaganda of such Augustan poets as Virgil and Propertius. Cleopatra was the drunken lascivious Oriental, worked over by her own house slaves . . . whoring after strange gods and foreign ways. . . . Inevitably, she was also portrayed as an indiscriminately sensual harlot, a charge that, as we have seen, was almost certainly false, though she did (it was claimed) derive a "really sensuous pleasure" from literature.

Antony became the target of more serious, and better founded, political accusations, for example that he had misused troops, acted without senatorial authorization, and given away territories that belonged to Rome. . . .

The exaggerated charges against Cleopatra also reveal fear; and though today the outcome may seem inevitable . . . at the time many must have believed that the New Isis would triumph, that Antony would indeed launch a dazzling new career of world conquest and imperial co-partnership from Alexandria. . . . Octavian's crushing naval victory at Actium, on 2 September 31—planned and won for him by his admiral Agrippa—finally put paid to Antony's ambitions. Less than a year later, after a halfhearted defense of Alexandria against Octavian's advancing army, Antony committed suicide. Cleopatra soon followed his example. . . . Once she was safely dead, admiring tributes to her noble end could be entertained without risk, while her heir Caesarion was butchered without compunction.

On 29 August, 30 B.C., Octavian officially declared the Ptolemaic dynasty at an end, thus writing finis—as we can see now—to the whole Hellenistic era of the Successors. . . .

The Successors' territories, meanwhile, were absorbed into the administrative efficiency of a semi-Stoicized universal empire. No room, there, for the New Isis. Yet Cleopatra achieved her dying wish. Unlike her forebears, she knew the country she ruled; and when she had the famous asp—in fact an Egyptian cobra—smuggled to her in a basket of figs, it was in the belief that, as Egyptian religion declared, death from snakebite would, the . . . cobra being sacred, confer immortality. She was not mistaken. Only Alexander—another Macedonian—could eclipse the mesmeric fascination that she exercised down the centuries, and still exercises, upon the European imagination: the perennial symbol of what, had Actium gone the other way, might have been a profoundly different world. We end, as we began, with a legend.

Epilogue

The Survival of Greek Culture

Turning Points
IN WORLD HISTORY

Rome Passes on the Greek Legacy

Sarah B. Pomeroy, Stanley M. Burstein, Walter Donlan, and Jennifer T. Roberts

Although by the end of the first century B.C. independent Greek political and military systems had given way to Rome's domination of the Mediterranean world, Greek culture survived and even flourished. By absorbing many aspects of that culture, before and after the demise of the Greek realms, the Romans became Hellenized, giving rise to the Greco-Roman fusion later termed "classical." And over time, the classical legacy came profoundly to affect the development of the medieval and modern Western worlds, as explained here by the authors of the absorbing *Ancient Greece: A Political, Social and Cultural History* (Sarah B. Pomeroy, of Hunter College; Stanley M. Burstein, of California State University, Los Angeles; Walter Donlan, of the University of California, Irvine; and Jennifer T. Roberts, of the City University of New York Graduate Center).

In many ways the early third century BC was the climax of ancient Greek history. For a brief period Macedonian power and Greek culture reigned supreme in the Near and Middle East. New Greek cities were founded at strategic points throughout this enormous region. A person could travel from Egypt to the borders of India speaking only Greek. The heyday of the Hellenistic kingdoms, however, was brief. Internal and external threats called their survival itself into question within a generation of their foundation. . . .

With total collapse of the Hellenistic state system virtually in sight, Antiochus III (223–187 BC) and Ptolemy V

(204–180 BC) launched vigorous counteroffensives that seemingly restored their dynasties' authority over most of their former territory. Before the Seleucids and Ptolemies could fully consolidate their hold on their kingdoms, however, disaster struck in the form of the Romans. Roman expansion into the eastern Mediterranean was so dramatic and unexpected that the [second-century B.C. Greek] historian Polybius could justifiably begin his great history with the deceptively simple question: How could anyone not be interested in knowing how the Romans overthrew the world created by Alexander in less than half a century?. . .

Greece's Influence on Rome

In the end, Rome . . . turned out to be the ultimate heir of Alexander's legacy, having extinguished the kingdoms of his successors. The demise of the Hellenistic state system did not mark the end of Greek civilization in the lands conquered by Alexander, but it did change its character and role. In the eastern portions of Alexander's empire, Greek civilization gradually disappeared as a coherent force. Macedonian and Greek rulers were responsible for the flowering of Greek culture in the Hellenistic East, and their patronage ended with the disappearance of their kingdoms in the late second and first centuries BC. . . . In the western part of the Hellenistic world, Greek culture did not merely survive. It flourished thanks to Roman support.

That Rome was the savior of Greek culture in the Near East is one of the paradoxes of history. A brutality that belied the promise of "freedom" the Romans had made to the Greeks in 196 BC after the defeat of Philip V marked the Roman conquest of the eastern Mediterranean. Incidents such as the enslavement of 150,000 people from Epirus by Aemilius Paulus in 168 BC, the destruction of Corinth in 146 BC, and Sulla's devastation of Attica in 86 BC made clear to the Greeks that the Romans had come to the East as masters, not liberators. Nevertheless, while the disruption of Greek life during the almost two centuries during which Rome consolidated its rule over the eastern Mediterranean was enormous, it was not the whole story.

Like their Macedonian predecessors, the Romans were no strangers to Greek culture. Greek influence on Rome dated from the beginning of the city's history and had become an integral part of Roman culture by the time Rome intervened in the affairs of the Hellenistic East. That influence continued long after Greece had ceased to be a political and military power and had become a minor province of the Roman empire. Not surprisingly, Greek literature and art were familiar to many upper-class Romans. Some senators, like Fabius Pictor (c. 220 BC), the father of Roman history, were sufficiently fluent in Greek to write books in the language. By the first century BC Roman aristocrats routinely acquired a Greek education. Roman culture was suffused with Greek influence. Rome's gods and myths had been recast in terms of Greek mythology. Latin writers constantly echoed their Greek predecessors, so that a work like Virgil's *Aeneid*, Rome's national epic, has to be read against the background of the *Iliad* and *Odyssey* for its artistry to be fully appreciated. The first-century-BC Roman poet Horace was only recognizing reality when he wrote that "Greece, though a captive, captured her fierce conqueror, and brought the arts to rustic Latium" (*Epistles* 2.1).

A Cultural Renaissance

One important result of the Hellenization of the Roman upper class was the Senate's adoption of the concept of Greek freedom as the framework for the exercise of Roman supremacy in the eastern Mediterranean. In spite of the suffering they inflicted on the cities and kingdoms of the Greek East, therefore, the Romans made the support of Greeks and Greek culture the linchpin of their rule of the region. Greeks enjoyed privileged status, and Greek cities provided the framework for Roman provincial administration. The result was a remarkable renaissance in the cultural life of the Greek cities of old Greece and the Near East during the first two centuries of the Christian era. Evidence of this renaissance is visible in the ruins of the splendid public buildings that everywhere in the eastern Mediterranean dominate the remains of Greek cities and in the innumerable honorary statues that crowd our museums.

Greek writers, such as the historian Appian and the orator Aelius Aristides, had good reason to celebrate the benefits of the *Pax Romana* ("Roman Peace"), although conscientious Roman governors like Pliny the Younger complained about the costs of the ambitious building projects undertaken by the Greek cities in their efforts to outdo each other in public splendor and distinction. The renaissance was not limited to architecture and the visual arts. The second and third centuries AD also saw a remarkable upsurge of Greek literary activity that historians of Greek literature call the Second Sophistic. The Second Sophistic is named after the great public orators such as Aelius Aristides who dominated the public culture of the period, but new works appeared in almost every genre of Greek literature. Many of these works such as the biographies and essays of the biographer and moralist Plutarch and the histories of Arrian were of considerable distinction and exercised significant influence on the development of later western thought.

Science and philosophy also flourished. Galen and Ptolemy compiled syntheses of Greek medicine, astronomy, and geography that remained authoritative for more than a millennium. Indeed, medical students still studied the works of Galen in the early nineteenth century AD. The Egyptian-born Neo-Platonist Plotinus created the last great philosophical system of antiquity, a philosophical mysticism based loosely on the works of Plato that was Christianity's most formidable intellectual rival. Only in one area of Greek life was there no renaissance: the civic and political culture of the Greek cities themselves. Instead, during these same two centuries, the last vestiges of the polis tradition of self-government disappeared.

Officially, the Romans treated the Greek cities of the eastern Mediterranean as self-governing entities. Epigraphical records of their government's activities are numerous, but the spirit was gone. City assemblies no longer met, and city councils were controlled by narrow aristocratic oligarchies. Even the freedom of action of these oligarchic regimes was increasingly limited by the Roman government's practice of employing officials such as Pliny the Younger to monitor their conduct of affairs. Plutarch candidly assessed the situation in an essay written in response to a young friend's request for advice about a possible political career. "Nowadays," he wrote, "when the affairs of the cities no longer include leadership in wars, nor the overthrowing of tyrannies, nor acts of alliances, what opening for a conspicuous and brilliant public career could a young man find?" Plutarch answered his own question by pointing out that "there remain the public lawsuits, and embassies to the Emperor" (*Precepts of Statecraft* 805a–b; Fowler). Greek patriots such as Plutarch, who considered holding the traditional magistracies in his home city of Chaeronea a sacred obligation, found the contrast with the freedom of fifth- and fourth-century BC Greece painful. Other Greeks were more pragmatic. Men such as Arrian, who was governor of Cappadocia under the emperor Hadrian (117–138 AD) and historian of Alexander, and Dio Cassius, a historian of Rome who held the offices of consul and praetorian prefect during the early third century AD, abandoned their poleis, and found rewarding careers in the service of Rome.

The Triumph of Hellenism

While Greeks and Greek culture prospered under Roman rule, the same was not true of the non-Greek cultures of Egypt and the Near East. The Roman emperors' patronage of the Greek cities of the eastern Mediterranean heightened the value of Greek culture and Roman citizenship. The former was the key to social and cultural prestige and the latter to a political career and its rewards. Non-Greek cultural traditions and institutions were not repressed, but they were devalued. In the second century AD the Syrian writer Lucian expressed the cultural priorities of the new regime in his autobiographical essay *The Dream*, stating that without a Greek education a man could only be an "artisan and commoner, always envying the prominent and fawning on the man who was able to speak," while the educated man was "honored and praised, in good repute among the best people, well regarded by those who are preeminent in wealth and breeding . . . and considered worthy of public office and precedence" (*The Dream* 9–11). Lucian's calculation was correct. His Greek education and literary skill brought him fame and a lucrative post on the staff of the Prefect of Egypt.

Some peoples, such as the Jews, resisted the assimilatory pressures of Roman imperial society, sometimes violently. Others found in the new Christian church opportunities for the satisfaction of the ambitions of their elites. Not surprisingly, however, over time increasing numbers of non-Greeks followed Lucian's example and sought to acquire the advantages of Greek status, especially after 212 AD when the emperor Caracalla erased the legal barriers between Greeks and non-Greeks by conferring Roman citizenship on virtually all inhabitants of the empire.

The process of assimilation was not always free of friction. Complaints of Greek prejudice and cultural chauvinism are frequent in the writings of Hellenized non-Greeks such as, for example, the Hellenized Syrian rhetorician Tatian, who urged Greeks not to despise non-Greeks and their ideas since most Greek practices "took their origin from barbarian ways" (*Address to the Greeks* 1.1). Nevertheless, by late antiquity a significant portion of the social and intellectual elite of the eastern provinces of the Roman empire consisted of Hellenized non-Greeks. The local languages of the region did not disappear. They survived in the vernacular speech of the urban lower classes and the countryside and even found new written expression in the literatures of Syriac and Coptic Christianity. But the traditional cultures of Egypt and the Near East died, as the native elites that had patronized them for millennia gradually deserted them. Harassed by the government of the Christian Roman emperors, they survived only in the esoteric knowledge of the priests of a few remote and impoverished temples before finally disappearing completely in late antiquity. Meanwhile, the dominant strand in the intellectual life of the eastern Mediterranean basin became what scholars call Hellenism, essentially a cosmopolitan form of Greek culture loosely based on the canon of Classical Greek literature. This literature formed the basis of both pagan and Christian education and thought, although the civic culture of the Greek city-states that had given birth to it almost a millennium earlier had disappeared. In this form Greek culture continued to flourish in the lands conquered by Alexander the Great and influenced the medieval civilizations of Byzantium and Islam and through them the culture of western Europe and the Americas.

Appendix of Documents

Document 1: Athens in the Opening Stage of the Peloponnesian War

This excerpt from Plutarch's biography of Pericles describes the reactions of his countrymen to his initial strategy. He ordered all the inhabitants to take refuge behind the Long Walls, where they were safe from the invading Peloponnesians (i.e., the Spartans and their allies), who freely ravaged the Attic countryside. Meanwhile, with free access to the sea, Athenian ships attacked enemy coasts.

He tried to pacify those who were longing to fight and were becoming restive at the damage the enemy were doing. He pointed out that trees, even if they are lopped or cut down, can quickly grow again, but that you cannot easily replace the men who fall in battle. He would not summon the Assembly for fear that he might be forced to act against his better judgement. Instead, he behaved like the helmsman of a ship who, when a storm sweeps down upon it in the open sea, makes everything fast, takes in sail and relies on his own skill and takes no notice of the tears and entreaties of the sea-sick and terrified passengers. In the same way Pericles closed the gates of Athens, posted guards at all the necessary points for security and trusted to his own judgement, shutting his ears to the complaints and outcries of the discontented. At the same time many of his friends continually pressed him to take the offensive, while his enemies threatened and denounced his policy, and the comic poets in their choruses taunted him with mocking songs and abused his leadership for its cowardice and for abandoning everything to the enemy. . . .

Pericles, however, remained immovable and calmly endured all the ignominy and the hatred which were heaped upon him without making any reply. He sent a fleet of 100 ships to the Peloponnese, but did not accompany it himself. Instead, he remained behind to watch affairs at home and keep the city under his control until the Peloponnesians withdrew. Then he set himself to placate the people, who were suffering severely from the war even after the departure of the Peloponnesians, and he won back some of his popularity by giving them various subsidies and proposing grants of conquered territories: he expelled, for example, the whole population of Aegina and divided up the island among the Athenians by lot. The people could find some consolation, too, in the damage which was being inflicted on the enemy. The fleet, as it sailed round the Peloponnese, ravaged a very large area and sacked a number of villages and small towns, while Pericles himself led an expedition into the Megarid and devastated the whole territory. It was clear from this that although the enemy did the Athenians a great deal of harm by land, they themselves were also suffering severely from the sea. In fact, they would never have carried on the war so long, but would soon have called off hostilities had not an act of heaven intervened to upset human calculations.

Plutarch, *Life of Pericles*, in *The Rise and Fall of Athens: Nine Greek Lives by Plutarch*. Trans. Ian Scott-Kilvert. New York: Penguin, 1960, pp. 200–201.

Document 2: Athens Surrenders, Ending the Great War

The fifth/fourth-century B.C. *Greek historian Xenophon tells here how Athens's state ship, the* Paralus, *arrived in Piraeus (in midsummer, 405) with dire news. The Spartan general Lysander had just decisively defeated the Athenian navy, cutting off the city's life-giving grain route. Xenophon goes on to describe the people's reactions and the terms of the surrender.*

It was at night that the *Paralus* arrived at Athens. As the news of the disaster was told, one man passed it on to another, and a sound of wailing arose and extended first from Piraeus, then along the Long Walls until it reached the city. That night no one slept. They mourned for the lost, but more still for their own fate. They thought that they themselves would now be dealt with as they had dealt with others. . . . Next day they held an Assembly at which it was decided to block up all the harbours except one, to repair and man the walls, and to take all other measures to put the city into a state of readiness for a siege.

While the Athenians were occupied in this way, Lysander . . . sent word to Agis at Decelea and also to Sparta that he was sailing to Athens with 200 ships. At the same time Pausanias, the other king of Sparta, the whole army of the Spartans and all the rest of the Peloponnesians . . . took the field. When the whole force was concentrated, Pausanias led them to Athens and camped in the Academy. Meanwhile Lysander arrived at Aegina and, gathering together as many of the people of Aegina as he could, gave the island back to them. He did the same thing for the people of Melos and for all the others who had been deprived of their own states. Then, after devastating Salamis, he anchored at Piraeus with 150 ships and closed the harbour to all merchant ships.

The Athenians were now besieged by land and by sea. They had no ships, no allies and no food; and they did not know what to do. They could see no future for themselves except to suffer what they had made others suffer, people of small states whom they had injured not in retaliation for anything they had done but out of the arrogance of power and for no reason except that they were in the Spartan alliance. They therefore continued to hold out. They gave back their rights to all who had been disfranchised and, though numbers of people in the city were dying of starvation, there was no talk of peace.

However, when their food supplies were entirely exhausted they sent ambassadors to Agis, saying that they were willing to join the Spartan alliance if they could keep their walls and Piraeus, and that they were prepared to make a treaty on these terms. . . .

Many Greek states, and in particular the Corinthians and Thebans, opposed making any peace with Athens. The Athenians, they said, should be destroyed. The Spartans, however, said they would not enslave a Greek city which had done such great things for Greece at the time of her supreme danger. They offered to make peace on the following terms: the Long Walls and the fortifications of Piraeus must be destroyed; all ships except twelve surrendered; the exiles to be recalled; Athens to have the same enemies and the same friends as Sparta had and to follow Spartan leadership in any expedition Sparta might make either by land or sea.

Theramenes and his fellow ambassadors brought these terms back to Athens. Great masses of people crowded round them as they entered the city, for it was feared that they might have come back unsuccessful and it was impossible to delay any longer because of the numbers who were dying of hunger. Next day the ambassadors reported to the Assembly the terms on which Sparta was prepared to make peace. Theramenes made the report and spoke in favour of accepting the Spartan terms and tearing down the walls. Sonic people spoke in opposition, but many more were in favour and so it was decided to accept the peace. After this Lysander sailed into Piraeus, the exiles returned, and the walls were pulled down among scenes of great enthusiasm and to the music of flute girls. It was thought that this day was the beginning of freedom for Greece.

Xenophon, *Hellenica*, published as *A History of My Times*. Trans. Rex Warner. New York: Penguin Books, 1979, pp. 104–108.

Document 3: The Rivalry Between Sparta and Thebes Reaches a Head

During the Spartan hegemony (supremacy) of Greece following the Pelo-ponnesian War, a period in which the Greeks continued to bicker, Thebes and Sparta were frequently at odds. This brief tract from Plutarch's life of the Spartan king Agesilaus recounts how, in 371 B.C., the Theban statesman Epaminondas stood up to Agesilaus in front of representatives from many Greek states, a confrontation that led to open warfare.

By this time [371 B.C.] both sides had come to favour a common peace, and ambassadors from all over Greece assembled in Sparta to negotiate a settlement. One of these was Epaminondas, a man who had already gained a reputation for his culture and learning, but had not yet given any proof of his military genius. It soon be-came clear to him that the rest of the delegates were overawed by Agesilaus, and he alone maintained the dignity and confidence to speak out freely. Accordingly he delivered a speech not on behalf of his fellow Thebans but of Greece as a whole: in this he declared that war made the Spartans strong at the expense of all the other states, and insisted that peace should be founded upon terms of justice and equality, and that it would only endure on condition that all the parties concerned were put on an equal footing.

Agesilaus noticed that all the Greek delegates listened to Epam-inondas with the greatest attention and admiration, and so he asked him whether he thought it just and equitable that the cities of Boeotia should be independent of Thebes [a reference to the Boeotian League, a group of cities of which Thebes was the dom-inant member]. Epaminondas promptly and boldly responded with another question—did Agesilaus think it just and equitable that the cities of Laconia should be independent of Sparta? At this Agesilaus grew angry, jumped to his feet and asked him to state un-equivocally whether he intended to make the cities of Boeotia in-dependent, whereupon Epaminondas merely repeated his question as to whether Agesilaus intended to make the cities of Laconia in-dependent. Agesilaus flew into a rage and seized upon this pretext to strike the name of Thebes out of the peace treaty and declare war upon her. He ordered the rest of the Greek delegates to de-part now that they had settled most of their disputes. Those dif-ferences which were capable of resolution should, he said, be left to the final terms of the peace: those which were not would have to be settled by war, since it was a hard task to remove all the causes of dissension between them.

Plutarch, *Life of Agesilaus,* in *The Age of Alexander: Nine Greek Lives by Plutarch.* Trans. Ian Scott-Kilvert. New York: Penguin, 1973, pp. 53–54.

Document 4: Uncertainty Reigns in Greece

Epaminondas defeated the Spartans at Leuctra in 371 B.C. Later, in 362, after several military forays into the Peloponnesus, he led the Theban army against a coalition of Spartans and others at Mantinea (in the central Peloponnesus). But as Xenophon states here, the Theban leader's death in the battle and the indecisive nature of the contest (the largest ever fought among Greeks up to that time) left the already war-weary Greeks more bewildered and exhausted than ever.

By overwhelming the force against which he struck, he [Epaminondas] caused the whole enemy army to turn and fly. But he himself fell in this attack, and after this those who were left, even though they had won, failed to take full advantage of the victory. The enemy phalanx was on the run, but the hoplites did not kill a single man of them, nor did they advance beyond the point where they had made their first impact. The enemy cavalry had also fled, but again the Theban cavalry did not pursue them and kill either cavalrymen or hoplites. Instead, they fell back timidly, like beaten men, through the routed lines of their enemies. The mixed force of infantry, cavalry and peltasts, who had shared in the victory of the cavalry, did indeed behave as though they had won and turned on the army's left wing, but here most of them were killed by the Athenians.

The result of this battle was just the opposite of what everyone expected it would be. Nearly the whole of Greece had been engaged on one side or the other, and everyone imagined that, if a battle was fought, the winner would become the dominant power and the losers would be their subjects. But God so ordered things that both parties put up trophies, as for victory, and neither side tried to prevent the other from doing so; both sides gave back the dead under a truce, as though they had won, and both sides received their dead under a truce, as though they had lost. Both sides claimed the victory, but it cannot be said that with regard to the accession of new territory, or cities, or power either side was any better off after the battle than before it. In fact, there was even more uncertainty and confusion in Greece after the battle than there had been previously.

Xenophon, *Hellenica*, published as *A History of My Times*. Trans. Rex Warner. New York: Penguin Books, 1979, p. 320.

Document 5: Philip Victorious over the City-States

In 338 B.C., after years of diplomacy, scheming, and outright aggression, Macedonia's King Philip (or Philippos) II confronted and defeated the leading city-states at Chaeronea (or Chaironeia), northwest of Thebes. This general account of the battle is by the first-century B.C. Greek historian Diodorus Siculus.

So Philippos, having failed to get the alliance of the Boiotians, nevertheless decided to fight both of them [Athens and Thebes] together. So he waited for the last of his allies to arrive and then marched into Boiotia, with more than 30,000 infantry and no less than 2,000 cavalry. Both sides were eager for the battle and were well matched in intention, zeal and courage, but the king had the advantage in numbers and in generalship. For he had fought many battles of different sorts and had been victorious in most cases, so that he had wide experience of military operations. On the Athenian side, the best of their *stratēgoi* [generals] were dead, Iphikrates, Chabrias and Timotheos too; and the best of those who were left, Chares, was no better than any ordinary soldier in the activity and counsel required of a *stratēgos*.

The armies deployed at dawn (i.e. at Chaironeia), and the king stationed his son Alexander, young in age but outstanding for his bravery and swiftness of action, on one wing, placing with him his best commanders, while he himself at the head of an élite corps exercised the command over the other; and he deployed individual units where the occasion required. On the other side, the Athenians, dividing the line according to nationality, assigned one wing to the Boiotians and commanded the other themselves. The battle was hotly contested for a long time and many fell on both sides, so that for a while the struggle permitted hopes of victory to both.

Then Alexander, eager to show his father his prowess and second to none in excess of zeal, and also with many good men at his side, first succeeded in breaking the solid front of the enemy line and, striking down many, he fought those opposite him into the ground. As the same success was won by his companions, gaps in the solid front were opened. Corpses piled up, until finally those with Alexander forced their way through and put their opponents to flight. Then the king also in person hazarded an advance, not conceding credit for the victory even to Alexander; he first forced back the troops stationed opposite him and then by compelling them to flee became the man responsible for the victory. More than 1,000 Athenians fell in the battle and no less than 2,000 were captured. Likewise, many of the Boiotians were killed and not a few taken prisoner. After the battle Philippos raised a trophy, gave up the dead for burial, gave sacrifices to the gods for victory, and rewarded according to their deserts those of his men who had distinguished themselves for bravery.

Quoted in Michael Crawford and David Whitehead, eds., *Archaic and Classical Greece: A Selection of Ancient Sources in Translation*. Cambridge: Cambridge University Press, 1983, pp. 614–15.

Document 6: Alexander's Character and Talents

This is the conclusion of the second-century A.D. Greek historian Arrian's account of Alexander's exploits, the Anabasis Alexandri *(Alexander's March Up-Country). Arrian discusses his subject's faults as well as his strong points and also suggests that Alexander desired to allow Persian customs and individuals to have roles in shaping the character of his new empire.*

Alexander died in the 114th Olympiad, in the archonship of Hegesias [June 10, 323 B.C.] at Athens. He lived, as Aristobulus tells us, thirty-two years and eight months, and reigned twelve years and eight months. He had great personal beauty, invincible power of endurance, and a keen intellect; he was brave and adventurous, strict in the observance of his religious duties, and hungry for fame. Most temperate in the pleasures of the body, his passion was for glory only, and in that he was insatiable. He had an uncanny instinct for the right course in a difficult and complex situation, and was most happy in his deductions from observed facts. In arming and equipping troops and in his military dispositions he was always masterly. Noble indeed was his power of inspiring his men, of filling them with confidence, and, in the moment of danger, of sweeping away their fear by the spectacle of his own fearlessness. When risks had to be taken, he took them with the utmost boldness, and his ability to seize the moment for a swift blow, before his enemy had any suspicion of what was coming, was beyond praise. No cheat or liar ever caught him off his guard, and both his word and his bond were inviolable. Spending but little on his own pleasures, he poured out his money without stint for the benefit of his friends.

Doubtless, in the passion of the moment Alexander sometimes erred; it is true he took some steps towards the pomp and arrogance of the Asiatic kings: but I, at least, cannot feel that such errors were very heinous, if the circumstances are taken fairly into consideration. For, after all, he was young; the chain of his successes was unbroken, and, like all kings, past, present, and to come, he was surrounded by courtiers who spoke to please, regardless of what evil their words might do. On the other hand, I do indeed know that Alexander, of all the monarchs of old, was the only one who had the nobility of heart to be sorry for his mistakes. Most people, if they know they have done wrong, foolishly suppose they can conceal their error by defending it, and finding a justification for it; but in my belief there is only one medicine for an evil deed, and that is for the guilty man to admit his guilt and show that he is sorry for it. Such an admission will make the consequences easier for the victim to bear, and the guilty man himself, by plainly showing his distress at former transgressions, will find good grounds of hope for avoiding similar transgressions in the future.

Nor do I think that Alexander's claim to a divine origin was a very serious fault—in any case, it may well have been a mere device to magnify his consequence in the eyes of his subjects. . . . Surely, too, his adoption of Persian dress was, like his claim to divine birth, a matter of policy: by it he hoped to bring the Eastern nations to feel that they had a king who was not wholly a foreigner, and to indicate to his own countrymen his desire to move away from the harsh traditional arrogance of Macedonia. That was also, no doubt, the reason why he included a proportion of Persian troops (the so-called 'Golden Apples', for instance) in Macedonian units, and made Persian noblemen officers in his crack native regiments. As for his reputed heavy drinking, Aristobulus declares that his drinking bouts were prolonged not for their own sake—for he was never, in fact, a heavy drinker—but simply because he enjoyed the companionship of his friends. . . .

It is my belief that there was in those days no nation, no city, no single individual beyond the reach of Alexander's name; never in all the world was there another like him, and therefore I cannot but feel that some power more than human was concerned in his birth; indications of this were, moreover, said to be provided at the time of his death by oracles; many people saw visions and had prophetic dreams; and there is the further evidence of the extraordinary way in which he is held, as no mere man could be, in honour and remembrance. Even today, when so many years have passed, there have been oracles, all tending to his glory, delivered to the people of Macedon.

In the course of this book I have, admittedly, found fault with some of the things which Alexander did, but of the man himself I am not ashamed to express ungrudging admiration. Where I have criticized unfavourably, I have done so because I wished to tell the truth as I saw it, and to enable my readers to profit thereby. Such was the motive which led me to embark upon this History: and I, too, have had God's help in my work.

Arrian, *Anabasis Alexandri*, published as *The Campaigns of Alexander.* Trans. Aubrey de Sélincourt. New York: Penguin Books, 1971, pp. 395–98.

Document 7: The Initial Division of Power Following Alexander's Death

As he himself attests in its first line, Arrian also wrote a work in ten books about the post-Alexander era (Events After Alexander*), the bulk of which is unfortunately lost. In the fragment excerpted here, the Successors, Perdiccas at first the most prominent among them, make Alexander's incompetent half-brother king strictly for appearances' sake, then begin assigning themselves various territorial niches.*

He [Arrian] also wrote an account in ten books of what happened after Alexander. They comprise the sedition in the army and the proclamation of Arrhidaeus, a son of Philip, Alexander's father . . . on the condition that the throne would be shared between him and Alexander, who was about to be born to Roxane from Alexander (the Great); and that is what happened when the child saw the light of day. They proclaimed Arrhidaeus king and changed his name to Philip. Strife broke out between the infantry and the cavalry; the most eminent of the cavalry and of the commanders were Perdiccas son of Orontes, Leonnatus son of Anteas and Ptolemy son of Lagus, after them Lysimachus son of Agathocles, Aristonous son of Pisaeus, Pithon son of Crateuas, Seleucus son of Antiochus and Eumenes of Cardia. These were the commanders of the cavalry, while Meleager commanded the infantry. They then sent numerous embassies to each other, and in the end the infantry who had proclaimed the king and the commanders of the cavalry came to an agreement, to the effect that Antipater should be general of Europe, Craterus protector (*prostates*) of the kingdom of Arrhidaeus, Perdiccas should hold the office of 'chiliarch' [commander of the king's bodyguards in Persia], which Hephaestion had held (this made him supervisor of the whole kingdom), while Meleager should be Perdiccas' lieutenant. On the pretext of purging the army Perdiccas arrested the most conspicuous leaders of the sedition, and had them put to death in his presence, alleging orders from Arrhidaeus; this struck terror in the rest of the army. Not long after he also put Meleager to death. As a result mutual suspicions were rife between Perdiccas and all the others. Nonetheless Perdiccas, pretending to act under the orders of Arrhidaeus, decided to appoint to the satrapies men who were suspected by him.

Accordingly Ptolemy's son of Lagus was appointed to rule Egypt and Libya and the parts of Arabia that lie close to Egypt, while Cleomenes who had been placed by Alexander in charge of this satrapy was to be Ptolemy's lieutenant; Laomedon was to rule Syria next to Egypt, Philotas Cilicia and Pithon Media; Eumenes of Cardia Cappadocia and Paphlagonia and the territory along the Black Sea as far as the Greek city of Trapezus, a colony of Sinope; Antigonus the Pamphylians, Lycians and Greater Phrygia; Asander the Carians; Menander the Lydians; Leonnatus Hellespontine Phrygia, which Calas had received from Alexander to govern, and which Demarchus had then ruled. Such was the distribution of provinces in Asia. In Europe, Thrace, the Chersonese and all the people who neighbour on the Thracians as far as the sea at Salmydessus on the Black Sea were entrusted to the rule of Lysimachus; the further parts of Thrace as far as the Illyrians, Triballians and Agrianians, Macedon itself and Epirus as far as the Ceraunian Mountains, and all the Greeks, were entrusted to Craterus and Antipater. Such was the distribution of provinces; but many parts remained unassigned, under the control of native rulers, as organised by Alexander.

Arrian, fragment of *Events After Alexander*, quoted in M.M. Austin, ed., *The Hellenistic World from Alexander to the Roman Conquest: A Selection of Ancient Sources in Translation.* Cambridge: Cambridge University Press, 1981, pp. 41–43.

Document 8: The Foundation of the Seleucid Kingdom

Appian was a Greek historian born in Alexandria circa A.D. 95. This excerpt from his Syrian Wars *first provides a useful thumbnail sketch of the early struggles among the Successors, then goes on to explain how one of them, Seleucus, managed to take control of a large slice of Alexander's now dismembered empire.*

After the Persians Alexander was king of the Syrians, as well as of all the people whom he saw. When he died leaving one very young son and another as yet unborn, the Macedonians, being deeply attached to the family of Philip, chose as their king Arrhidaeus, Alexander's half-brother, although he was believed to be dim-witted, and changed his name from Arrhidaeus to Philip. While the children of Alexander were growing up (they even placed the pregnant mother under guard), his friends divided the peoples of the empire into satrapies [provinces], which Perdiccas shared out among them in the name of King Philip. Not long after, when the kings were put to death, the satraps became kings. The first satrap of the Syrians was Laomedon of Mytilene, appointed by Perdiccas and then Antipater, who after Perdiccas was guardian of the kings. Ptolemy, the satrap of Egypt, sailed against Laomedon and sought to bribe him to hand over Syria, which protected Egypt's flank and was a good base to attack Cyprus. He failed and so arrested him, but Laomedon bribed his guards and escaped to Alcetas in Caria. For some time Ptolemy ruled Syria; he sailed back to Egypt after leaving garrisons in the cities. Antigonus was satrap of Phrygia, Lycia and Pamphylia, and was appointed overseer of the whole of Asia by Antipater when he returned to Europe. He besieged Eumenes, satrap of Cappadocia, whom the Macedonians had voted an enemy, but Eumenes escaped and seized control of Media. Eventually Antigonus captured Eumenes and put him to death, and on his return was received in great pomp by Seleucus the satrap in Babylon. One day Seleucus insulted an officer without consulting Antigonus, who was present, and Antigonus out of spite asked for accounts of his money and his possessions; Seleucus, being no match for Antigonus, withdrew to Ptolemy in Egypt. Immediately after his flight, Antigonus deposed Blitor the governor of Mesopotamia for letting Seleucus escape, and took over personal control of Babylonia, Mesopotamia and all the peoples from the Medians to the Hellespont (Antipater was dead by now). With so much territory in his power he became at once an object of jealousy to the other satraps. And so an alliance was formed between Seleucus, the chief instigator of the coalition, Ptolemy, Lysimachus satrap of Thrace, and Cassander son of Antipater, who ruled the Macedonians in his father's name. They sent a joint embassy to Antigonus to demand that he share out between them and other Macedonians, who had been expelled from their satrapies, the territory he had acquired and his money. Antigonus treated them with scorn, and so they went to war jointly against him, while he made counter-preparations, expelling the remaining garrisons of Ptolemy in Syria and laying his hands on the parts of Phoenicia and Coele Syria, as it is called, that were still under Ptolemy. Crossing the Cilician Gates he left his son Demetrius, then about 22 years old, at Gaza with his army to meet the attacks of Ptolemy from Egypt. Ptolemy won a brilliant victory over him at Gaza and the young man took refuge with his father. Ptolemy immediately sent Seleucus to Babylon to recover his rule, giving him for the purpose 1,000 infantry and 300 cavalry. With such a small force Seleucus recovered Babylon, where the inhabitants received him enthusiastically, and within a short time he greatly extended his empire [which he later reckoned as officially beginning in October

312 B.C.]. Antigonus defeated an attack by Ptolemy, winning a brilliant victory over him at sea off Cyprus; his son Demetrius was in command. This splendid achievement caused the army to proclaim both Antigonus and Demetrius kings; the other kings were dead by this time, Arrhidaeus the son of Philip, Olympias and the sons of Alexander. Ptolemy's own army also proclaimed him king, so that his defeat should not place him in a position of inferiority vis-à-vis the victors. And so for these men different circumstances led to similar results; the rest immediately followed their example and from satraps they all became kings.

And so it was that Seleucus became king of Babylonia, and also of Media, after he had killed in battle with his own hand Nicanor who had been left by Antigonus as satrap of Media. He waged many wars against Macedonians and barbarians; the two most important were against Macedonians, the latter war against Lysimachus king of Thrace, the former at Ipsus in Phrygia against Antigonus, who was commanding his army and fighting in person although over 80 years old. After Antigonus had fallen in battle, the kings who had joined with Seleucus in destroying him shared out his territory. Seleucus obtained then Syria from the Euphrates to the sea and inland Phrygia. Always lying in wait for the neighbouring peoples, with the power to coerce and the persuasion of diplomacy, he became ruler of Mesopotamia, Armenia, Seleucid Cappadocia (as it is called), the Persians, Parthians, Bactrians, Areians and Tapurians, Sogdiana, Arachosia, Hyrcania, and all other neighbouring peoples whom Alexander had conquered in war as far as the Indus. The boundaries of his rule in Asia extended further than those of any ruler apart from Alexander; the whole land from Phrygia eastwards to the river Indus was subject to Seleucus. . . .

He founded cities throughout the whole length of his empire; there were sixteen called Antioch after his father, five Laodicea after his mother, nine named Seleucia after himself, four called after his wives, three Apamea and one Stratonicea. Of these the most famous up to the present are the two Seleucias, by the sea and on the river Tigris, Laodicea in Phoenicia, Antioch under Mt Lebanon and Apamea in Syria. The others he called after places in Greece or Macedon, or after his own achievements, or in honour of Alexander the king. That is why there are in Syria and among the barbarians inland many Greek and many Macedonian place-names.

Appian, *Syrian Wars*, quoted in M.M. Austin, ed., *The Hellenistic World from Alexander to the Roman Conquest: A Selection of Ancient Sources in Translation*. Cambridge: Cambridge University Press, 1981, pp. 86–88.

Document 9: Demetrius Loses Control of Macedonia

The incessant warfare among the successors, characterized by shifting alliances and the devastation of lands and cities, especially those in Macedonia, is well illustrated in this excerpt from Plutarch's life of Demetrius, "the Besieger." In 285 B.C., three years after the desertion of his army, chronicled here, Demetrius was captured by Seleucus and imprisoned (dying in 283). By that time, the successor kingdoms were more or less firmly established.

Nothing comparable to this great expedition against Asia had been assembled by any man since the days of Alexander, but as it was preparing to sail, the three kings, Seleucus, Ptolemy and Lysimachus formed an alliance against Demetrius. Next they sent a combined delegation to Pyrrhus urging him to attack Macedonia. He should consider himself at liberty to disregard his treaty with Demetrius, in which the latter had given no guarantee of leaving him unmolested, but had claimed for himself the right to make war upon the enemy of his choice. Pyrrhus responded to their appeal and Demetrius thus found himself drawn into a war on several fronts before his preparations were complete. While Ptolemy sailed to Greece with a powerful fleet and incited various cities to revolt, Lysimachus invaded Macedonia from Thrace and Pyrrhus from Epirus, each of them plundering the country as he advanced. Demetrius left his son in command in Greece, while he hurried back to relieve Macedonia and marched against Lysimachus. On his way news reached him that Pyrrhus had captured Verroia. The report quickly spread to the Macedonians and Demetrius could no longer control his army. The whole camp resounded with tears and lamentations mingled with shouts of anger and execration against their commander. The men refused to stay with Demetrius and insisted on dispersing, ostensibly to return to their homes, but in reality to desert to Lysimachus. In this situation Demetrius determined to remove himself as far from Lysimachus as he could and to march against Pyrrhus. He reckoned that Lysimachus might be popular with the Macedonians because he was a fellow-countryman and on account of his association with Alexander, while Pyrrhus was a newcomer and a foreigner whom they would be unlikely to prefer to himself. But these calculations proved quite unfounded. When he approached his adversary's camp and pitched his own close by, the admiration which his men had felt in the past for Pyrrhus' brilliant feats of arms quickly revived, and besides this their traditions had accustomed them to believe that the man who proved himself the best fighter was also the best ruler. Besides, the soldiers also learned that Pyrrhus dealt leniently with his prisoners and since they were now anxious to transfer their allegiance either to Pyrrhus or to another master, but in any event to rid themselves of Demetrius, they began to desert him. At first they came over stealthily and in small groups, but presently the climate of disorder and sedition spread through the whole camp. At last some of the soldiers plucked up courage to go to Demetrius and told him to clear out and save himself, for the Macedonians were tired of fighting wars to pay for his extravagances. Demetrius thought this very reasonable advice compared to the hostility shown him by the others, and so he went to his tent, and just as if he were an actor rather than a real king, he put on a dark cloak in place of his royal robe and slipped away unnoticed. Most of his men at once fell to tearing down his tent, and while they were looting it and fighting over the spoils, Pyrrhus came up and finding that he met no resistance immediately took possession of the camp. After this the whole kingdom of Macedonia, which Demetrius had ruled securely for seven years, was divided between Lysimachus and Pyrrhus.

Plutarch, *Life of Demetrius*, in *The Age of Alexander: Nine Greek Lives by Plutarch*. Trans. Ian Scott-Kilvert. New York: Penguin, 1973, pp. 374–75.

Document 10: Pyrrhus a Talented but Shortsighted Leader

This brief but insightful observation by Plutarch, about the way the Epirote general Pyrrhus squandered his considerable talents and potential, could be applied just as fittingly to most of the other Hellenistic rulers.

Pyrrhus' hopes of the conquest of Italy and Sicily were finally demolished. He had squandered six years in his campaigns in these regions, but although he had been worsted in all his attempts, his spirit remained undaunted in the midst of defeat. The general opinion of him was that for warlike experience, daring and personal valour, he had no equal among the kings of his time; but what he won through his feats of arms he lost by indulging in vain hopes, and through his obsessive desire to seize what lay beyond his grasp, he constantly failed to secure what lay within it. For this reason Antigonus compared him to a player at dice, who makes many good throws, but does not understand how to exploit them when they are made.

Plutarch, *Life of Pyrrhus*, in *The Age of Alexander: Nine Greek Lives by Plutarch*. Trans. Ian Scott-Kilvert. New York: Penguin, 1973, pp. 414–15.

Document 11: The Treaty Between Macedonia and Carthage

The troubles between Rome and the Hellenistic kingdoms originated mainly with the alliance made between Philip V and Hannibal in 215 B.C., during the opening years of the Second Punic War. Fortunately for posterity, Polybius later had access to and recorded the treaty, excerpted here.

'This is a sworn treaty between Hannibal the general, Mago, Myrcan, Barmocar, such other members of the Carthaginian Senate as were present with him, and all Carthaginians serving under him on the one side, and on the other side Xenophanes, son of Cleomachus the Athenian, the envoy whom King Philip of Macedon, son of Demetrius, sent to us to represent him, together with the Macedonians and their allies.

The oath is taken in the presence of . . . all the gods who rule Carthage; in the presence of all the gods who rule Macedonia and the rest of Greece; in the presence of all the gods of war who preside over this oath.

Hannibal the general and those with him and all the Carthaginian senators with him and all the Carthaginians serving in his army propose that in respect of what seems good to you and to us we should make this sworn treaty of friendship and goodwill and become as friends, kinsmen and brothers on the following conditions.

First, that King Philip and the Macedonians and those of the rest of the Greeks who are their allies should protect the Carthaginians, the sovereign people, Hannibal their general and all those peoples who live under Carthaginian rule and observe the same laws. . . .

Second, that King Philip and the Macedonians and those of the rest of the Greeks who are their allies shall be protected and guarded by the Carthaginians . . . and by such others as may hereafter enter into alliance with us in Italy and the adjacent regions.

Third, that we shall form no plots, nor set ambushes against one another, but with all sincerity and goodwill, and without subterfuge or secret design we shall be the enemies of those who make war against the Carthaginians, always excepting those kings, cities and nations with whom we have sworn treaties and friendships.

Fourth, that we shall likewise be the enemies of those who make war against King Philip, always excepting the kings, cities and peoples with whom we have sworn treaties and friendships.

Fifth, that you will be our allies in the war in which we are now engaged against the Romans, until such time as the gods grant victory to us and to you, and you will give us such help as we may need or as we shall mutually determine.

Sixth, that when the gods have granted us victory in the war against the Romans and their allies, if the Romans shall request the Carthaginians to make terms of peace, we shall make such an agreement as shall include you too, and on the following conditions:

That the Romans shall never be permitted to make war on you;

That the Romans shall no longer rule over Corcyra, Apollonia, Epidamnus, Pharos, Dimale, the Parthini, or Atintania, and that they shall hand back to Demetrius of Pharos those of his friends who are at present in territory under the rule of Rome.

Seventh, if the Romans ever make war upon you or upon us, we shall give help to one another in this conflict as may be required on either side.

Eighth, the same action shall follow if any other nation makes war upon you or upon us, always excepting those kings, cities, or peoples with whom we have sworn treaties of alliance.

Ninth, if we decide to remove from or add to this sworn treaty, we shall remove or add only such clauses as both of us may determine.'

Quoted in Polybius, *Histories*, published as *Polybius: The Rise of the Roman Empire*. Trans. Ian Scott-Kilvert. New York: Penguin Books, 1979, pp. 358–59.

Document 12: An Urgent Call for Greek Unity

In 213 B.C., an Aetolian orator named Agelaus made this impassioned, moving, and, as it turned out, prophetic plea for the Greeks to present a united front against the rising Roman threat. Unfortunately for Greece, his words fell largely on deaf ears.

'It would be best if the Greeks never went to war with one another, if they could regard it as the greatest gift of the gods for them all to speak with one voice, and could join hands like men who are crossing a river; in this way they could unite to repulse the incursions of the barbarians and to preserve themselves and their cities. But if we have no hope of achieving such a degree of unity for the whole country, let me impress upon you how important it is at least for the present that we should consult one another and remain on our guard, in view of the huge armies which have been mobilized, and the vast scale of the war which is now being waged in the west. For it must already be obvious to all those who pay even the slightest attention to affairs of state that whether the Carthaginians defeat the Romans or the Romans the Carthaginians, the victors will by no means be satisfied with the sovereignty of Italy and Sicily, but will come here, and will advance both their forces and their ambitions beyond the bounds of justice. I therefore beg you all to be on your guard against this danger, and I appeal especially to King Philip. For you the safest policy, instead of wearing down the Greeks and making them an easy prey for the invader, is to take care of them as you would of your own body, and to protect every province of Greece as you would if it were a part of your own dominions. If you follow this policy, the Greeks will be your friends and your faithful allies in case of attack, and foreigners will be the less inclined to plot against your throne, because they will be discouraged by the loyalty of the Greeks towards you. But if you yearn for a field of action, then turn your attention to the west, keep it fixed on the wars in Italy, and bide your time, so that when the moment comes, you may enter the contest for the sovereignty of the whole world. Now the present moment is by no means unfavourable to such hopes. But you must, I entreat you, put aside your differences with the Greeks and your campaigns against them until times have become more settled, and concern yourself first and foremost with this aspect of the situation which I have just mentioned, so that you retain the power to make peace or war with them as you think best. For if you wait until the clouds which are now gathering in the west settle upon Greece, I very much fear that these truces and wars and games at which we now play may have been knocked out of our hands so completely that we shall be praying to the gods to grant us still this power of fighting or making peace with one another as we choose, in other words of being left the capacity to settle our own disputes.'

Quoted in Polybius, *Histories*, published as *Polybius: The Rise of the Roman Empire*. Trans. Ian Scott-Kilvert. New York: Penguin Books, 1979, pp. 299–300.

Document 13: The Superiority of the Roman Military System

In this portion of his history, titled "On the Phalanx," Polybius discusses the strengths of the Macedonian phalanx, but also its fatal weaknesses, and then goes on to explain why Roman battle formations are more efficient.

In the past the Macedonian formation was proved by operational experience to be superior to the others which were in use in Asia and Greece, while the Roman system overcame those employed in Africa and among all the peoples of Western Europe. In our own times we have seen both the two formations and the soldiers of the two nations matched against one another, not just once but on many occasions. It should prove a useful exercise, and one well worth the trouble, to study the differences between them, and to discover the reason why on the battlefield the Romans have always proved the victors and carried off the prize. If we examine the matter in this way we shall not, like the ignorant majority of mankind, speak merely in terms of chance, and congratulate the victors without giving the reasons, but shall be able to pay them the praise and admiration they deserve because we have come to understand the causes of their success. . . .

There are a number of factors which make it easy to understand that so long as the phalanx retains its characteristic form and strength nothing can withstand its charge or resist it face to face. When the phalanx is closed up for action, each man with his arms occupies a space of three feet. The pike he carries was earlier designed to be twenty-four feet long, but as adapted to current practice was shortened to twenty-one, and from this we must subtract the space between the bearer's hands and the rear portion of the pike which keeps it balanced and couched. This amounts to six feet in all, from which it is clear that the pike will project fifteen feet in front of the body of each hoplite when he advances against the enemy grasping it with both hands. This also means that while the pikes of the men in the second, third, and fourth ranks naturally extend further than those of the fifth rank, yet even the latter will still project three feet in front of the men in the first rank. I am assuming of course that the phalanx keeps its characteristic order, and is closed up both from the rear and on the flanks. . . .

At any rate if my description is true and exact, it follows that each man in the front rank will have the points of five pikes extending in front of him, each point being three feet ahead of the one behind.

From these facts we can easily picture the nature and the tremendous power of a charge by the whole phalanx, when it advances sixteen deep with levelled pikes. Of these sixteen ranks those who are stationed further back than the fifth cannot use their pikes to take an active part in the battle. They therefore do not level them man against man, but hold them with the points tilted upwards over the shoulders of the men in front. In this way they give protection to the whole phalanx from above, for the pikes are massed so closely that they can keep off any missiles which might clear the heads of the front ranks and strike those immediately behind them. Once the charge is launched, these rear ranks by the sheer pressure of their bodily weight greatly increase its momentum and make it impossible for the foremost ranks to face about.

I have described both in general terms and in detail the composition of the phalanx. I must now for purposes of comparison explain the special features of Roman equipment and tactical formation, and the differences which distinguish the two. With the Romans each soldier in full armour also occupies a space three feet wide. However, according to the Roman methods of fighting each man makes his movements individually: not only does he defend his body with his long shield, constantly moving it to meet a threatened blow, but he uses his sword both for cutting and for thrusting. Obviously these tactics require a more open order and an interval between the men, and in practice each soldier needs to be at least three feet from those in the same rank and from those in front of and behind him if he is to perform his function efficiently. The result of these dispositions is that each Roman soldier has to face two men in the front rank of the phalanx, and so has to encounter and fight against ten spear points. It is impossible for one man to cut through all of these once the battle lines are engaged, nor is it easy to force the points away; moreover, in the Roman formation the rear ranks do not support the front, either in forcing the spears away or in the use of their swords. It is easy to understand then, as I mentioned at the beginning, how nothing can withstand the frontal assault of the phalanx so long as it retains its characteristic formation and strength.

What then is the factor which enables the Romans to win the battle and causes those who use the phalanx to fail? The answer is that in war the times and places for action are unlimited, whereas the phalanx requires one time and one type of ground only in order to produce its peculiar effect. Now if the enemy were compelled to position themselves according to the times and places demanded by the phalanx whenever an important battle was imminent, no doubt those who employ the phalanx would always carry off the victory for the reasons I have given above. But if it is quite possible, even easy, to evade its irresistible charge, how can the phalanx any longer be considered formidable? Again, it is generally admitted that its use requires flat and level ground which is unencumbered by any obstacles such as ditches, gullies, depressions, ridges and watercourses, all of which are sufficient to hinder and dislocate such a formation. There is general agreement that it is almost impossible, or at any rate exceedingly rare, to find a stretch of country of say two or three miles or more which contains no obstacles of this kind. But even assuming that such an arena could be found, if the enemy refuses to come down into it, but prefers to traverse the country sacking the towns and devastating the territories of our allies, what purpose can the phalanx serve? If it remains on the ground which suits it best, not only is it unable to assist its allies, but it cannot even ensure its own safety, for the transport of its supplies will easily be stopped by the enemy when they have undisputed command of the open country. On the other hand, if it leaves the terrain which favours it and attempts an action elsewhere, it will easily be defeated. Or again, supposing that the enemy does decide to descend into the plain and fight there, but, instead of committing his entire force to the battle when the phalanx has its one opportunity to charge, keeps even a small part of it in reserve at the moment when the main action takes place, it is easy to forecast what will happen from the tactics which the Romans are now putting into practice.

The outcome indeed does not need to be demonstrated by argument: we need only refer to accomplished facts. The Romans do not attempt to make their line numerically equal to the enemy's, nor do they expose the whole strength of the legions to a frontal attack by the phalanx. Instead they keep part of the forces in reserve while the rest engage the enemy. Later in the battle, whether the phalanx in its charge drives back the troops opposed to it or is driven back by them, in either event it loses its own peculiar formation. For either in pursuing a retreating enemy or falling back before an oncoming one, the phalanx leaves behind the other units of its own army; at this point the enemy's reserves can occupy the space the phalanx has vacated, and are no longer obliged to attack from the front, but can fall upon it from flank and rear. When it is thus easy to deny the phalanx the opportunities it needs and to minimize the advantages it enjoys, and also impossible to prevent the enemy from acting against it, does it not follow that the difference between these two systems is enormous?

Besides this, those who rely on the phalanx are obliged to march across and encamp on ground of every description; they must occupy favourable positions in advance, besiege others and be besieged themselves and deal with unexpected appearances of the enemy. All these eventualities are part and parcel of war, and may have an important or a decisive effect on the final victory. In all these situations the Macedonian formation is sometimes of little use, and sometimes of none at all, because the phalanx soldier cannot operate either in smaller units or singly, whereas the Roman formation is highly flexible. Every Roman soldier, once he is armed and goes into action, can adapt himself equally well to any place or time and meet an attack from any quarter. He is likewise equally well-prepared and needs to make no change whether he has to fight with the main body or with a detachment, in maniples or singly. Accordingly, since the effective use of the parts of the Roman army is so much superior, their plans are much more likely to achieve success than those of others. I have felt obliged to deal with this subject at some length, because so many Greeks on those occasions when the Macedonians suffered defeat regarded such an event as almost incredible, and many will still be at a loss to understand why and how the phalanx proves inferior by comparison with the Roman method of arming their troops.

Polybius, *Histories*, published as *Polybius: The Rise of the Roman Empire*. Trans. Ian Scott-Kilvert. New York: Penguin Books, 1979, pp. 508–73.

Document 14: The Last Hellenistic Ruler Defeated

This dramatic account of the victory of Octavian and his talented general, Marcus Agrippa, over Antony and Cleopatra at Actium (in western Greece) in 31 B.C. is from Plutarch's biography of Antony. After escaping the battle, Cleopatra returned to Alexandria. The following year, she committed suicide there, bringing the Ptolemaic dynasty, as well as Greece's last period of large-scale political autonomy, to a close.

On the fifth day the wind dropped, the sea grew calm, and the two fleets met. Antony together with Publicola took command of the right wing, Coelius was in charge of the left, and Marcus Octavius and Marcus Insteius of the centre. Octavius Caesar [Octavian] posted Agrippa on the left and took the right wing himself. Antony's army was commanded by Canidius and Octavius's by Taurus, but both generals drew up their forces along the shore and remained inactive. As for the two commanders, Antony made the round of all the ships in a small rowing boat. He urged the soldiers to rely on the weight of their vessels and to stand firm and fight exactly as if they were on land, and at the same time he ordered the sea captains to receive the shock of the enemy's warships as if they were lying quietly at anchor, and to hold their positions at the mouth of the gulf which was a narrow and difficult passage. . . . About noon a breeze sprang up from the sea. By this time Antony's men had become impatient at waiting so long for the enemy, and since they felt confident that the height and the size of their ships made them invincible, they got the left wing of the fleet under way. Octavius Caesar was overjoyed to see this and ordered the rowers of his right wing to back water, so as to lure the enemy out of the gulf and its narrow entrance. His plan was to surround them with his more agile craft and fight at close quarters, where he was confident that he would have the advantage over his opponents' large and undermanned galleys which were slow and difficult to manoeuvre.

When the opposing battle lines first met, the ships did not attempt to ram or crush one another at all. Antony's vessels, because of their great weight, were not making the speed which is required to stave in an opponent's timbers. Octavius Caesar's, on the other hand, deliberately avoided a head-on collision with their enemies' bows, which were armoured with massive plates and spikes of bronze, nor did they even venture to ram them amidships, since their beaks would have been easily snapped off against hulls which were constructed of huge square timbers bolted together with iron. And so the fighting took on much of the character of a land battle, or, to be more exact, of an attack upon a fortified town. Three or four of Octavius's ships clustered round each one of Antony's and the fighting was carried on with wicker shields, spears, poles, and flaming missiles, while Antony's soldiers also shot with catapults from wooden towers. Agrippa then began to extend his left wing, so as to feel his way round the enemy's flank. Publicola to counter this manoeuvre was obliged to advance against him and so became separated from the centre, which was thrown into confusion and was promptly engaged by Arruntius, who commanded the centre of Octavius's fleet. At this moment, while neither side had gained a decisive advantage, Cleopatra's squadron of sixty ships was suddenly seen to hoist sail and make off through the very midst of the battle. They had been stationed astern of the heavy ships, and so threw their whole formation into disorder as they plunged through. The enemy watched them with amazement, as they spread their sails before the following wind and shaped their course for the Peloponnese. And it was now that Antony revealed to all the world that he was no longer guided by the motives of a commander nor of a brave man nor indeed by his own judgement at all: instead, he . . . allowed himself to be dragged along after the woman, as if he had become a part of her flesh and must go where-ever she led him. No sooner did he see her ships sailing away than every other consideration was blotted out of his mind, and he abandoned and betrayed the men who were fighting and dying for his cause. He got into a five-banked galley and . . . he hurried after the woman who had already ruined him and would soon complete his destruction.

Cleopatra recognized him and hoisted a signal on her ship, whereupon Antony came up and was taken on board, but he neither saw her, nor was seen by her. Instead he went forward by himself into the bows and sat down without a word, holding his head between his hands. . . . For three days he stayed by himself in the bows of the ship; all this time he felt either too angry or too ashamed to see Cleopatra, and he then put in at Taenarum [on the southern coast of the Peloponnesus]. It was here that Cleopatra's waiting women first persuaded the two to speak to one another, and then later to eat and sleep together. . . .

At Actium his fleet continued to hold out for several hours against Octavius, and it was only after the ships had been severely battered by a gale, which blew head on against them, that his men unwillingly surrendered at about four in the afternoon.

Plutarch, *Life of Antony*, in *Makers of Rome: Nine Lives by Plutarch*. Trans. Ian Scott-Kilvert. New York: Penguin Books, 1965, pp. 330–33.

Chronology

ca. 508
The Athenian statesman Cleisthenes and his supporters establish a democracy, the world's first, in Athens.

ca. 500–323
Greece's Classic Age, in which Greek arts, architecture, literature, and democratic reforms reach their height.

490
The Athenians defeat a force of invading Persians at Marathon, northeast of Athens.

480
The Athenian statesman-general Themistocles engineers a major naval victory over the Persians at Salamis, southwest of Athens.

ca. 450
Birth of the infamous Greek traitor Alcibiades.

431
The disastrous Peloponnesian War, which will engulf and exhaust almost all the city-states, begins.

429
A deadly plague strikes Athens, killing a large number of residents, including its most able leader, Pericles.

415
At Alcibiades' urging, the Athenians send a large military expedition to Sicily in hopes of conquering the Greek city of Syracuse; when the ships arrive in Sicily, Alcibiades deserts his countrymen, leaving Nicias, a far less capable general, in charge of the expedition.

413
The Athenians are disastrously defeated in Sicily; most of the survivors are condemned to slave labor in the local quarries.

410
The renowned Theban general Epaminondas is born.

404

Athens surrenders to Sparta, ending the great war; the Spartan hegemony of Greece begins.

395

A temporary coalition of Greek city-states, including Thebes, Athens, and Corinth, challenges Sparta, whose heavy-handed policies are universally unpopular.

382

The Spartans occupy the Cadmea (the Theban acropolis), an aggressive move most Greeks condemn; Philip, the Macedonian king destined to conquer and briefly to unite the Greeks, is born.

371

Epaminondas defeats the Spartans at Leuctra, near Thebes, forever shattering the myth of Spartan invincibility; soon afterward he leads troops into the Peloponnesus (the region traditionally dominated by Sparta), initiating a period of Theban supremacy.

362

Epaminondas dies in battle at Mantinea, in the central Peloponnesus, signaling the end of the short-lived Theban supremacy of Greece.

359

Philip takes charge of the disunited, culturally backward Macedonia; within just a few years he will turn it into a strong nation with a formidable standing army.

338

Philip and his teenaged son, Alexander, defeat a temporary Greek alliance led by Athens and Thebes at Chaeronea, in central Greece.

336

Philip is assassinated and Alexander, who will one day be called "the Great," ascends Macedonia's throne; one of the leading Macedonian generals, Antigonus "the One-eyed," has a son, Demetrius, who will eventually become known as "the Besieger."

334

Alexander invades Persia; in the next few years he overruns Persian territories, spreading Greek language, ideas, and political administration across the Near East.

323

After creating the largest empire the world has yet seen, Alexander dies in the former Persian capital of Babylon.

ca. 323–30
Greece's Hellenistic Age, in which Alexander's generals, the so-called "Successors," war among themselves and carve up his empire into several new kingdoms, which then proceed also to fight among themselves; during the second half of this period, Rome gains control of the Greek world.

ca. 319
Birth of Pyrrhus, a prince of the small Greek kingdom of Epirus, who will become one of the leading military strongmen of the age and the first important Greek general to confront the Romans.

305
Demetrius lays siege to the city of Rhodes, but fails to take it.

301
Antigonus and Demetrius are decisively defeated by a coalition of the other Successors at Ipsus, in central Asia Minor.

280
Three large Greek monarchies (the Macedonian, Seleucid, and Ptolemaic kingdoms) have by now emerged from the chaos of the long wars of the Successors; Pyrrhus answers a call for help from Tarentum, a Greek city in southern Italy that has been threatened by Rome; Pyrrhus narrowly defeats the Romans at Heraclea, near Tarentum.

275
Having failed to make decisive headway against the Romans, Pyrrhus abandons Italy.

241
The Romans defeat the maritime empire of Carthage, ending the First Punic War.

213
Agelaus of Aetolia, a Greek orator, warns of the impending threat of Roman imperialism and calls for the Greeks to unite; but his call is largely ignored.

201
The Second Punic War ends with another resounding Roman victory.

200–197
Rome prosecutes and wins the Second Macedonian War against Macedonia's King Philip V, who had allied himself with Carthage in the Second Punic War.

189
The Romans defeat the Seleucid ruler, Antiochus III, at Magnesia, in western Asia Minor.

171–168
Rome wins the Third Macedonian War and dismantles the Macedonian Kingdom.

148
The Romans turn the former Macedonian Kingdom into a province of their growing empire.

146
A Roman general destroys the once-great Greek city of Corinth as an object lesson to any Greeks contemplating rebellion against Rome.

69
Birth of Cleopatra VII, daughter of Ptolemy XII, ruler of the Ptolemaic Kingdom (consisting mainly of Egypt), now a third-rate power hovering precariously in Rome's orbit.

48
Aided by the Roman strongman Julius Caesar, Cleopatra ascends the Egyptian throne.

44
Caesar is assassinated in the Roman Senate.

31
Cleopatra and her second Roman lover/ally, Mark Antony, are defeated by another powerful Roman, Octavian, at Actium, in western Greece; the following year, the legendary queen, last of the Hellenistic and independent Greek rulers of antiquity, takes her own life.

For Further Research

Ancient Sources in Translation

Appian, *Roman History*. 4 vols. Trans. Horace White. Cambridge, MA: Harvard University Press, 1964. Contains descriptions of some of the Greek Hellenistic Kingdoms eventually conquered by Rome.

Archimedes, *Works*. Trans. Thomas L. Heath, in *Great Books of the Western World*, vol. 11. Chicago: Encyclopedia Britannica, 1952.

Arrian, *Anabasis Alexandri*, published as *The Campaigns of Alexander*. Trans. Aubrey de Sélincourt. New York: Penguin Books, 1971.

Kenneth J. Atchity, ed., *The Classical Greek Reader*. New York: Oxford University Press, 1996.

M.M. Austin, ed., *The Hellenistic World from Alexander to the Roman Conquest: A Selection of Ancient Sources in Translation*. Cambridge: Cambridge University Press, 1981.

Morris R. Cohen and I.E. Drabkin, *A Source Book in Greek Science*. Cambridge, MA: Harvard University Press, 1948. A collection of writings by ancient Greek scientists, including many from the Hellenistic Age, with useful commentary.

Michael Crawford and David Whitehead, eds., *Archaic and Classical Greece: A Selection of Ancient Sources in Translation*. Cambridge: Cambridge University Press, 1983.

Livy, *History of Rome from Its Foundation*, Books 21–30 excerpted in *Livy: The War with Hannibal*. Trans. Aubrey de Sélincourt. New York: Penguin Books, 1972. Contains descriptions of Roman interaction with the Greek Hellenistic kingdoms.

———, *History of Rome from Its Foundation*, Books 31–45 excerpted in *Livy: Rome and the Mediterranean*. Trans. Henry Bettenson. New York: Penguin Books, 1976. Contains descriptions of Roman interaction with the Greek Hellenistic kingdoms.

Pausanias, *Guide to Greece*. 2 vols. Trans. Peter Levi. New York: Penguin Books, 1971.

Plutarch, *Parallel Lives*, excerpted in *The Rise and Fall of Athens: Nine Greek Lives by Plutarch*. Trans. Ian Scott-Kilvert. New York: Penguin, 1960.

————, *Parallel Lives*, excerpted in *Makers of Rome: Nine Lives by Plutarch*. Trans. Ian Scott-Kilvert. New York: Penguin Books, 1965.

————, *Parallel Lives*, excerpted in *The Age of Alexander: Nine Greek Lives by Plutarch*. Trans. Ian Scott-Kilvert. New York: Penguin, 1973.

Polybius, *Histories*, published as *Polybius: The Rise of the Roman Empire*. Trans. Ian Scott-Kilvert. New York: Penguin Books, 1979.

Diodorus Siculus, *Library of History*. 12 vols. Various trans. Cambridge, MA: Harvard University Press, 1962–1967.

Thucydides, *The Peloponnesian War*. Trans. Rex Warner. New York: Penguin Books, 1972.

————, *The Peloponnesian War*, published as *The Landmark Thucydides: A Comprehensive Guide to the Peloponnesian War*. Trans. Richard Crawley, ed. Robert B. Strassler. New York: Simon & Schuster, 1996.

Xenophon, *Hellenica*, published as *A History of My Times*. Trans. Rex Warner. New York: Penguin Books, 1979.

Modern Sources

City-State Rivalry and Warfare in the Fifth and Fourth Centuries B.C.

J.K. Anderson, *Military Theory and Practice in the Age of Xenophon*. Berkeley: University of California Press, 1970.

John Buckler, *The Theban Hegemony*. Cambridge, MA: Harvard University Press, 1980.

Walter M. Ellis, *Alcibiades*. New York: Routledge, 1989.

Michael Grant, *The Classical Greeks*. New York: Scribner's, 1989.

Donald Kagan, *The Outbreak of the Peloponnesian War*. Ithaca, NY: Cornell University Press, 1969. This and the following three sequels by Kagan collectively constitute the most thorough examination of the Peloponnesian War presently available.

————, *The Archidamian War*. Ithaca, NY: Cornell University Press, 1974.

————, *The Peace of Nicias and the Sicilian Expedition*. Ithaca, NY: Cornell University Press, 1981.

————, *The Fall of the Athenian Empire*. Ithaca, NY: Cornell University Press, 1987.

Robert J. Littman, *The Greek Experiment: Imperialism and Social Conflict, 800–400 B.C.* London: Thames and Hudson, 1974.

Malcolm F. McGregor, *The Athenians and Their Empire.* Vancouver: University of British Columbia Press, 1987.

Christian Meier, *Athens: Portrait of a City in Its Golden Age.* Trans. Robert and Rita Kimber. New York: Henry Holt, 1998.

Russell Meiggs, *The Athenian Empire.* Oxford: Clarendon Press, 1972.

Claude Mosse, *Athens in Decline, 404–86 B.C.* London: Routledge & Kegan Paul, 1973.

Don Nardo, *The Age of Pericles.* San Diego: Lucent Books, 1996.

G.E.M. de Ste. Croix, *The Origins of the Peloponnesian War.* Ithaca, NY: Cornell University Press, 1972.

Barry S. Strauss, *Athens after the Peloponnesian War: Class, Faction and Policy, 403–386 B.C.* London: Croom Helm, 1986.

Philip II, the Rise of Macedonia, and Alexander's Conquests

Eugene N. Borza, *In the Shadow of Olympus: The Emergence of Macedon.* Princeton, NJ: Princeton University Press, 1990.

J.R. Ellis, *Philip II and Macedonian Imperialism.* New York: Thames and Hudson, 1977.

J.F.C. Fuller, *The Generalship of Alexander the Great.* New Brunswick, NJ: Rutgers University Press, 1960.

Peter Green, *Alexander of Macedon, 356–323 B.C.: A Historical Biography.* Berkeley: University of California Press, 1991.

N.G.L. Hammond, *The Genius of Alexander the Great.* Chapel Hill: University of North Carolina Press, 1997.

———, *Philip of Macedon.* Baltimore: Johns Hopkins University Press, 1994.

Don Nardo, *Philip II and Alexander the Great Unify Greece.* Springfield, NJ: Enslow Publishers, 2000.

Nick Sekunda and John Warry, *Alexander the Great: His Armies and Campaigns, 334–323 B.C.* London: Osprey, 1998.

Hellenistic States, Leaders, and Political Developments

John Boardman et al., *Greece and the Hellenistic World.* New York: Oxford University Press, 1988.

Max Cary, *History of the Greek World from 323 to 146 B.C.* London: Methuen, 1968.

Petros Garouphalias, *Pyrrhus.* London: Stacey International, 1979.

Michael Grant, *From Alexander to Cleopatra: The Hellenistic World.* New York: Charles Scribner's Sons, 1982.

Peter Green, *Alexander to Actium: The Historical Evolution of the Hellenistic Age.* Berkeley: University of California Press, 1990.

————, ed., *Hellenistic History and Culture.* Berkeley: University of California Press, 1993.

N.G.L. Hammond, *Epirus.* Oxford: Oxford University Press, 1967.

E.V. Hansen, *Attalids of Pergamum.* Ithaca, NY: Cornell University Press, 1971.

Lucy Hughes-Hallett, *Cleopatra: Histories, Dreams and Distortions.* New York: HarperCollins, 1991.

Naphtali Lewis, *Greeks in Ptolemaic Egypt.* Oxford: Clarendon Press, 1986.

————, *Life in Egypt Under Roman Rule.* Oxford: Clarendon Press, 1983.

Jack Lindsay, *Cleopatra.* London: Constable and Company, 1970.

Don Nardo, *The Collapse of the Roman Republic.* San Diego: Lucent Books, 1998.

————, *Cleopatra.* San Diego: Greenhaven Press, 2001.

F.W. Walbank, *The Hellenistic World.* Cambridge, MA: Harvard University Press, 1993.

Hellenistic Society, Arts, and Culture

Margarete Bieber, *The History of Greek and Roman Theater.* Princeton, NJ: Princeton University Press, 1961.

Frank J. Frost, *Greek Society.* Lexington, MA: D.C. Heath, 1980.

Arnaldo Momigliano, *Alien Wisdom: The Limits of Hellenization.* Cambridge: Cambridge University Press, 1975.

Don Nardo, *Greek and Roman Science.* San Diego: Lucent Books, 1997.

J.J. Pollitt, *Art in the Hellenistic Age.* Cambridge: Cambridge University Press, 1986.

Sarah B. Pomeroy, *Goddesses, Whores, Wives, and Slaves: Women in Classical Antiquity*. New York: Schocken Books, 1995.

———, *Women in Hellenistic Egypt: From Alexander to Cleopatra*. New York: Schocken Books, 1989.

Rex Warner, *The Greek Philosophers*. New York: New American Library, 1958.

F.A. Wright, *A History of Later Greek Literature, from the Death of Alexander in 323 B.C. to the Death of Justinian in 565 A.D.* London: Routledge & Kegan Paul, 1951.

Hellenistic Warfare and the Coming of Rome

F.E. Adcock, *The Greek and Macedonian Art of War*. Berkeley: University of California Press, 1957.

Arthur E.R. Boak and William G. Sinnegin, *A History of Rome to A.D. 565*. New York: Macmillan, 1965.

Brian Caven, *The Punic Wars*. New York: Barnes and Noble, 1992.

Peter Connolly, *Greece and Rome at War*. London: Greenhill Books, 1998.

Michael Crawford, *The Roman Republic*. Cambridge, MA: Harvard University Press, 1992.

G.T. Griffith, *Mercenaries of the Hellenistic World*. New York: AMS, 1977.

Erich Gruen, *The Hellenistic World and the Coming of Rome*. Berkeley: University of California Press, 1984.

Archer Jones, *The Art of War in the Western World*. New York: Oxford University Press, 1987.

William L. Rodgers, *Greek and Roman Naval Warfare*. Annapolis, MD: Naval Institute Press, 1964.

John Warry, *Warfare in the Classical World*. Norman, OK: University of Oklahoma Press, 1995.

General Greek History, Geography, and Culture

Lesly Adkins and Roy A. Adkins, *Handbook to Life in Ancient Greece*. New York: Facts On File, 1997.

Hermann Bengtson, *History of Greece, from the Beginnings to the Byzantine Era*. Trans. Edmund F. Bloedow. Ottawa: University of Ottawa Press, 1988.

William R. Biers, *The Archaeology of Greece*. Ithaca, NY: Cornell University Press, 1996.

George W. Botsford and Charles A. Robinson, *Hellenic History*. New York: Macmillan, 1956.

C.M. Bowra, *The Greek Experience*. New York: New American Library, 1957.

J.B. Bury, *A History of Greece to the Death of Alexander*. Rev. Russell Meiggs. London: Macmillan, 1975.

M.I. Finley, *The Ancient Greeks: An Introduction to Their Life and Thought*. New York: Viking Press, 1964.

Charles Freeman, *Egypt, Greece, and Rome: Civilizations of the Ancient Mediterranean*. New York: Oxford University Press, 1996.

Michael Grant, *The Founders of the Western World: A History of Greece and Rome*. New York: Scribner's, 1991.

———, *The Rise of the Greeks*. New York: Macmillan, 1987.

Peter Levi, *Atlas of the Greek World*. New York: Facts On File, 1984.

Thomas R. Martin, *Ancient Greece: From Prehistoric to Hellenistic Times*. New Haven, CT: Yale University Press, 1996.

Don Nardo, *Greek and Roman Sports*. San Diego: Lucent Books, 1999.

———, *Life in Ancient Athens*. San Diego: Lucent Books, 2000.

———, *The Parthenon*. San Diego: Lucent Books, 1999.

———, *The Trial of Socrates*. San Diego: Lucent Books, 1997.

———, ed., *Ancient Greek Drama*. San Diego: Greenhaven Press, 2000.

Sarah B. Pomeroy et al., *Ancient Greece: A Political, Social, and Cultural History*. New York: Oxford University Press, 1999.

Chester G. Starr, *The Ancient Greeks*. New York: Oxford University Press, 1971.

———, *A History of the Ancient World*. New York: Oxford University Press, 1991.

Alfred Zimmern, *The Greek Commonwealth: Politics and Economics in Fifth-Century Athens*. New York: Oxford University Press, 1931 (fifth edition). Revised and reprinted, 1961.

Index

About the Editor

Historian Don Nardo has written or edited numerous volumes about the ancient Greek world, including *The Age of Pericles*, *Greek and Roman Sports*, *The Parthenon*, *The Trial of Socrates*, *Life in Ancient Athens*, and literary companions to the works of Homer and Sophocles. He resides with his wife Christine in Massachusetts.